D0154247

# International Dictionary of Insurance and Finance

## John Clark

**Glenlake Publishing Company, Ltd**

Chicago ● London ● New Delhi

**Fitzroy Dearborn Publishers**

Chicago and London

© The Chartered Institute of Bankers 1999
ISBN: 1-888998-69-5

Library Edition: Fitzroy·Dearborn Publishers, Chicago and London
Library Edition ISBN: 1-57958-161-7

All rights reserved. No part of this book may be reproduced in any form or by any means electronic, mechanical, photocopying, recording, or otherwise without the prior written permission of the publisher.

GPCo
1261 West Glenlake
Chicago, Illinois 60660
Glenlake@ix.netcom.com

# Preface

This book is intended to provide access to the specialist terms of insurance and general finance for students and professionals in the growing world of insurance, and its interaction with pensions, savings and the stock exchange. It should also assist private investors and people who read financial journals and the financial pages of daily newspapers. Like its companion volume the *Dictionary of Banking and Finance Terms*, it does not limit itself merely to well-established terms. It also includes definitions of the everyday jargon, acronyms and newly adopted words (many from the United States) that are now common in national and international financial dealings.

# A

**A1**  The best. The term originates in marine insurance, where A1 denotes a vessel that is in perfect condition, the letter referring to the condition of the hull and the number to the condition of the ship's trappings.

*The ship was registered A1 at Lloyd's.*

*See also* **Lloyd's of London.**

**AAA**  *See triple-A*

**AAR**  Abbreviation of *against all risks.*

**abandonment**  Act of passing ownership of insured property to the insurer in the event of total loss. This takes place in certain circumstances, if the loss is unavoidable or the cost of repair exceeds the value of the property. In the latter case, the property is written off. Abandonment occurs most often in marine insurance when a vessel is declared dangerous or unseaworthy.

*The ship was stranded on a reef and could not be salvaged, so the owners declared a constructive total loss and gave the underwriters notice of abandonment.*

*See also* **underwriter.**

**ABC agreement**  In a US brokerage company, an agreement with an employee detailing the rights of the company if it buys a membership of the New York Stock Exchange on his or her behalf.

**ABC code**  *See commercial code*

**ABI**  Abbreviation of *Association of British Insurers.*

**ability-to-pay taxation**  Theory of taxation whereby those who are able to pay more are taxed at a higher rate. Ability-to-pay taxation may be applied to luxury goods, which therefore attract a high rate of tax.

**above par**  Normally used of a share that has a market value above denomination or *par value.*

*The shares of G & B Electronics were traded above par for the first time today.*

**above the market**  Describing a price that is higher than the usual market price.

**absolute advantage**  Argument in favour of international trade, put forward by Adam Smith (1723-90). Absolute advantage applies where, for example, two countries can both produce two commodities they need, but country A is more efficient at producing commodity X and country B is more efficient at producing commodity Y, so they would both profit by concentrating on the particular commodity each produces best and trading them.

**absolute bill of sale**  *Bill of sale* by which goods are transferred to the possession of another.

**absolute efficiency**  Efficiency that depends on discovering and putting into effect the most effective possible combination, distribution, allocation or utilization of limited resources.

**absolute liability**  Principle that whomever causes loss or damage is legally liable in all cases (whether or not negligence or wrongdoing occurred).

**absolute monopoly**  Total monopoly, occurring where there is only one manufacturer of a product or supplier of a service and therefore no competition for the commodity or service in question.

**absorbed account**  Account that has been consolidated with other similar accounts and so ceases to exist.

**absorbed business**  Company that is merged with or taken over by another company and so ceases to exist.

**absorbed cost**  Production cost that is taken into general expenses and not charged to the customer.

**abusive shelter**  Investment instrument that gives little in the way of return but allows the investor to reduce income tax liabilities.

**a/c**  Abbreviation of *account*.

**ACA**  Abbreviation of Associate of the Institute of Chartered Accountants.

**acc**  Abbreviation of *account*.

**ACCA**  Abbreviation of Associate of the Chartered Association of Certified Accountants.

**accelerated accrual**  Pension benefits built up at a faster rate than 60ths. For post-1989 pension schemes, the Inland Revenue permits benefits to accrue at a rate of $^{1}/_{30}$ of final remuneration for each year of service.

**accelerated depreciation**  In accounting, practice of depreciating an *asset* at a rate greater than the actual decline in its value in order to gain *tax concessions*. Accelerated depreciation need not occur throughout the life of an asset; a substantial proportion of its total value is often written off in the first year, and reduced allowances for depreciation are made thereafter.

**acceleration** Increase in the rate of a price trend, or provision for the early repayment of the amount due in a *swap* agreement.

**accelerator principle** Theory that growth in production is directly related to the level of investment.

**acceptance** Broadly, the act of agreeing to do something. In business and finance it can be taken in various ways:

1. Acceptance is one of the two stages in negotiating a *contract: offer* and acceptance. A contract is complete only when the offer has been formally accepted by the *acceptor*.
2. It is the act of writing on a *bill of exchange*, by which the acceptor accepts the bill and agrees to pay the *drawer*.
3. It is used to denote a bill that has been endorsed in the above way and has thereby been accepted.

**acceptance by intervention** *See acceptance for honour.*

**acceptance for honour** Situation that occurs when a *bill of exchange* is turned down (or protested) and is then accepted by another party, thereby saving the honour of the *drawer*. It is also termed acceptance supra protest or acceptance by intervention.

**acceptance market** Part of the *money market* that deals in accepted *bills of exchange*.

**accepting** (US **acceptance**) **house** Financial institution whose business is concerned mainly with the negotiation of *bills of exchange*, by either guaranteeing or accepting them.

**Accepting Houses Committee** Committee that represents the London *accepting houses*. Its members get preferential terms on bills sold to the Bank of England.

**accepting office** Insurance company that accepts a policy for reinsurance from another company. It may itself share part of the *risk* with yet a third insurance company.

**acceptor** Person who accepts either the terms of a *contract*, or a *bill of*

*exchange.* When a bill of exchange is accepted, the *drawee* becomes the acceptor.

**accident, sickness and unemployment insurance** (ASU insurance) *See loan protection insurance.*

**accident year** In insurance, the accounting year (or calendar year) in which an accident has occurred.

**accidental death benefit** Insurance policy that pays out in the event of accidental loss of life. It is often an additional feature of another financial package, and usually requires no medical examination of the insured.

**ACII** Abbreviation of Associate of the *Chartered Insurance Institute.*

**accommodation** Money that is lent to someone for a brief period.

**accommodation bill** *Bill of exchange* signed by one person in order to help another to raise a loan. The signatory (or accommodation party) is acting as guarantor, and normally does not expect to pay the bill when it falls due. Accommodation bills are also known as kites, windbills or windmills.

**accord and satisfaction** When one party has discharged its obligations under a *contract*, it may elect to release the other party from its obligations. When this is done in return for a new *consideration*, the release is known as accord and satisfaction.

**account** Very generally, a note kept of any financial transaction. It is abbreviated to a/c, acc or acct. The term has three broad meanings:

1. It is used in banking to designate an arrangement made to deposit money with a bank, building society or a number of other financial institutions. An account may be of many differing types, usually indicated by a qualifying word, depending on the conditions of withdrawal, level of interest, minimum amount of money in the account, or other factors.

2. On the London Stock Exchange, before 1996, it was a period of two weeks in which trading was carried out. This method of working meant that transactions were made with deferred payment, enabling *speculation* to take place. The account system was abandoned in 1996.

3. It is a record of financial transactions, and in this sense, often termed *accounts.* It can be in written form (*e.g.* in a ledger) or held on computer.

*He spent three days preparing his accounts for the Inland Revenue.*

**accountancy** Body of knowledge relating to financial matters. Also the work done by an *accountant*, involving knowledge of the law as it affects financial matters (*e.g.* the *tax* laws), *book-keeping*, and the preparation of *annual accounts*.

**accountant** Any person practising accountancy, whether qualified or not. The term may be prefixed with various other terms, denoting the specialism of the accountant (*e.g.* *cost accountant, management accountant*), that accountant's position within a business (*e.g.* *chief accountant*), or his or her professional qualifications (*e.g.* *certified accountant, certified public accountant, chartered accountant*).

**account day** Formerly the Monday ten days or six business days after the end of each stock exchange *account*, on which all settlements must be made. It was also known as settlement date or day. The account system used by the London Stock Exchange was abandoned in 1996.

**account executive** In the UK, most commonly used for a person in advertising responsible for service to one client. In the USA, it is an alternative term for *stockbroker*.

**accounting** Very broadly, the activity of recording and verifying all monies borrowed, owed, paid or received.

**accounting concepts** Basic concepts by which sets of accounts are made up. The four generally accepted accounting concepts are the *accruals concept, consistency concept*, going concern concept and *prudence concept*.

**accounting cost** Total expenditure required to undertake an activity. *See also economic cost.*

**accounting equation** Principle that the capital plus the liabilities equal the total resources of a company.

**accounting period** Time for which accounts are prepared, such as a year for a company's financial accounts or a month for internal management accounts.

**accounting principles** Another term for *accounting concepts.*

**accounting ratio** One of several ratios that are considered important in assessing the financial viability of a project or company.

**accounting standards** Standards by which *annual accounts* are made up, set by professional bodies such as the *Accounting Standards Board* (ASB) in the UK.

**Accounting Standards Board** (ASB) Organization established in the UK in 1990 to set up and improve standards in the world of accountancy

**accounts payable** Accounts on which a company owes money (for which it has been invoiced), also termed trade creditors.

**accounts receivable** Accounts on which money is owed to a company (for which it has issued invoices), also called trade debtors.

**account stated** Account consisting of items that both parties concerned have agreed as being correct; any balance is thereby also agreed.

**accredited** Describes someone who is authorized to act on behalf of a company or individual.

**accrual** Gradual increase by addition over a period of time. *See also accrued benefits.*

**accrual rate** Method of calculating an employee's retirement *pension* as a fraction of his or her final salary, *e.g.,* 60ths accrual is where a person with 30 years service is entitled to $^{30}/_{60}$ (or ½) salary at retirement. *See also accelerated accrual.*

**accruals concept** Principle used in *accounting* by which *income* and *expenditure* are taken into the profit and loss account for the period in which they occur. This method of accounting is useful in that it pulls together *receipts* and the *costs* incurred in generating them, avoiding the time lag between the time *income* is received and the time *liabilities* become due. *See accounting concepts; consistency concept; profit-and-loss account; prudence concept.*

**accrued benefits** Under a company *pension* scheme, accrued benefits are those pension benefits to which a person is entitled up to a certain point in time, regardless of whether or not he or she stays in the job.

**accrued dividend** Dividend payment due to shareholders but not paid, the capital being retained by the company to fund expansion.

**acct** Abbreviation of *account.*

**accumulated depreciation** In accounting, the total value of an asset that has been written off so far. *See write off.*

**accumulation** Term with two meanings:

1. Something that is allowed to increase in value, such as retained profit that accumulates if a company's dividend payments are always less than the total profit made.

2. In insurance, many losses that occur during one event due to a concentration of risks in the particular area.

**accumulation units** In unit trusts or life assurance, an accumulation unit is one for which the dividend is ploughed back into the investment to produce higher earnings.

**accumulator funds** Offshore funds on which interest and other payments accumulate (no dividends are paid). *Capital gains tax* and *income tax* are payable on the "profit" when the funds are disposed of.

**acid-test ratio** Ratio of a company's assets (not including stock) to its current liabilities. It is also called the liquidity ratio or the quick ratio (because it gives a quick assessment of the company's financial state).

**acquisition** The takeover of control of one company by another or by an individual is known as an acquisition of the target company. The purchase of an *equity* stake in the target company is the usual method of acquisition.

**acquisition costs** Costs to an insurance company of seeking business and drawing up policies.

**acquisition trail** Course embarked upon when a company becomes *acquisitive*.

*A & C Electronics reported improving finances after its takeover of BD Small Electronics, indicating a possible return to the acquisition trail.*

*See also **takeover**.*

**acquisitive** Describing a company that is always on the lookout to grow by taking over other companies. *See also **takeover**.*

**ACT** Abbreviation of *advance corporation tax*.

**active bond crowd** New York Stock Exchange members who do most of the trading.

**act of bankruptcy** There are three specific acts of bankruptcy: attempting to leave the country to avoid creditors; giving away property in order to defraud creditors; failing to comply with a bankruptcy notice filed by a *creditor*. By acting in any of these ways, a person may make himself or herself liable to bankruptcy charges.

**act of God** Event caused by nature that is so unpredictable as to be unavoidable, *e.g.* the timing and location of earthquakes or floods. Acts of God are normally insured against as a matter of course.

**action** Equity stake.

*The company seemed to have a great deal of potential and so she bought herself a piece of the action.*

**actionnaires** French term, referring to the holders of shares in a French public company (*société anonyme*). See **public limited company**.

**active** Busy, in action, constantly changing, as in, *e.g.*, active patner, active stock.

**active money** Money in circulation.

**active partner** Partner working for a firm. *See also* **nominal partner**; **sleeping partner**.

**actively at work** Condition imposed imposed by underwriters of **group life assurance**, whereby only those members of the scheme "actively at work" at the commencement date are allowed to join. Anyone not actively at work can join on return to work, but will be subject to underwriting.

**active stock** Shares that are frequently traded on the exchange.

**Act-only policy** Type of *motor insurance* that provides only the minimum cover required by law.

**actuals** Physical commodities that may be purchased on the commodities market and delivered immediately; also known as spot goods. *See also* **futures**.

**actual total loss** Insured item that has been lost or completely destroyed. The full insured value is payable by the insurer.

**actuarial age** Person's age at his or her nearest birthday (before or after the present date).

**actuarial analysis** Analysis carried out by an *actuary* on behalf of an insurance company.

**actuarial value** Valuation of future liabilities, used in insurance and pensions schemes, based on likely probabilities as calculated by an *actuary*.

**actuary** Person who assesses probabilities on the basis of reliable statistical information. Most often employed in insurance, an actuary works out the likelihood of an event happening, and this information determines the level of a *premium* for an insurable risk.

**added years** Method of providing additional pension benefits on top of the members' main occupational scheme benefits. This type of *additional voluntary contribution* (AVC) guarantees an additional fraction of final pensionable salary on retirement.

**additional personal allowances** For *taxation* purposes, the additional amount allowed against a married woman's *income* over and above the personal *allowance*. *See also* *tax relief*.

**additional premium** Extra *premium* charged against an insurance policy if its terms are amended after the initial premium has been paid.

**additional voluntary contribution** (AVC) Extra sum paid into an *occupational pension scheme* by an employee, to increase the size of the pension. *See also* *free-standing additional voluntary contribution*.

**address commission** In shipping, commission paid to a shipping *agent* in return for seeing that the cargo is loaded onto the vessel.

**adjudication** Act of giving judgement. Adjudication may be the act of resolving a legal problem, industrial dispute or of declaring *bankruptcy*. *See also* *adjudication order*.

**adjudication of bankruptcy** *See adjudication order*.

**adjudication order** Order of court, declaring someone bankrupt. It is also known as adjudication of bankruptcy. *See also* **bankrupt**.

**adjustable peg** System that allows exchange rates to vary between certain narrowly defined limits. *See also* *crawling peg*.

**adjustable-rate mortgage** (ARM) Mortgage whose rate of *interest* rises and falls along with interest rates in general.

**adjuster** (US **adjustor**) Person who calculates losses in insurance claims, also called a loss adjuster.

**administered price** Price set and partly controlled by the seller, and based on his or her knowledge of the costs of production and estimates of *demand* and *competition*. An administered price lies between *monopoly* and free market prices, and characterizes a state of imperfect competition. *See also* *free market*.

**administration** Broadly, the sum of actions involved in the organization or management of a company. *See administration expenses*.

In law, however, administration is either the winding-up of the estate of a deceased person in the absence of an executor or in the event of intestacy, or it is the winding-up of a company. Both cases involve the court appointment of someone to act as *administrator*.

**administration expenses** One of the general expenses. In company accounting, this is a blanket term covering expenses incurred in the overall management of a company, but not positively attributable to any particular department or operating arm.

**administration order** County Court order requiring the administration of the estate of a debtor, who usually has to pay the debts by instalments in order to avoid bankruptcy.

**administrative receiver** Person appointed by the court to manage a company's assets on behalf of debenture holders or other secured creditors.

**administrator** Term with two meanings:

1. Person appointed (usually by the court) to manage someone else's property.

2. Person appointed by the court to manage the affairs of someone who has died without making a will (intestate). Proof of his or her authority is a letter of administration issued by the court.

**ad referendum** When referring to a contract, ad referendum indicates that while the contract has been agreed and signed, there are still some matters to be discussed.

**ad valorem** In *taxation*, ad valorem (literally according to the value) indicates that tax is calculated as a percentage of the value of the transaction, rather than charged at a fixed rate, *e.g.* value-added tax is paid as a percentage of the goods or services sold and is therefore "ad valorem", whereas car road tax in the UK is paid at a fixed rate. *See value-added tax.*

**ad valorem duty** Duty charged as a percentage of the total value of the goods or services being taxed. Value added tax is a form of ad valorem duty. *See value-added tax.*

**advance** Part-payment for work contracted made ahead of total payment, before the goods or services contracted for have been rendered. Sometimes, if payment depends on sales, the advance is set against those sales. It is used for annuities as the regular income payment is made, *e.g.* "yearly in arrears", *i.e.* at the start of the year.

**advance corporation tax** (ACT) Corporation tax is often levied in two parts. The first part is levied on the distribution of profits and is known as advance corporation tax. The second half of the tax is estimated on the company's earnings. *See corporation tax.*

**advance documentation** One of two sets of documents sent to a potential borrower by a loan provider. After a *cooling-off period* of seven days, a second similar set, called original documentation, must be sent.

**adverse** Bad or, at the very least, unhelpful.

**adverse balance** In general, an account balance that shows a *loss* or *liability*. More especially, it is short for adverse *balance of trade*.

**adverse selection** Concept of disproportionate *risk*: those who are more prone to suffer loss or to make claims than the average risk.

**advice note** Notice from a supplier giving details of goods ordered or delivered. It either accompanies or precedes the shipment, and precedes the invoice. *See also delivery note.*

**advisery board** Group of specialists who advise others.

**advisery client** Person a stockbroker gives advice to; the client then makes his or her own decisions. *See also discretionary client.*

**AE** Abbreviation of *account executive.*

**AFBD** Abbreviation of *Association of Futures Brokers and Dealers.* Previously a self-regulating organization (SRO) under the 1986 Financial Services Act, it has been replaced by the *Securities and Futures Authority* (SFA).

**affidavit** Statement or declaration made in writing and witnessed by a commissioner for oaths (such as a *solicitor*), often for use in legal proceedings.

**affreightment** Carriage of goods by sea.

**after-acquired property** Possessions obtained by a bankrupt after bankruptcy has been declared.

**after date** Written on a *bill of exchange*, after date indicates that the bill will become due a certain (specified) period after the date on the bill. Hence, the bill might read, "60 days after date, we promise to pay…" *See also after sight; at sight.*

**after hours dealing** Alternative term for *early bargain.* This is a transaction made on the London Stock Exchange after its official close. Such a deal is treated as part of the next day's trading.

**aftermarket** Trading in *stocks* and *shares* after they have made their initial debut on the *market*. The aftermarket may also be the market in components and services arising after a product has been sold. This is also known as the add-on market.

*The flourishing computer aftermarket is created by enthusiasts who soup up old models in preference to buying new ones.*

**after-sales service** Acts performed by a manufacturer or supplier after the goods or service has been sold. After-sales service packages are frequently put together as inducements to buy.

**after sight** Written on a *bill of exchange*, term that indicates that the period for which the bill is drawn is to be calculated from the date on which the *acceptor* first saw (or accepted) it. This date is normally written on the bill by the acceptor. *See also* **after date**; **at sight**.

**after-tax profit** Profit calculated after all tax deductions have been made.

**AG** Abbreviation of the German *Aktiengesellschaf*.

**against all risks** (AAR) In marine insurance, term indicating that a vessel and its cargo have been insured against all possible insurable eventualities. It is roughly equivalent to *comprehensive insurance* of motor vehicles.

**age admitted** In a *life assurance* policy, a term that indicates that the assurer has seen a birth certificate or other evidence of the age of the assured. No further proof of age is needed in the event of a claim.

**age allowance** Tax allowance available to a person over the age of 65 or a married couple where one partner is over that age.

**agency** Term with two meanings:

1. It is a person or *company* that represents another in a particular field.

2. It is a contractual *agreement*, by which one party agrees to represent another, the agent's word becoming as binding in the affairs of the other as if the latter had acted on his or her own behalf.

**agency bill** *Bill of exchange* that is accepted by the London branch of a foreign bank.

**agency fee** Fee paid each year to an *agent*. It is also termed a facility fee.

**agency of necessity** Situation that arises when an *agent* acts to safeguard the principal's interests, without the principal's permission. This situation can only arise when (a) the principal cannot be reached, (b) there is a *contract* of agency already in existence between the two parties and, (c) immediate action is absolutely necessary. If these conditions exist, then the agent's actions are legally binding on the principal.

**agenda** List of matters to be discussed at a meeting. An agenda can constitute a legal document.

**age not admitted** In a *life assurance* policy, a term which indicates that proof of the age of the assured has not been seen by the assurer at outset. Proof will therefore be requested at claim stage.

**agent** Person or company that has entered into a contract of *agency* with another party, and acts as its representative, usually in buying and selling goods or services.

**agent de change** Stockbroker in France, particularly on the Bourse in Paris.

**aggregate** Sum total.

**aggregate deductible** In reinsurance, the total loss the reinsured bears on top of normal retention before the reinsurer is liable.

**aggregate exposure** In insurance and reinsurance, the upper limit of claims relating to a single event (or linked events).

**aggregation** Under *excess of loss* reinsurance, the accumulation of claims which defines the amount that can be recovered.

**AGM** Abbreviation of *annual general meeting*.

**agreed additional costs** Costs in addition to indemnity which the insurer agrees to pay for in some property policies, *e.g.* architects fees, removal of debris and hotel accommodation.

**agreed-value policy** Insurance policy that states the sum to be paid out in the event of a claim. It is often used for antiques, jewellery and classic cars.

**agreement** Verbal or written contract between two or more parties to explain the way they intend to act in respect of each other.

**aids to trade** Activities (often services) that assist other businesses, such as advertising, banking, insurance and transport.

**AIM** Abbreviation of *Alternative Investment Market.*

**air bills all risk** Certificated insurance policy that covers risks pertaining to goods sent by air.

**air-pocket stock** Stock whose price suddenly falls, usually after rumours of the company's poor performance.

**AITC** Abbreviation of *Association of Investment Trust Companies.*

**Aktiengesellschaft** Equivalent of a *public limited company* (plc) in Austria, Germany or Switzerland. It is abbreviated to AG.

**alien insurer** US term for any insurance company based outside the USA.

**Allfinanz** German term for *bancassurance.*

**alligator spread** Profit made on an *option* that is instantly snapped up by the broker as commission, leaving nothing for the investor.

**allocated capacity** Proportion of *Lloyd's of London* member's premium limit allocated to *syndicates.*

**allocatur** *Certificate* of approval of *costs* incurred in an action (*e.g.* *liquidation*) for *taxation* purposes.

**allonge** Slip attached to a *bill of exchange* that provides extra space for the noting of *endorsements*. Allonges were most useful when bills of exchange moved freely from one holder to another, but now are less common.

**allotment** Broadly, the sharing out of something, usually funds, among a group of people.

**allotment of shares** When a company issues *shares* by publishing a *prospectus* and inviting applications, allotment is the assignment of shares to each applicant. In cases where the issue is oversubscribed, shares are allotted in proportion to the quantity requested and so applicants do not always receive the number of shares they originally requested. *See also* **application and allotment**; *oversubscribed.*

**allowable expenses** Expenses that are tax-deductible.

**allowance** Term with two meanings:
1. It is money that is allotted (allowed) to individuals for a specific reason, or a provision made for unusual or uncertain events.
2. It is the amount deducted for one of various reasons before *income* is calculated for *tax* purposes. Examples include personal allowance and married couple's allowance.

**all-risks policy** Insurance policy that covers personal possessions against loss or damage, usually anywhere in the country. All-risks policies are frequently extended to cover possessions in other parts of the world, and are therefore often used to insure small moveable items. Despite the term "all-risks", there are usually some important exclusions.

**ALM** Abbreviation of *Association of Lloyd's Members.*

**alphabet brokers** Colloquial US term for major insurance brokers (because of the habit of calling them by their initials).

**alpha** Stock Exchange categorization of the top 100 most actively traded shares with a large capitalization value.

**alternate director** Person who acts in place of a named director in his/her absence.

**alternative accommodation** Provision allowed for in most *household insurance* policies of the cost of somewhere else to stay if a property is rendered unhabitable (usually because of a fire).

**Alternative Investment Market** (AIM) Replacement for the Unlisted Securities Market, which closed at the end of 1996, aimed at helping smaller companies to raise capital.

**amalgamation** The coming together or unification of two or more companies. *See also* **merger**; **takeover.**

**ambulance stock** Securities recommended to a client whose investment portfolio has done badly. The practice is especially common in Japan.

**American Stock Exchange** (AMEX) New York stock exchange that deals in *stocks* and *bonds* of smaller companies.

**AMEX** Abbreviation of *American Stock Exchange.*

**amortize** To pay off a *debt* by means of payments over a period of time. More specifically, in *accounting*, the cost of a fixed *asset* is written into the profit-and-loss account over a period of years, rather than being taken into account when it is first bought. The cost of the asset has been amortized when this period is over.

*The capital cost of the packaging equipment will be amortized over 5 years.*

*See* **depreciation**; **profit-and-loss account.**

**amortizing mortgage** *Mortgage* in which all the principal and interest has been repaid, usually by equal payments, by the end of the mortgage term. Although the payments are equal, early payments are made up mostly interest, whereas later payments are mostly repayments of the principal.

**amount at risk**   On an insurance policy, the amount payable minus the amount covered by reserves. It is also the "death risk" covered by risk premium reassurance.

**analysis**   Determination of the composition or the significance of something. In business and finance, an analysis can be a detailed study or investigation of a particular subject, often culminating in a report, upon which executives may base their decisions.

**analysis-paralysis**   What happens when managers ask for more and more information, and spend their time having endless meetings and writing interminable reports, but never making any decisions.

**analyst**   Person who undertakes *analysis.*

**anchor-and-chain clause**   In marine insurance, a clause in a policy that frees the insurer from the responsibility of retrieving an anchor and chain lost in bad weather.

**ancillary credit business**   Business that does not directly provide credit but is engaged in credit brokerage, debt adjusting, debt counselling, debt collection or the operation of a credit reference agency. *See **debt collection agency**.*

**& Co**   Abbreviation of "and company".

**annual accounts**   Report submitted annually, showing the current financial state of a company and the results of its operations for that year. *See also **annual report**.*

**annual bonus**   Amount added each year to a ***with-profits policy***, also called a reversionary bonus.

**annual charges**   For *taxation* purposes, that part of a person's or company's income that has been paid after tax has been deducted, *e.g.* a *covenant* to a person is deemed by the Inland Revenue to have been paid net of tax.

**annual general meeting** (AGM)   *Shareholders'* meeting, required by law to be held yearly by every public company. An AGM is normally used to discuss the ***annual report*** and accounts, to announce ***dividends*** and to elect ***auditors*** and ***directors***. This is often the only opportunity the shareholders have to air their views. *See **public limited company**. See also **EGM**; **gadfly**.*

**annual increment** Amount by which money (often a salary) or goods increase in the course of one year.

**annual percentage rate** (APR) Also known as annualized percentage rate, the rate of *interest* charged on a monthly basis (*e.g.* on a *hire purchase* transaction) shown as a yearly *compound* rate. The true cost of borrowing including any costs and charges.

**annualized premium income** (API) Amount earned by a *life assurance* office from the sales of new policies (a measure of the office's performance).

**annual report** Document required by law to be released annually by public companies, describing the company's activities during the previous year. It usually includes the company's balance sheet for the year.

**annual return** Document that in the UK must be submitted to Companies House each year by every company with share capital, detailing such items as the address of the registered office, a list of current members, charges on the company, etc.

**annual value** Income that accrues annually from the possession of, say, property or a portfolio of shares. A distinction is normally made between net annual value and gross annual value, the former being the annual income from a possession after expenses of ownership have been deducted, and the latter being the income before expenses have been taken into account.

**annuitant** Person receiving an *annuity*.

**annuity** Contract whereby a person pays a certain amount of money to an insurance company, either as a lump sum or in instalments, and receives periodic payments in return for life or a specified period. *See also annuity certain; pension; purchased life annuity.*

**annuity certain** *Annuity* that is payable over an agreed period, such as 10 or 15 years, irrespective of life or death of the *annuitant*.

**annul** To make void in law, to cancel.

*The contract was annulled by the courts.*

**antedate** To put on a document, *e.g.* an *invoice*, a date which is already past.

*The invoice was antedated to 1 December last year.*

*See also postdate.*

**anti-trust laws** Legislation in the USA enacted to prevent the formation of *monopolies*. It is similar to the Monopolies and Mergers Act in the UK.

**AOB** Abbreviation of any other business. AOB normally appears at the end of an agenda and provides an opportunity for discussion of any matters not already dealt with or arising too late for inclusion on the formal agenda.

**APCIMS** Abbreviation of *Association of Private Client Investment Managers and Stockbrokers.*

**API** Abbreviation of *annualized premium income.*

**APP** Abbreviation of *appropriate personal pension.*

**application and allotment** System whereby a company may issue *shares*. This is done by publishing a *prospectus*, inviting applications from institutions and individuals to buy shares, and then allotting shares to those who take up the offer. *See also* **allotment; stag.**

**apportion** To share out. The term is normally applied to *costs*.

*They decided to apportion start-up costs equally between the members of the co-venture.*

**appreciation** Increase in value. In *accounting*, appreciation is an increase in value of (fixed) *assets*.

*Over the years the company directors were pleased to see their office block appreciate.*

*See also* **depreciation**

**appropriate personal pension** (APP) *Pension* plan whereby the planholder can *contract out* of the *State Earnings-Related Pension Scheme* (SERPS). Full *National Insurance contributions* are still paid by both the employer and employee, and a rebate is paid by the Department of Social Security directly into the plan.

**appropriation** Practice of putting aside (funds) for a special reason.

*They decided to appropriate funds from the production budget to set up a marketing department.*

There are three specialist meanings of the term:

1. In company accounting, it is the division of pre-tax *profits* between corporation *tax*, company *reserves* and *dividends* to shareholders. The term works in the same sense in a *partnership* situation.

2. In the shipping of produce, the appropriation is the document by which the seller identifies to the buyer the relevant unit in the shipment.

3. If a *debtor* makes a payment to a *creditor* and does not specify which debt the payment is in settlement of, the creditor may appropriate it to any of the debts outstanding on the debtor's account. This is often known as appropriation of payments.

*See also appropriation account.*

**appropriation account**   Account that shows net profits (current and carried forward) and how they are split between dividends and reserves.

**APR**   Abbreviation of *annual percentage rate.*

**arb**   Shortened form of *arbitrage.*

**arbitrage**   Practice of dealing on two markets almost simultaneously in order to profit from differing *exchange rates.* Arbitrage may take place when dealing in *commodities, bills of exchange* or currencies. It also occurs in situations where prices and returns are fixed and in this sense arbitrage may be contrasted with *speculation* in that there is little risk involved. In the USA, often shortened to arb. *See also reverse arbitrage; soft arbitrage.*

**arbitrager** (or **arbitrageur**)   Person who practises *arbitrage.*

**arbitration**   In disputes arising out of a *contract*, the parties involved may either go to court or appoint someone (an arbitrator) to settle the dispute. The agreement to go to arbitration does not preclude either of the parties taking legal proceedings if it desires. *See also umpirage.*

**ARBs**   Abbreviation of *arbitragers.*

**arrangement**   Generally, the settlement of any financial matter. More specifically, a deed of arrangement is an agreement between a *debtor* and some or all of his *creditors*, reached in order to avoid the debtor's *bankruptcy.* Arrangement may be encountered in various forms: as a letter of licence, deed of inspectorship, *assignment* of property or a deed of composition. It may take place either before or after a bankruptcy petition has been presented to the courts.

**arrears**   Money owed but not yet paid. Annuities can be paid in arrears, *e.g.* "yearly in arrears" means the first annuity payment is made in one year's time.

*See also advance.*

**arrestment** Scottish term for *attachment*.

**articled clerk** Kind of apprentice, generally working in one of the professions, such as law or accounting.

**articles of association** *See memorandum of association.*

**ASB** Abbreviation of *Accounting Standards Board*.

**A-shares** Shares with rights different from those legally attached to *ordinary shares*. There are also B-shares, C-shares, etc. The term is frequently used to describe *non-voting shares*.

**as origin** In reinsurance, describing a reinsurance policy whose terms are the same as the original insurance policy.

**as per advice** Term normally found as a note on a *bill of exchange*, indicating that the *drawee* has already been notified that the bill has been drawn on him.

**assay** Testing of a metal or ore to determine the proportion of precious metal it contains. Assay most often applies to metals used in coinage, and to gold and silver. Metals assayed are stamped with a hallmark and an assay mark.

**assay master** Official who is responsible for the testing and grading of metals in the above way.

**ASSC** Abbreviation of Accounting Standards Steering Committee. *See accounting standards.*

**assented** In a situation where a company is threatened with a *takeover*, assented *stocks* or *shares* are those whose owner is in agreement with the takeover. In these circumstances, there may arise separate markets in assented and non-assented stock. Assented stock may also be stock whose owner is in agreement with a proposed change in the conditions of issue.

**assessment** Act of calculating *value*.

*I am waiting for my Income Tax assessment..*

**asset** Something which belongs to an individual or company and which has a *value*, e.g. buildings, plant, stock, but also *accounts receivable*.

There are several types of assets for business purposes, and they are usually classified in terms of their availability for *exchange*.

**asset-backed** Term that refers to investments which are related to tangible assets, *e.g.* property, so that the investment participates in **growth** which can easily be determined. *See* **tangible assets**.

**asset-based financing** Loans secured on a company's assets, especially its accounts receivable or its stock.

**asset management** Broadly, the efficient control and exploitation of a firm's assets, most commonly used to describe the management of any *fund* by a fund manager.

**assets-to-equity ratio** Value of assets owned by a company compared to the value of investment.

**asset stripping** Practice, normally frowned upon, whereby a company is bought so that the buyer may simply sell off its assets for immediate gain.

**asset value** Value of the assets of a company.

**asset value per share** Value of the assets of a company, minus its liabilities, divided by the number of shares.

**assignee** Person or company to whom rights in an asset (such as a *life assurance* policy) are assigned. *See* **assignment**; **assignor**.

**assignment** Legal transfer of a property, right or obligation from one party to another. Life assurance policies can be assigned.

**assignor** Person who assigns a *life assurance* policy (perhaps as security for a loan) to a third party, the assignee.

**associate** Term prefixed adjectivally to indicate a company or individual linked in some way to another, as in, *e.g.*, associate company.

**associate company** Company that is partly owned by another.

**associate director** Director who is a member of the *board* but lacks full voting powers. The position is normally held by able but comparatively junior managers; it rewards their enthusiasm and reinforces their commitment without giving them real power.

**associated operation** Operation that is somehow linked to another within a company. Associated operations within a company may, *e.g.*, manufacture similar products or use similar production methods.

**association** Group of people or companies with a common interest, *e.g.* a trade association is a group of companies operating in the business, who come together to provide information and services to each other. Association is also what happens when a company is formed.

**Association of British Insurers** (ABI)  Trade body that represents UK insurance companies and issues their codes of practice. It was formed in 1985 by a merger of the British Insurance Association, the Accident Offices Association, the Life Office Association and the Industrial Life Office Association.

**Association of Futures Brokers and Dealers** (AFBD)  Former *self-regulating organization* (SRO), established in 1986, which regulated the activities of brokers and dealers on the London futures market. In 1991 it became part of the *Securities and Futures Authority* (SFA).

**Association of Investment Trust Companies** (AITC)  Organization that provides information about the activities of UK investment trust companies.

**Association of Lloyd's Members** (ALM)  Voluntary organization of the *external members* of *Lloyd's of London* that represents them on the Lloyd's market.

**Association of Private Client Investment Managers and Stockborkers** (APCIMS)  Organization established in 1990 that represents the interests of private-client investment managers and stockbrokers in the UK.

**Association of Unit Trusts and Investment Funds** (AUTIF)  Trade association for UK *unit trust* companies.

**assurance**  Insurance that provides for an event that will certainly happen (such as death), as opposed to an event that may happen (*see insurance*). There are many types of assurance policy. *See endowment assurance; life assurance; term assurance; unit-linked assurance policy.*

**assured**  Person who receives the proceeds of an *assurance* policy when the policy matures or the person assured dies. *See also grantee.*

**AST**  Abbreviation of *automated screen trading.*

**at and from**  In marine insurance, description of a policy that covers the vessel and its cargo both in port and at sea.

**at best**  Instruction to a *broker* to buy or sell *shares* or *commodities* at the best possible price. *See at limit.*

**at call**  Money at call has been borrowed but must be repaid on demand. *See also at short notice.*

**at limit**  Instruction to a *broker* to buy or sell *shares* or *commodities* with a limit on the upper and lower prices.

**at par**  Equal, indicating a share price equal to the paid-up or nominal value. *See also parity; par value.*

**at short notice**  Describing money that is borrowed for a very short period of time, say twenty-four or forty-eight hours, usually at a low *interest* rate. *See also at call.*

**at sight**  Note on a *bill of exchange* indicating that the payment is due on presentation of the bill. *See also after sight.*

**attachment**  Act of court whereby the court is able to recover money owed by a debtor in order that the creditor may in turn pay the court. *Arrestment* is the equivalent of attachment in Scottish law.

**at-the-money-option**  Call or put option where the price of the security on the market is the same as the *exercise price.*

**attorney**  In the UK, someone who is legally authorized to act for another, or a person practising at the bar. In the USA, however, the term is more often used to denote a *lawyer.*

**attractive stock**  Ordinary shares that promise a good return.

**attritional loss**  In reinsurance, a small loss that is usually retained by an insurer and not passed on to the reinsurer.

**at warehouse**  *Goods* or *commodities* that are waiting at a warehouse either to be bought or delivered to a customer. A price at warehouse (or ex-warehouse) does not normally include freight charges. *See also futures; spot goods.*

**auction**  Method of selling goods in public. The auctioneer acts as an agent for the seller, offers the goods and normally sells to the highest bidder (for which service the auctioneer charges a *commission).*

**audit**  Examination of the *accounts* of a company. It is a legal requirement in the UK that the accounts of all companies over a certain size (in terms of annual turnover) be scrutinized annually by a qualified *auditor.*

**auditor**  Person appointed by a company or other organization to perform an *audit.*

**audit trail**  System whereby each stage of a transaction is formally re-corded.

**authenticate**  To state that something is true, *e.g.* an *auditor* signs a company's *accounts*, thereby authenticating them.

**authority**  Broadly, authority is the given power to act in a certain way. Hence, an *agent* receives authority to act in such a way on behalf of his or her principal, or a banker receives an authority from a client to operate the account in a certain way.

**authorized capital**  Amount of capital a company is authorized to raise through the issue of shares, as set down in the company's articles of association.

**authorized clerk**  Employee of a *stockbroker*, who is authorized to make transactions on his or her behalf.

**authorized insurer**  Organization legally authorized in the UK to run an insurance business under the 1982 Insurance Companies Act.

**AUTIF**  Abbreviation of *Association of Unit Trusts and Investment Funds.*

**automated screen trading** (AST)  System that uses computers to display prices and deal in securities (in real time).

**automatic debit transfer**  Service provided in the UK by Girobank that, for a small charge, allows a business to collect regular sums of money from a large number of customers.

**automatic sum insured**  Method of quickly determining the cover (sum insured) to be provided by a *household contents insurance* based on the type of property and the number of bedrooms.

**AVC**  Abbreviation of *additional voluntary contribution.*

**average**  Term with two meanings:
1. In general, it is a single number or value that indicates the general tendency of a collection of numbers or value. The average of *n* values is the sum of the values divided by *n*. It is also called the mean.
2. In insurance, it is a method used to apportion losses in case of underinsurance. A property policy may include an average clause which reduces the claim payment by the percentage that the insured value relates to its actual value. *See* **general average**.

**average adjuster**  Person who calculates the loss: how much money is to be paid on an insurance claim.

**average available earnings**  *Profit* available for distribution to shareholders.

**average clause**  In marine and commercial insurance and some fire insurance policies, a clause in the policy that stipulates certain items shall be subject to *average* if there is underinsurance.

**average cost pricing**  Determination of a price in accordance with the average cost of producing a good. The manufacturer makes neither a profit nor a loss.

**average due date**  If the due date falls within a range of days, the average due date is the mid-point of that range. *See* *due date*.

**average price**  Alternative term for *target price*.

**average revenue**  Total amount of money received divided by the number of units of a product sold.

**aviation insurance**  Insurance of aircraft (aeroplanes, gliders, helicopters) or their cargoes, usually with cover for own damage and third party claims. All risks cover is also available.

**axe**  Used as a verb, the term means to stop abruptly or to cut back (normally for financial reasons).

*The R & D department was the first to be axed when the company found it was in financial trouble.*

# B

**baby bonds** Bonds offered by registered *friendly societies* to minors. The funds are tax-exempt.

**back** Term with two meanings:

1. It is used adjectivally to refer to the past.
2. To back is to lend money to a project to enable it to start or continue operating.

*He finally found a bank to back his idea. It is lending him £50,000.*

**backdate** To date a document with a date previous to that on which it was actually signed. Back dating indicates that the provisions of the document became effective on the back date rather than the date on which the document was signed.

**back duty** Also known as back tax, a retrospective tax levied on profits or goods on which no tax was paid at the time.

**backer** Person or institution that backs projects or operations.

*She found it relatively easy to find a backer for such an interesting business proposition.*

**back-in** *Poison pill* tactic sometimes used by the shareholders of a company threatened by *takeover*, whereby the shareholders sell their holdings back to the company at a price agreed by the board.

**backing away** Failure of a securities dealer to carry through a deal at the price he or she has quoted. Backing away is usually frowned upon in all markets.

**back month** On financial *futures* markets, those contracts that are being traded for the month that is furthest in the future.

**backroom** Informal name given to the department in a stockbroking firm that deals in matters other than the buying or selling of shares, *e.g.* share *dividends*, shareholder registrations, and payment.

**backroom backlog** Delay in processing stockbroking transactions, caused by a large volume of business.

*A huge backroom backlog followed the deregulation of the London market.*

**back tax** Also known as back duty, payment of tax on income that was not paid at the time it was earned or first claimed. *See also tax evasion.*

**back-to-back** Term with two meanings.

1. Form of *credit* by which a finance house acts as an intermediary between a foreign seller and a foreign buyer, concealing the identity of the seller. The seller passes to the finance house the documents relevant to the sale.

2. In insurance, a back-to-back policy is a combination of a temporary annuity and an endowment or whole life plan.

**back-to-back loan** Type of *loan* between companies in different countries (and perhaps in different currencies) employing a bank or finance house which uses funding from a third party to provide the loan.

**back-to-back policy** A combination of two *life assurance* policies which are packaged together to form one investment plan. Commonly, the policies are a temporary annuity and an endowment of whole life.

**backwardation** Two meanings are possible:

1. In a commodity market, it is the situation in which the future price is lower than the spot price, because of excessive present demand, which is expected to fall as time passes. Opposite, in commodity terms, to *contango*.

2. In stock markets, the situation in which the highest bid price is higher than the lowest offer price, making it theoretically possible to buy from one market maker and sell to another immediately, at a profit. *See also choice price; touch.*

**backward integration** Amalgamation of a company that operates at one stage of production with another that is located farther back in the chain, *e.g.* a manufacturing company amalgamates with a company that provides raw materials.

**bad debt** Debt which has not been, and is not expected to be, paid. Such losses are practically unavoidable in business (and allowances are almost always made for such instances), although some bad debts may be sold to a *factoring* company which attempts to recover the debt on its own account.

**bad paper** *Bill of exchange* that is never likely to be honoured.

**bagging the Street** Concealment of information about the sale of *stock* from dealers and specialists by institutional investors or *brokers*. Such information may include reasons why the stock is being sold off, and the number and price of the shares in question.

**bail bond** Extension to *motor insurance*, taken out in the UK, that can be used to pay the bail of a UK motorist taken into custody in Spain (which frequently happens in cases of injury to a third party in an accident).

**bailee** Person to whom goods are entrusted for safe keeping. *See* **bailment**.

**bailment** Act of placing goods into the care (but not possession) of someone else. The person who places the goods is the bailor and must be the rightful owner. The bailee is the person who receives the goods.

**bailor** Person who leaves goods with somebody (the bailee) for safe keeping. *See* **bailment**.

**bailout** Government intervention in the affairs of a public company to prevent it going bankrupt, providing loans at low interest, or tax concessions. Bailout also means the withdrawal of capital from a public company by its founders before the public has a chance to do so.

**bail out** To go to the rescue of a company that is experiencing financial difficulties by providing it with *capital*.

**balance** Quite apart from its general applications, the term is used, primarily in double-entry book-keeping, to refer to the sum owed or owing when an *account* has been reckoned. Hence, the phrase to balance the books means to add in this sum to the relevant side of the account so that both columns show the same total.

**balance of payments** Account of all recorded financial exchanges made between the residents of a country and those of other countries. The balance of payments is divided into current and capital accounts. The current account takes stock of all invisible and visible trade (the *balance of trade* is part of the balance of payments current account), and the capital account includes all movements of *capital* in or out of the country.

**balance of trade** Also known as the visible balance, the difference between the value of a country's *visible imports* and *visible exports*. When the value of visible imports totals more than the value of visible exports, it is known as an adverse balance of trade. *See* **balance of payments**.

**balance sheet** Statement that shows the financial position of a company in respect of its assets and liabilities at a certain time.

**balance ticket** Alternative term for *certification of transfer*.

**balloon** Large irregular part-payment of a loan, made when funds are available. Such an arrangement is termed a balloon loan.

**balloon mortgage** Mortgage in which a lump sum has to be paid at the end of the mortgage period to pay off outstanding principal and interest. It is also called a non-amortizing mortgage.

**ballot** While in general terms a ballot is a method of voting by marking a paper, it more specifically refers to a method of allotting *shares* to applicants in the event a share issue is *oversubscribed*. All applications are entered for the ballot and those drawn at random receive some or all of the shares applied for. *See application and allotment.*

**bancassurance** Involvement of banks in the traditional insurance market.

**band earnings** Earnings between the lower earnings limit and the upper earnings limit for National Insurance purposes, also called middle-band earnings. Benefits under the State Earnings-Related Pension Scheme (SERPS) are based on band earnings.

**bank rate** Official rate of interest charged by a central bank (such as the Bank of England) to other banks in the system. The term has fallen out of use in the UK and is now commonly known as the *base rate*.

**bankrupt** Person who is unable to pay his or her debts, as determined by the court.

**bankruptcy** State of being unable to pay debts, as determined by the court.

**bankruptcy debt** Debt owed by a bankrupt at the beginning of bankruptcy or for which he or she becomes liable after the beginning of bankruptcy because of an obligation that pre-dates it.

**bankruptcy level** Amount of money owed for which a person can be made bankrupt as specified in a statutory instrument by the Secretary of State.

**bankruptcy order** Order of the court adjudging someone bankrupt.

**bankruptcy petition** Application to the court to be declared bankrupt or to have someone else declared bankrupt.

**bar** Term with three meanings:

1. It is the profession of a barrister.

*In 1976 she was called to the bar.*

2. It is an obstacle that prevents something happening.

*His inadequate knowledge of accounting acted as a bar to his career progress.*

3. It is an informal term meaning one million.

**bar code**  Code printed onto goods in the form of black bars of different widths on a white background. The bar code is capable of being read and deciphered by computer. Most commonly used at checkout points in retailing, the system is capable of reading price and product details, of charging the customer and updating stock records.

**bargain**  In Stock Exchange jargon, any deal struck involving the buying and selling of *shares*.

**bargaining**  Act of negotiating a price or other terms.

**bargaining theory**  Theory whereby wage levels are seen as the result of talks between management and the labour-force rather than of supply and demand in the labour market.

**barrier**  Obstacle that prevents entry or makes it difficult.

**barrier to entry**  Set of economic and other conditions that make it difficult to set up a business, *i.e.* to enter the market.

**base**  Lowest or starting point from which calculations are made, especially calculations of relative stock price movements.

**base date**  Alternative term for *base year*.

**base period**  Time period selected as the base for an *index* number series. The index for a base period is usually 100, and changes in prior or subsequent periods are expressed relative to it.

**base rate**  Term with two meanings:
1. It is the minimum amount of interest a bank charges on a loan. The base rate is normally augmented in actual circumstances, according to current market pressures and the risk involved in the loan.
2. Another term for the rate at which the Bank of England lends to discount houses and other banks in the system.

**base stock (method)**  Method of stock valuation whereby stock levels are assumed to be constant and the goods are valued at their original cost.

**base year**  Sometimes also known as the *base date*, the time from which an index (*e.g.* the Financial Times All Share Index) is calculated. *See also index*.

**basic rate of income tax** Rate of income tax between lower and higher rates. In 1998/99 it was 23% in the UK.

**basic state pension** Flat-rate pension paid by the the Government to people who reach State Pension age and have paid sufficient National Insurance contributions (NICs).

**basic sum assured** For a *life assurance* policy, the minimum sum payable on death or survival beyond a specified date.

**basis** Value of an *asset* for *tax* purposes.

**basis point** Unit used to measure the rate of change of investment payments for bonds or notes. Each basis point is equal to 0.01 per cent.

**bear** Stock Exchange dealer or analyst who believes that prices or investment values will go down.

**bear closing** Situation that occurs when a dealer has sold shares or commodities he does not yet own and then buys them back, at a lower price, thus making a profit.

**bearer bill** Bill of exchange, cheque or other negotiable instrument that is payable to the bearer (or has no payee named).

**bearer bond** Bond payable to the bearer rather than to a specific, named individual. *See also registered bond.*

**bearer note** Another name for a *bearer bill*.

**bearer securities** Securities that are payable to the bearer and thus easily transferable.

**bearer scrip** Temporary document acknowledging acceptance of an offer form and cheque for a new issue, exchanged for a bearer bond when the bond is available (or when all instalments have been paid).

**bearer stocks** Like bearer bonds, securities that are payable to the bearer, not to a named holder.

**bear hug** In corporate finance, an informal term for notice given to the board of a *target* company that a *takeover* bid is imminent.

**bearish** Someone or something (*e.g.* a market) with the qualities of a *bear*.
*Some market analysts believe that reaction to this week's money-supply figures will not be so bearish after all.*

**bear market** Condition in which share prices are falling. *Bears* are speculators who sell shares in anticipation of falling prices.

**bear position** Position of an investor whose sales exceed his or her purchases, and who therefore stands to gain in a falling or bear market. *See bear.*

**bear raid** Vigorous selling in concert in order to force down the price of a particular commodity or share. *See also concert party.*

*After the 1929 crash, massive bear raids on stocks were recognized as an activity that must be stopped.*

**bear slide** What happens when stock and share prices move towards a bear market situation.

**bear squeeze** Situation in which bears who have been *short selling* are faced with a price rise rather than a fall.

**bed-and-breakfast deal** Transaction formerly used to minimize the impact of *capital gains tax*. A *shareholder* sold his or her holding at a *loss* after trading closed for the day, and registered the loss for tax purposes. Next morning, the shareholder bought his or her holding back. The tax advantages of bed-and-breakfasting in the UK were withdrawn from March 1998. The US term for a bed-and-breakfast deal is swap.

**bed and PEP** Transaction used to buy shares in a PEP. A shareholder sells his or her holding after trading closes for the day and buys it back next morning with a *personal equity plan* (PEP).

**bells and whistles** Extras added to a financial product to make it more attractive. *Options* are a typical incentive.

**below par** Share price that has fallen below the nominal value at which the share was issued.

**below-the-line accounts** Those items included in company accounts that refer to the distribution of profits. Details of e.g. *dividends* would thus be included in below-the-line accounts.

**below-the-line expenditure** Alternative term for *capital expenditure,* because such expenditure is listed below the line recording the total in a statement of account and is regarded as an additional cost.

**below the market** Describing a price that is lower than the usual market price.

**benchmark** Point on an *index* that has a significance and is used as a reference point.

**B**

**beneficial interest** Possession or involvement that gives a person the right to take some form of benefit (*e.g.* profit or use) from a property.

**beneficial owner** Term with two meanings:

1. When a shareholding is held by a *nominee* such as a stockbroker, the nominee's name appears on the register of shareholders. The real owner is known as the beneficial owner. *See nominee shareholder.*

2. The owner of the beneficial interest in a property. It may not be the legal owner, but he or she has a right in the benefits.

**beneficiary** Person who gains money or property from something; *e.g.* from a financial transaction such as a life assurance policy, a will or a trust.
*She was surprised to find herself the principal beneficiary of the will.*

**benefit** Term with two possible meanings:

1. It is a payment made under an *insurance* or social security scheme.

2. It is a payment to a worker, either in kind or in cash, apart from his or her wages.

**benefit policies** Insurance policies that provide a specified level of benefit as opposed to indemnity. Examples include life assurance, permanent health insurance and personal accident and sickness insurance.

**benefits in kind** Benefits that an employee receives instead of or in addition to salary or wages. Examples include company cars, mobile telephones and medical insurance. Many of such benefits are assigned a value and assessed for income tax.

**benefit taxation** Theory of taxation by which taxes to cover public services are paid by those who use them, rather than by the general public at large.

**Benjamin method** Actuarial system that projects ultimate loss ratios by applying formulas to paid loss ratios.

**Besloten Vennootschap** (BV) Dutch equivalent of private *limited company* (Ltd).

**best advice** Term reflecting the fact that legally a financial adviser must recommend a suitable product to meet a client's needs. An Independent Financial Adviser must offer best advice from all of the financial products available in the marketplace. A *tied agent* must offer best advice from the range of products on offer by his or her company.

**best execution rule** Requirement that a stockbroker must obtain the best available price when buying or selling securities on behalf of a client.

**best price**  Order to buy or sell something at the best price available at the time.

**beta factor** (or **coefficient**)  Measurement of the volatility of a company's shares, *i.e.* how sensitive the stock is to market fluctuations. The beta is denoted in figures, *e.g.* 1.5, which means that this share will rise 15% in a market that has risen 10%. Shares that under-perform the market are rated below 1.

**beta shares** (US **stocks**)  Second-line shares, as opposed to the less numerous highly-capitalized alpha (first-line) or more numerous gamma (third-line).

**betterment**  In insurance, an improvement made to the standard of insured property when it is repaired following damage.

**betterment clause**  In an insurance policy, a clause stating that the insurer can ask the insured for money towards the cost of repair or replacement of an article that was rebuilt or repaired to an improved standard.

**better than best advice**  Requirement under the Financial Services Act that an independent financial adviser who is a "connected person" recommends the absolute best product in the market.

**BIIBA**  Abbreviation of *British Insurance and Investment Brokers Association.*

**bid**  Offer to buy something, (*e.g.* shares) at a certain price. A seller may make a certain offer and a prospective buyer may make a bid. The bid cancels out the offer. More especially, a bid is an offer by one company to buy the shares of another, a *takeover bid. See also bid-offer spread; bid price.*

**bidder**  Someone who makes a bid for something.

*At the auction, many of the bidders remained anonymous.*

**bidding ring**  Group of stock market or antique dealers acting in concert in order to drive prices up or down. This practice is illegal. *See also concert party.*

**bid-offer spread**  Difference between the *offer price* and the *bid price, i.e.* the price at which units in a unit trust or unit-linked life assurance are bought and sold (encashed). Usually the spread is 5% or 6% and it represents an initial charge to the plan.

**bid price**  Term with two meanings:

1. It is the price a market maker is prepared to pay to buy securities. *See also bid-offer spread; offer price.*
2. It is the price at which *unit trusts* or *unit-linked assurance policies* are sold.

**bid rate** Rate of interest offered for deposits.

**Big Bang** Popular term for the deregulation of the London Stock Exchange on 27 October 1986. Among the changes implemented were the admission of foreign institutions as members of the Exchange, the abandonment of rigid distinctions between *stockbrokers*, *jobbers* and bankers, and the abolition of fixed *commissions*. *See also Little Bang; single capacity.*

**Big Blue** Nickname for IBM (International Business Machines).

**Big Board** Nickname for the New York Stock Exchange.

**Big Eight** Nickname for the eight largest firms of accountants: Arthur Anderson, Arthur Young, Cooppers and Lybrand, Deloitte Haskins and Sells, Ernst and Whinney, Peat Marwick Mitchell, Price Waterhouse and Touche Ross.

**Big Four** Nickname for the four main commercial banks in the UK: Barclays, Lloyds TSB, Midland and NatWest. The largest banks now include Halifax and Abbey National, who changed status from building societies. Big Four is also the name given to Japan's largest stock marketing companies: Dalwa, Nikko, Nomura and Yamaichi.

**bigger fool theory** Justification for buying shares that are over-priced, which runs that there is always a bigger fool somewhere on the market who will buy them from you at an even higher price.

**bilateral netting** System in which two companies offset their payments and receipts with each other each month and then make a single payment and receipt, thus reducing paperwork and bank charges.

**bill** There are four possible meanings:
1. It is a list of charges to be paid on goods or services. In this sense the usual US term is check.

   *The supplier presented an exorbitant bill which we refused to pay.*

2. It is a document promising to pay someone a certain amount of money. It is in this sense that the US meaning of the term is a banknote.

3. It is a document describing goods, most often used in dealings with customs.

4. It is short for *bill of exchange.*

**bill broker**  Person or company that buys or sells *bills of exchange*, either on their own account, or as an intermediary.

**billion**  One thousand million, 1,000,000,000. Formerly in the UK a billion was a million million.

**bill of exchange**  Document indicating that one party (the drawee) agrees to pay a certain sum of money on demand or on a specified date, to the drawer. Two very familiar bills of exchange are cheques and banknotes. Another form of bill of exchange is used by the government to regulate the *money supply.*

**bill of imprest**  Order that entitles its bearer to have money paid in advance.

**bill of lading**  Document detailing the transfer of goods from a (foreign) supplier to a buyer. It may be used as a document of *title.*

**bill of sale**  Document certificating the transfer of goods (but not real estate) to another person. Goods transferred in this way may not become the property of the receiving party and may be redeemed when the bill is paid.

**bill of sight**  Document passed to a customs inspector by an importer who is unable to describe in detail the imported goods. When the goods are landed a full description must be given, known as perfecting the sight.

**bill rate**  Rate at which a *bill of exchange* is discounted. *See* **discounting.**

**bills in a set**  Foreign *bills of exchange* are normally made out in triplicate and sent to the drawee separately to prevent loss. These copies are known as bills in a set.

**Bills of Exchange Act**  Act of 1882 that defines bills of exchange, cheques and promissory notes and the responsibilities of the parties to them.

**bills payable**  In accounting, *bills of exchange* that are held and must be paid at some future date. These are effectively liabilities. *See also* **bills receivable.**

**bills receivable**  In accounting, *bills of exchange* that are held and are due to be paid at some future date. These are effectively assets. *See also* **bills payable.**

**BIMBO** Abbreviation of buyin management buyout, a type of *management buyout* that involves also venture capital from outside.

**binding authority** *See binding cover.*

**binding cover** Mandate received by a *coverholder* from an *underwriter* allowing him or her to do insurance business up to a certain limit of cover. It is also termed binding authority.

**black** To forbid or boycott trade in certain goods or with certain trading partners.

An account that is said to be in the black is in credit. *See also red.*

**black book** Company's pre-planned strategy to be put into action in the event of a hostile *takeover bid.*

**black economy** Illegal economic activity conducted largely for cash by companies and individuals who pay no taxes on the proceeds. *See also moonlighting; tax evasion.*

**blacklist** List of companies, products or people that are undesirable and to be avoided.

In the USA the term means more specifically the denial of work to certain people on the grounds of their past beliefs or actions.

*John Smith believes he has been blacklisted by management because of his prominence during the 1991 strike.*

**black market** Wholly illegal market; one that is illicit and uncontrolled. Black markets deal in scarce or stolen goods, and frequently come into existence in wartime, because the goods concerned are rationed, or because the market is exceptionally high – in which case counterfeit or imitation goods often appear. Trading is often in kind, one valued commodity being exchanged for another.

**Black Monday** Monday 19 October 1987. The phrase was coined shortly after the huge losses sustained on the equities markets on that day.

**black money** Money obtained illegally, usually through the international drug trade.

**Black Wednesday** 16 September 1992, the day sterling left the *Exchange Rate Mechanism* (ERM). The result was a fall of 15% in sterling against the Deutschmark.

**blank** In general, any form that has not been filled in or not filled in completely, such as a blank cheque.

**blank bill** *Bill of exchange* on which the payee is not specified.

**blank credit** Credit facilities with no upper limit.

**blank endorsement** Term with two meanings:
1. It is a blank cheque endorsed on the reverse.
2. It is a reference that may be freely used by the endorsed person, *e.g.* a statement given by a referee for distribution with a *curriculum vitae*.

**blanket** Something that covers all eventualities, as in, *e.g.*, a blanket policy.

**blanket agreement** Agreement that covers many, if not all, items concerning one party's relationship with another.

**blanket certificate** In *motor insurance*, a certificate with standard wording that allows the policyholder to drive any vehicle he or she owns (or is buying on hire purchase). The insurer usually requires knowledge of the vehicle's identity.

**blanket commercial guarantee insurance** Type of *fidelity guarantee insurance* that gives cover against dishonesty of any member of staff without the staff having to be named.

**blanket policy** Insurance policy that covers all the property at a specific location, or all examples of a specified property, or possessions at several locations, but always under one sum insured.

**blanket rate** Fixed charge that covers a series of transactions or services, and unchanging.

**blank transfer** In the transfer of shares, a transfer form that is left blank as regards the name of the transferee, *e.g* if the shares are to be put up as security to a mortgage, the transfer form will be left blank, as the mortgagor has the right to take possession of the shares if the mortgagee defaults.

**block** Group of something (*e.g.* shares); or an obstruction of prevention of entry or exit, as in a blocked account.

**blocked currency** Currency that may not be removed from a country, sometimes for political reasons.

**B**

**blowout** Informal term referring to unexpectedly strong sales of something, *e.g.* goods sold at retail.

*Traders regard the Eurobond issue as a blowout because it sold quickly and sparked real excitement on launch.*

**Blue Book** Popular term for a UK government publication entitled *National Income and Expenditure*, best described as the national annual report and accounts.

**blue-chip** Describing an investment that is regarded as extremely safe, without being a *gilt-edged security*. It also describes a company whose shares are regarded as an extremely safe investment.

*Analysts believe that blue-chip stocks will continue strong, but that other shares will continue to drift.*

**blue-chip investment** Investment in the *stock* of one of the blue-chip companies; hence, a safe but conservative investment. *See blue-chip.*

**blue-collar worker** Alternative term for a manual worker.

**blue month** Month with the greatest trading activity in products such as *futures* and *options*.

**blue-sky** *Security* that is worthless or highly speculative, or something with no specific aim.

*Along with its research and development programme, the company invested in a certain amount of blue-sky research.*

**blue-sky laws** Laws in some US states intended to protect investors, including supervision of the isue of securities and broker licensing.

**blurb** Short piece of advertising copy, especially publisher's copy on the jacket or cover of a book.

**board** Group of people who run a company, society or trust; *see board of directors*.

**board of directors** Decision-making group comprising all the directors of a company, who are legally responsible for their actions. The board of directors is specifically charged with the management of the company and in the case of a *public limited company* is elected by the shareholders at the company's *annual general meeting* (AGM). In the USA, the board of directors draws up company policy and appoints executives to run the company. It is sometimes also known simply as "the board".

**board meeting** Meeting of a *board of directors*.

**bogus** Fake or counterfeit.

*The police are investigating reports of a con man posing as a salesman, carrying a bogus identity card.*

**boiler insurance**  Type of engineering insurance that covers damage to a boiler and damage or injury to third parties by a boiler explosion.

**boiler room**  Little-known firm of brokers or dealers which sells securities over the telephone.

**bona fide**  Latin for "in good faith". It usually appears in reference to contracts, especially contracts of *insurance*. All parties to a contract are expected to reveal all information relevant to the contract in hand, that is, they are expected to contract in good faith. It is also used simply to mean honest or trustworthy. *See also* **mala fide**.

*After completing an in-depth investigation, the authorities decided that the company was bona fide after all.*

**bona vacantia**  Property such as real estate or shares that has no owner and no obvious claimant, *e.g.* property that remains in the hands of a liquidator after the creditors have been paid.

**bond**  Term with four meanings:

1. It is a security issued at a fixed rate by central government, local authorities or occasionally by private companies. It is essentially a contract to repay money borrowed, and as such represents a debt. Normally, bonds are issued in series with the same conditions of repayment and denominations. It is also known as a fixed-interest security.

2. In insurance, it is a single premium investment which can offer either growth income or a combination of both.

3. It refers to the importing of goods from abroad. If goods are imported and import duty is not paid immediately, the goods are placed in a bonded warehouse (*i.e.* they are held in bond) until all customs formalities are completed.

4. It is a firm tie or agreement between individuals. "My word is my bond" is the motto of the London Stock Exchange.

**bonded**  Held in *bond*.

**bonded warehouse**  Type of warehouse for goods on which excise duty need not be paid until the goods are removed.

**bond note**  Document indicating that imported goods held in bond may be released, because all import formalities have been completed.

**bond-washing** Practice of buying bonds *cum dividend* and selling them *ex dividend*, to reduce the rate of tax payable on the transaction. The dividend on the bond becomes a capital gain, on which a lower rate of tax is payable than if tax were paid on the proceeds as dividend income. Because of changes in the tax laws in the UK, there is no longer scope for this kind of manoeuvring, although it still happens in the USA.

**bonus** Additional payment. In insurance, it is the amount added to the sum assured under with-profits policies. It can be a reversionary or *terminal bonus*.

**bonus dividend** Unexpected extra *dividend* paid to a shareholder.

**bonus issue** Issue of *shares* made by a company wishing to reduce the average price of its shares. Shareholders receive a number of extra shares in proportion to the number already held. It is also known as a capitalization issue.
*A & T Publications has announced a three-for-one bonus issue.*

**book** In business, the books most frequently referred to are the books of account in which business transactions are recorded. Books of account are normally held to be legal documents.

**book debt** Debt recorded in an account book.

**book-keeping** Business of keeping records of financial transactions.

**book of original entry** Alternative term for *book of prime entry*.

**book of prime entry** Account book in which transactions are recorded from day to day before being transferred to the main *ledger*.

**book rate** In *motor insurance*, standard rate an insurer applies to a certain type of risk.

**book value** Alternative term for written down value. See *write down*.

**boom** Popular term for a period when employment, prices and general business activity are at a high level and resources are being used to the full. Booms have a nasty habit of turning into *slumps*. See also *recession*.

**bootstrap** Mostly used in the USA where *takeover* activity is most prevalent, to describe a cash offer for a controlling interest in a company which, if accepted, is followed by another offer (usually at a lower price) for the remainder of the shares.
*The tycoon found bootstrapping a very cost-effective method of taking over other companies.*

**bordereau** List, schedule, memorandum or account, especially one joined to a policy or document. The term is also used to describe a list of risks presented for reinsurance by an insurer.

**borrowing** Most widely used in the sense of accepting money that is not one's own on the understanding that it will be repaid, usually with interest, at a later date.

**Borse** Stock exchange in Europe

**bottom** Generally refers to the lowest point of something. In shipping, however, the term refers to a ship, and bottomry is anything to do with shipping.

**bottoming out** Informal term for a very sudden and serious fall in market prices.

**bottom line** Last line of an *account*, showing either *profit* or *loss*. In this sense the phrase has come to mean the "brutal truth" in general usage.

**bought** Something that comes into one's possession through some kind of exchange (usually cash) is said to have been bought. *See **bought deal**.*

**bought deal** Practice common in the USA, and becoming more common in the UK, of a major financial institution purchasing a large *portfolio* of *securities* which it then passes on to its clients piecemeal.

**bought ledger** Account book in which a business records purchases and, by extension, the credit-control department of an organization.

**bounce** Sudden rise in the value of a share that has been peforming badly.

**bounty** In a modern business context, a government *subsidy* given to aid particular industries. It may be in the form of *tax* concessions or a cash handout.

**bourse** Stock exchange in France; "the Bourse" is the Paris stock exchange.

**boutique** Relatively new form of financial services company, operating in much the same way as a High Street shop, into which customers may walk to seek investment advice and services. It is also known as a financial supermarket.

**box** Informal name for the desk at which *underwriters* sit to do business with brokers in *Lloyd's of London*.

**boycott** Refusal to trade with a certain company or nation or in certain goods.

**bracket**  Broadly, a group of people or things that are in some way similar to each other, *e.g.*, the term is applied to a group of banks involved in an issue of new shares.

**bracket creep**  What happens when *inflation* forces groups of people into the next tax or income bracket. Normally brackets are fixed annually to account for inflation, but bracket creep can occur if inflation runs at a higher level than anticipated. *See income bracket; tax bracket.*

**brain-drain**  Popular term describing the migration of specialists (usually scientists or technologists) from their home country to another country, often lured by higher salaries and more sympathetic research grants.

**branch**  Part of a business, such as a building society or shop, that functions apart from but under the overall control of the central organization.

**brand**  To put a name (the brand name) on something or to design and package a product so that it is easily recognizable by a consumer. A brand name can be protected by law against misuse by competitors hoping to benefit from the reputation associated with a particular branded product.

**branded goods**  Goods that are packaged by the manufacturer with the brand name clearly visible. Branded goods may often be sold at a higher price than others because of the selling power of the name.

**brand leader**  Brand of a certain type of goods that has the largest share of the market. A brand leader may often be seen as a company's most valuable *asset.*

**brand loyalty**  Marketing concept by which consumers continually purchase certain gods which they identify by brand name (and associate with quality and value for money).

**break**  When prices have been rising steadily over a period, the break is a sudden and substantial drop in prices.

**break even**  To cover one's costs, making neither a *profit* or *loss.*

**break-even chart**  Graph showing the relationship between total fixed costs, variable costs and revenues for various volumes of output.

**break-even point**  Point at which fixed and variable costs are exactly covered by sales revenue. At greater volumes of output an operation would normally expect to make a *profit.*

**breaking an account**  Closing an account and transferring the balance to another one.

**B**

**breakout**  What happens when a share or commodity price breaks a previously fixed, or at least, stable pattern.

**break-up**  Term with two meanings:

1. In real estate, a tenanted property is worth less on the property market than a vacant one. A property with some tenanted and some vacant apartments may be bought and then broken up, so that the tenanted flats may be sold to the tenants and the vacant flats may be sold to outsiders at a much higher rate.

2. In corporate terms, break-up occurs when several or all of the operating arms of a company are sold off, usually after a *takeover*.

*See also* **asset stripping**; **break-up value**.

**break-up value**  Value of a share or company on the assumption that the company is being disbanded or broken up. The break-up value of a share is calculated by dividing the probable net proceeds from the sale of the company's assets by the number of shares. Sometimes, the term is used as a loose synonym for asset value per share.

**Bretton Woods Conference**  Held in 1944 in Bretton Woods, New Hampshire, this conference between the USA, Canada and the UK formed a new system of international monetary control and resulted in the setting up of the *International Monetary Fund* (IMF) and the International Bank for Reconstruction and Development.

**bricks and mortar**  Informal term for the *fixed assets* of a company.

**bridge financing**  Any form of short-term funding in anticipated arrival of funds, whether for a venture company on the verge of raising new capital, or a bridging loan for a home buyer who needs to pay for a house before receiving the proceeds on the sale of the former property.

**bridging loan**  Also called bridging advance, *see* **bridge financing**.

**British Insurance and Investment Brokers Association** (BIIBA)  Trade organization established in 1977, which extended its activities from insurance only to include investment advisers when it changed to its present name in 1988.

**British Insurance Brokers Association**  Former trade association of insurance brokers, now replaced by the *British Insurance and Investment Brokers Association* (BIIBA).

**B**  **British Venture Capital Association** (BVCA)  Trade association of companies that deal in *venture capital*.

**broad money** Alternative term for M3. *See money supply.*

**broadside** Informal term for a publicity leaflet or handout.

**broken chain of events** Break in a sequence of events such that the principle of cause and effect cannot be applied to all of them. In insurance terms, the final loss does not result from the original peril. *See also* **direct chain of events**; **proximate cause.**

**broker** Broadly, an intermediary between a buyer and a seller. There are several forms of broker, the job title referring to what it is that a particular broker deals in; *e.g.* an insurance broker deals in insurance.

**brokerage** Payment made to a *broker* for services rendered. Also known as a broker's *commission.*

**brokerage account** Record kept by a stockbroker of sales and purchases of securities.

**brokerage house** US term for a firm of brokers.

**broker-dealer** Firm that acts in the dual capacity of share broker for its clients and as dealer for its own account.

**broker pool** Group of insurers who use one broker to negotiate reinsurance business.

**broker's open cover** Reinsurance broker able to arrange automatic reinsurance cover.

**broker-trader** On the London International Financial Futures Exchange, a firm that acts as both broker and trader for its own account. It is similar to a *broker dealer.*

**bubble** Industry or trend with no substance in it. A bubble usually bursts with more-or-less disastrous consequences for those involved. Probably the most famous bubble was the South Sea Bubble which burst in 1720.

**bubble company** Company formed with no real business to undertake, sometimes as a vehicle to defraud the public.

**bucket shop** Popular phrase describing brokers of *stocks, shares* and commodities who are not recognized as members of any *exchange.*

**budget** Plan that details expected future income and outgoings, normally over a time span of a year. It is also the sum of money set aside for a given activity or project.

The Budget is a government's financial plan for the forthcoming financial year, announced as a statement by the Chancellor of the

**B**

Exchequer, and concerned principally with the raising of revenue by *taxation*.

**budget-day value** (BDV)  Value of an asset on Budget Day (6 April) 1995, used to calculate *capital gains tax*, which was introduced on that day.

**budget deficit**  Budgetary imbalance, caused by excess of *expenditure* over *income*. In the case of the British government budgets, the deficit is generally funded by the authorization of an increase in the **National Debt**.

**buffer stock**  In manufacturing industries, a stock of raw materials held as an insurance against shortages or sudden price rises.

On the commodity markets, buffer stocks are held for release at certain strategic times in order to stabilize prices and markets.

**buildings insurance**  Insurance of the fabric of a building plus any permanent fitted items, such as kitchen or bedroom fitments. *See household insurance.*

**built-in obsolescence**  Practice of manufacturers who design a product so that it needs to be replaced by the consumer in a relatively short time, resulting either from fast deterioration or changes in fashion.

**bulk transfer**  Transfer of value from one pension arrangement to another pension arrangement in respect of a group of members. It is usually paid following a business reorganization.

**bull**  Stock exchange dealer or analyst who believes that prices or investment values will increase. On this conviction, the dealer buys now and profits by selling later at a higher price.

**bulldog bond**  Sterling-denominated bond issued by foreign governments for sale on the UK market.

**bullet**  Term with two meanings:

1. It is the final payment of a loan consisting of the whole principal (previous payments being of interest only).
2. It is a security that pays a guaranteed (fixed) interest at a specific date.

**bullet loan**  Loan in which all early payments are of interest only; the final payment (bullet) includes the principal.

**bullish**  Describes a market or person with the qualities of a *bull*.

**B**

**bull market**  Condition in which share prices are rising. *Bulls* are speculators who buy shares in anticipation of rising prices.

**bull position** Position of an investor whose purchases exceed his or her sales, and therefore stands to gain in a rising or bull market. *See bull.*

**bumping** Situation that occurs when a senior person takes the place of a junior.

**bunny bond** *Bond* with the option of yielding interest or additional bonds instead of interest.

**burden of debt** When a *debt* is passed on to successive generations, the burden of debt is the *interest* payments on the accumulated debt.

**bureau** Office that specializes in a certain form of business, *e.g.* an employment bureau specializes in supplying temporary or permanent staff to employers for a *commission.*

**bureau de change** Office at which currencies may be exchanged on payment of a *commission.* Some bureaux offer additional services, such as the encashment of personal cheques.

**burning costs** Method of calculating reinsurance premiums based on previous claims experience.

**burn rate** When a new company begins trading on venture capital, the burn rate is the rate at which the company consumes capital in financing fixed overheads. *See venture capital.*

**business all risks** Type of insurance that provides a business with cover against loss or damage to capital equipment (whether caused by fire, theft or accidental damage by a member of staff).

**business development loan** Loan made for buying fixed assets such as plant and premises, usually over a five-year term.

**Business Expansion Scheme** (BES) Former government scheme that encouraged investment in unlisted companies by granting tax relief on such investment. In January 1994 it was replaced by the *Enterprise Investment Scheme* (EIS).

**business insurance** Any of the many kinds of insurance that relate to business activities. They include *blanket commercial guarantee insurance, buildings insurance, business interruption insurance, key person insurance, liability insurance, motor insurance* and *public liability insurance.*

**business interruption insurance** (BI insurance) Insurance that provides compensation for the policyholder if his or her business activities are interrupted by a mishap such as a fire. The amount insured covers loss of net profits, fixed costs and any additional expenses incurred. The policy is subject to a material damage warranty, *i.e.* a claim for matching damage must have been paid for the BI cover to be effected. It is also known as consequential loss insurance.

**business property relief**  Relief on inheritance tax that is available on some kinds of business property.

**bust**  Informal term meaning bankrupt.

*After as bad a year as this one has been, I would not be surprised if a large number of small companies went bust.*

**busted bond**  Bond whose issuer has defaulted on the loan raised to finance the issue. Valueless except as collectors' items, busted bonds are also called old bonds.

**buy**  To gain title to something in exchange for money.

**buy back**  A company that is originally financed by venture capital may pay back the capital invested either by seeking a *quotation* or by being taken over. In either case, it will be buying itself back from the venture capitalist. *See* **venture capital**.

**buy earnings**  To buy earnings is to invest in shares that have a low yield but a good earnings growth record.

**buyer credit**  System in which a seller makes a cash contract with an overseas buyer, who pays up to 20% of the price and funds the rest through a long-term loan with a UK bank. The repayment of the loan to the bank is guaranteed by the Export Credits Guarantee Department (ECGD).

**buyer's market**  Market in which there are too many sellers and not enough buyers, so that buyers are in a position to influence prices or conditions of purchase.

**buyers over**  On the Stock Exchange, a situation in which there are more buyers than sellers. The opposite is *sellers over*.

**buy forward**  To buy shares, commodities, etc. for delivery at a later date. In essence, buying forward is a gamble on the current price, *i.e.* that it will rise in the future and the buyer will then be able to sell at a profit. *See also* **selling short**.

**B**

**buy in**  Refers to a situation where a seller of shares, etc. fails to deliver on the agreed date, which sometimes happens if the seller is *selling short*. In this case the buyer is entitled to buy shares from another source and to charge the seller with any expenses incurred. This process is known as buying in.

**buy on close**  Buying contracts on a financial *futures* market at a price within the *closing range*. *See also* **buy on opening**.

**buy on opening**  Buying contracts on a financial futures market at a price within the *opening range*. *See also* **buy on close**.

**buyout**  The purchase of an entire company.

**buyout bond**  Also known as a Section 32 policy, a pension transfer vehicle that preserves any *guaranteed minimum pension*.

**buyout policy**  Occupational pension scheme whereby the subscriber (the employee of the company offering the scheme) may buy out of the scheme if he or she wishes to leave the company.

**buy recommendation**  Recommendation to buy.

*Two market analysts today changed their recommendations on A & G shares from attractive to outright buy.*

**BV**  Abbreviation of *Besloten Vennootschap*.

**BVCA**  Abbreviation of *British Venture Capital Association*.

**B**

# C

**CA** Abbreviation of *chartered accountant*.

**cabinet crowd** Members of the New York Stock Exchange who deal in rarely traded bonds.

**cable transfer** An alternative term for *telegraphic transfer*.

**CAC** Abbreviation of *Compagnie des Agents de Chance*.

**CAD** Abbreviation for *cash against document*.

**call** Act of demanding payment for *shares* or *stocks*, or repayment of a *debt*. A lender may advance money on condition that it is repaid on call (without notice).

**callable bond** Bond that may be called for payment before its *maturity date*.

**called-up capital** Sum of money that has been paid to a company by its shareholders. *See also partly-paid shares; uncalled capital*.

**call option** Option to by shares, commodities or financial futures at an agreed price on or before an agreed future date.

**callover** Method of trading on a stock exchange whereby the securities listed are called out in order, and dealers make bids or offers for each *security* according to their instructions.

**callover price** Price for a security verbally agreed at *callover*.

**call provision** Condition attached to a *bond* by which the issuer is entitled to redeem the bond at a fixed price after a specified period of time.

**call up** Alternative for *call*, especially with respect to *partly-paid shares*.

**Calvo clause** Contract clause regarding foreign investment. It states that, in the event of a dispute, the parties agree to abide by the law of the foreign country.

**cancellation** Voiding of an agreement, either in due course (such as the discharge of a *bill of exchange*).

**cancellation notice** Statutory notice sent for most life policies, allowing the proposer to cancel the policy within 14 days of receipt of the notice if he or she decides not to continue with the policy. A full refund of premium is given.

**cancellation price** Lowest price a unit trust manager can accept for units on any one day.

**C & F** Abbreviation of *cost and freight*.

**cap** Interest rate *option* that enables the investor to hedge against the possibility of *interest* rates rising to the investor's disadvantage. *See hedging*.

**capacity** Measurement of the ability of a company to produce goods or services. In insurance, it specifically means the amount of insurance business an insurer is able to write.

**cap and collar mortgage** Mortgage with fixed upper and lower limits of the variable interest rate.

**capital** Vague term that most often requires a qualification. Unqualified, it usually refers to the resources of an organization or person (*e.g.* equipment, skill, cash).

**capital account** Part of the *balance of payments*, which refers to international movements of *capital*, including intergovernmental loans.

**capital adequacy** Total capital that a financial institution must hold to cover potential risks.

**capital allowances** Amounts deducted from a company's *profits* before tax is calculated, to take into account *depreciation* of capital *assets* (such as vehicles, plant and machinery, and industrial buildings).

**capital assets** Another term for *fixed assets*.

**capital bond** Full name National Savings Capital Bond, a 5-year UK bond dating from 1989, issued by the Department of National Savings. It is sold in units of £100 and has a fixed rate of interest, which is not taxed at source.

**capital budget** Forward planning of forward capital movement, involving larger sums of money and longer timescales than a *cash budget*.

**capital clause** In the *memorandum of association* of a company, that section setting out the details of the company's *capital*.

**capital duty** Former tax paid by companies on profits gained from a new share issue. It ceased to be levied in 1988.

**capital employed** Capital that a company uses to finance its assets. It is taken to be the sum of shareholders' funds, loans and deferred taxation.

**capital expenditure** Expenditure on capital goods *e.g. fixed assets* such as plant or on trade investments and *current assets*. Capital expenditure is classed as below-the-line for accounting purposes. *See also trade investment*.

**capital gain** Gain made from a capital transaction, *e.g.* the buying and selling of *assets*.

**capital gains tax** (CGT) Tax paid on *capital gains*.

**capital goods** Goods (such as machines) that are used for the production of other goods. Ships are also sometimes regarded as capital goods.

**capital growth** Increase in the value of an investment over a period of time.

**capital guarantee investment** Investment, such as those offered by *National Savings*, that cannot fall in value (because of a guarantee given by a bank, building society, government or other institution).

**capital-intensive** Describing a business in which *capital* is the most important and costly factor of production. Thus, an industry in which the major cost is the purchase and maintenance of machinery (*fixed capital*) is capital-intensive.

**capitalism** Economic and political system in which people are entitled to trade for profit on their own account. It is also known as free or private enterprise. *See also communism*.

**capitalist economy** Economy in which business is conducted for the profit of the companies and persons engaged in it.

**capitalization** Term with two meanings:
1. It is the conversion of a company's reserves into share capital by issuing more shares.
2. It is the total amount of capital available to a company in the long term.

**capitalization issue** Alternative term for *bonus issue*.

**capital/labour ratio** Proportion of capital to labour used in an economy.

**capital market** Market made up of the various sources of *capital* for investment (medium- or long-term) in new and already existing companies. It is centred on the London Stock Exchange and the *Alternative Investment Market* (AIM).

**capital outlay** Expenditure on *fixed assets* such as machinery. *See also capital*.

**capital profit** Profit generated by selling capital goods (*fixed assets*), rather than by trading.

**capital protected annuity** *Annuity* that provides an income for life, but if death occurs before the *annuitant* has received a sum equal to the purchase price, the balance is paid to the annuitant's estate. This results in a lower annuity rate when the annuity is bought.

**capital redemption** Feature of an insurance policy that pays a lump sum when it matures (*see **maturity date***).

**capital reserves** Profits from a company's trading that represent part of the company's capital and so may not be repaid to shareholders until the company is wound up.

**capital saturation** Situation in a company or industry in which there is such a proportion of capital to labour that any increase in capital would have no significant positive effect on output.

**capital stock** Value of all capital goods owned by a company, industry or nation, after *depreciation* has been taken into account.

**capital transfer tax** (CTT) Tax paid on the transfer of capital, *e.g.* in the form of a gift or bequest. Capital transfer tax covers the former form of inheritance tax.

**capped mortgage** Mortgage with a fixed upper limit to its variable interest rate.

**captive fund** Fund for venture capital held by a large financial services group. *See **venture capital***.

**captive insurance company** Insurance company, totally owned by a *parent company*, which insures the parent company's risks. It may be managed by a capital management company.

**captive market** Market in which there is a monopoly of production, allowing the consumer no option but to buy that company's product.

**CAR** Abbreviation of *compound annual return*.

**car** Alternative term for a *futures* contract.

**cargo insurance**  Insurance for cargo during transit, which may be taken out by the exporter or the importer (or both).

**carnet**  Document valid internationally that allows the passage of dutiable goods without duty having to be paid until the goods reach their destination.

**carry**  Money borrowed or lent in order to finance trading in *futures*. The process of borrowing and lending in this way is known as carrying.

**carry back**  Method by which a person making contributions to a *personal pension scheme* may gain tax relief for a previous year (if the premium is paid in the current year). Contributions can be carried back for one year only in most circumstances.

**carry forward**  Method by which a person making contributions to a *personal pension scheme* may carry forward unused pension relief from a previous year to the current year (if maximum contributions have not been made during the previous years). The maximum period for carry forward of unused relief is the previous six years. Carry forward can be used with *carry back*. The term also refers to a tax rebate that is paid because a company has gone into the *red* for a period of time.

**carry over**  To postpone payment on a bargain traded on a stock exchange from one settlement day to the next.

**cartel**  Group of companies that come together to monopolize a market, agreeing between them which company presides over which area of operation. Cartels are illegal in the UK and the USA.

**cascade tax**  Tax imposed at each stage of production, *e.g.* a product may pass from one country to the next as each stage of production is carried out, and would thus attract several taxation stages, and the price of the finished product would be higher than if it had been produced in one country.

**case of need**  Endorsement made on a *bill of exchange*. It is followed by the name of a person or company to whom the holder of the bill may apply in the event that the bill is not paid.

**cash against document**  (CAD)  Method of payment for goods for export, whereby the documentation for a shipment is sent to an agent or bank at the destination. These are passed to the consignee, who makes the payment. The consignee is free to take delivery of the shipment when it arrives. Cash against document is a process of payment that is also used by large UK investment houses.

**cash agent** *Agent* who is paid a one-off *commission* for getting new business for an insurance company, which generally thereafter deals with renewals, etc.

**cash and carry** Popular term for a wholesale warehouse, from which retailers buy their goods and transport them away. More and more frequently, cash and carries are used by members of the general public.

**cash and new** On a stock exchange, a method of postponing payment on a *bargain* until the next settlement day. The investor begins with a bargain for which he or she would like to postpone payment. Towards the end of the *account*, a deal is made that is opposite to the first (*i.e.* the investor either buys or sells a similar *instrument*). The original position is then restored by yet another purchase or sale, to be settled on the next settlement day. In effect, the investor negates the original position and then returns to it in the next account.

**cash book** In *book-keeping*, a book in which all receipts and payments are recorded in the first instance.

**cash bonus** Additional sum added to the normal payment on an assurance policy because of increased profits that have been earned.

**cash budget** Forward plan of day-to-day income and expenditure.

**cash cow** Product that continues to provide a healthy *revenue* after its initial launch, with relatively little extra investment.

**cash deal** Agreement or transaction concluded with a cash payment; on the stock exchange, a deal to be completed on the next trading day.

**cash dealings** Stock exchange deals that must be settled on the following day. Such bargains are said to be for cash settlement rather than account settlement.

**cash discount** Reduction in the price of goods in return for payment in cash.

**cash dividend** *Dividend* paid in cash (rather than as shares).

**cash flow** Movement of money through a company from the time it is received as income (or borrowing), to the time it leaves the company as payments (*e.g.* for raw materials, salaries, etc.). A negative cash flow is the situation in which there is too little money coming in to pay for outgoings. Conversely, a positive cash flow occurs when a company receives income before it is due to pay outgoings. *See also* **discounted cash flow**.

**cash in advance** Method of payment in which the purchaser pays for good or services before delivery.

**cash investment** Investment that provides immediate or short-notice withdrawal of funds at minimum risk; the funds invested are guaranteed. They include a current account, deposit account, National Savings and various building society accounts.

**cash lump sum** *See lump sum.*

**cash on delivery** (COD) Distribution system whereby the person in receipt of goods makes payment for them on the spot to the deliverer. Such a system is operated by the UK Post office, where it is the postman or postwoman who takes receipt of payment.

**cash position** State of the finances of a person or business at a given time, particularly whether there are funds available (cash positive) or unavailable (cash negative).

**cash price** Price at which goods may be bought using cash. The price paid in cash is usually different from the *hire purchase* price in that the latter usually includes interest.

**cash settlement** Payment for *cash dealings*.

**CASS** Abbreviation of *Claims Advice and Settlement System*.

**CAT** Abbreviation of *computer-assisted trading*.

**catastrophe cover** Type of reinsurance on an excess of loss basis to protect against an accumulation of losses arising from one event.

**catastrophe risk** In insurance, an exceptional loss (*e.g.*, resulting from a flood or earthquake).

**Catmark** Government scheme announced in 1998 for checking Charges, Access and Terms of *Individual Savings Accounts* (ISAs), due for introduction in 1999.

**CATS** Abbreviation of *Certificate of Accrual on Treasury Securities*, a form of *zero-coupon bond*.

**caution** Term with two meanings:
1. It is any warning.
2. It is a notice lodged with the Land Registry that places a condition on any pending action.

*See also caveat.*

**caveat** Caution or warning.

**caveat emptor**  Latin for "buyer beware". In legal terms this maxim means that a buyer of goods should use his or her own common sense, and that the law is not prepared to aid someone who buys goods foolishly.

**caveat subscriptor**  Latin for "signer beware", meaning that anyone who signs a document is bound by its contents, regardless of whether or not he or she has read it, or understood its legal implications.

**CBD**  Abbreviation of cash before delivery.

**CBI**  Abbreviation of Confederation of British Industry.

**CCA**  Abbreviation of *current cost accounting*.

**cedant**  Insurer who provides *reinsurance*, sometimes called a ceding company.

**cede**  To reinsure.

**ceding company**  See *cedant*.

**CeFA**  Professional qualification awarded to financial advisers who pass the examinations of The Chartered Institute of Bankers (CIB).

**census**  National survey that provides information on population, economics and social matters. In the UK and the USA a national census is taken every ten years.

**Census of Distribution**  Survey taken every five years of wholesale and retail distribution services.

**Census of Production**  Survey taken annually of industrial production and public utility services.

**central bank**  Bank that provides banking services for a government; *e.g.* the Bank of England in the UK.

**Central Fund**  Fund at *Lloyd's of London* used to pay claims if an underwriter fails financially. The money for the fund is raised by a levy imposed on each *syndicate*.

**Central Gilts Office**  (CGO)  Computerized book-entry transfer system for gilt-edged stock established in 1986 by the Bank of England and the Stock Exchange. It ensures automatic "same-day" payments for the electronic transfer of stock.

**Central Government Borrowing Requirement**  (CGBR)  Amount calculated by deducting private sector borrowing (by public companies and local authorities) from the *Public Sector Borrowing Requirement* (PSBR).

**central purchasing**  Practice of making all purchases required by a company through one department.

**Central Unit**  UK Treasury department that co-ordinates economic information from other departments, and manages the government's economic strategy.

**CentreWrite**  *Lloyd's of London* subsidiary, established in 1991, that provides *reinsurance to close* for underwriters' *syndicates*.

**CEO**  Abbreviation of chief executive officer.

**certificate**  Document that proves something, *e.g.* right of ownership or that an insurance is valid and its premium has been paid.

**certificated**  Describing something that has documentary evidence to prove that it is genuine.

**Certificate of Accrual on Treasury Securities** (CATS)  In the USA, a *zero-coupon bond* issued by the Treasury Department.

**certificate of bonds**  Document issued to a registered bond holder confirming that the bonds are registered in his or her name.

**certificate of deposit** (CD)  Essentially, a document (originally issued by merchant banks) declaring that a certain sum had been deposited with a bank. Sterling certificates of deposit refer to long-term fixed deposits of sums over £10,000 and therefore offer high interest rates.

**certificate of incorporation**  Document issued to a company when it has completed legal incorporation procedures and satisfied the terms of the Companies Acts.

**certificate of insurance**  Documentary proof that insurance cover exists. It is needed for compulsory insurances such as motor and employer's liability. *See certificate of motor insurance.*

**certificate of origin**  Import-export document that declares the country of origin of goods.

**certificate of motor insurance**  Document that confirms the existence of a valid motor insurance policy. It must state the name of the policyholder, the registration number of the vehicle, dates of commencement and expiry of the insurance, the person or persons insured to drive the vehicle, and any limitations on use.

**certification** *Inland Revenue* rules require that certain pension transfers require a certificate to confirm that the pension, or cash, is limited to a specified amount.

**certification of transfer** Act of signing a transfer deed in order to transfer stocks from one owner to another. The transfer is further made official by reporting it to the registrar.

**certified accountant** Accountant who has passed the examinations of the Chartered Association of Certified Accountants.

**certified copy** Copy of a document that is certified as being identical to the original.

**certified public accountant** Accountant who has passed US professional accounting examinations.

**cession** Business that a *reinsurance* company receives from a *cedant*.

**CET** Abbreviation of *common external tariff*.

**ceteris paribus** Latin for "other things remaining equal". It is used in economic analysis to study the effects of economic variants while assuming that other factors remain the same.

**CGBR** Abbreviation of *Central Government Borrowing Requirement*.

**CGT** Abbreviation of *capital gains tax*.

**chairman** A person who chairs a meeting, also called a chairperson or merely "chair", or the most senior director of a company, full title Chairman of the *Board of Directors*.

**chamber of commerce** Organization that promotes and represents the interests of those involved in commerce in a particular geographical area.

**CHAPS** Abbreviation of *Clearing House Automated Payments System*.

**Chapter 11** Clause in US company law that enables a company to continue to operate after it has been declared bankrupt (under the direction of the court), so that it may find a way to pay its creditors. The rough equivalent in Britain is *administration*.

**charge** Term with three meanings:
1. It is a sum of money that must be paid on goods or services or the act of requesting that sum.
2. It is an obligation to meet a debt.

3. It is a legal or equitable interest in land to secure payment of a debt.

**chargeable** Something that may be charged for, most usually a sum of money on which *tax* is liable to be paid.

**chargeable asset** Asset that is liable to give rise to a charge for *capital gains tax* (CGT).

**chargeable event** Any event that gives rise to liability to income or capital gains tax.

**chargeable gain** Gain, or more specifically capital profit, on which tax is payable.

**chargeable transfer** Lifetime gift that gives rise to *inheritance tax*.

**charge off** Alternative term for *write off*.

**charges forward** When goods are delivered, a notice that all charges must be paid at the time the goods are delivered.

**charges register** Part of the certificate issued by the UK Land Register that details all *mortgages* and *charges* in respect of a certain piece of land.

**charge card** Credit card that allows purchases from certain retail outlets up to set limits.

**charging order** Court order that allows a debtor's goods to be "earmarked" for the creditor. If the debt is not repaid, the goods become the property of the creditor.

**charitable trust** Trust set up for charitable purposes, usually exempt from tax.

**charter** Term with two meanings:

1. It is the granting in writing of a title, right or privilege.

2. It is the practice of hiring out a ship or aircraft for commercial or private use.

**chartered** Term applied to a person or institution that has been granted a *charter*, such as a chartered accountant or chartered company.

**chartered accountant** In England and Wales, an accountant who has passed the examinations of the Institute of Chartered Accountants and is either an associate or fellow of the Institute. In Ireland and Scotland, a chartered accountant is a fellow or associate of the Institute of Chartered Accountants in Ireland, and Scotland, respectively. The main difference between a chartered and a certified accountant is that the training of the former normally involves a period of time working with a firm of accountants and that of the latter does not.

**chartered company** Company that is incorporated by Royal Charter. The main difference between a chartered company and an ordinary company is that the former is treated as an individual person in law.

**Chartered Insurance Institute** (CII) Organization of insurance companies and brokers established in 1873 (granted a Royal Charter in 1912). It sets standards for the insurance industry, provides training and examinations, and grants diplomas (associateships and fellowships).

**chartist** Stock market or economic analyst who believes that trends (*e.g.* in price movements, etc.) follow recognizable patterns and so predicts future trends with the aid of charts. *See also* **fundamentalist**.

**chattels** Moveable property, as opposed to *fixtures* (property that cannot be moved).

**cheap jack** Person who buys goods at very low prices (*e.g.* from bankrupt companies or goods that are of poor quality) and sells them at below normal price, sometimes in the street or on a market. *See also* **caveat emptor**; *mock auction*.

**cheap money** Alternative term for *easy money*.

**checking** Computer process that takes place on the London Stock exchange between trading sessions, by which the records of brokers and market makers are reconciled. *See also* **reconciliation**.

**check sample** Sample taken from a consignment of goods and examined to determine whether or not the consignment is acceptable.

**cherry picking** Informal term for the policy of a financial institution that chooses only one type of business, usually one that is very secure or that makes a direct contribution to profitability. In insurance, it describes the activities of an insurer who only insures the "best" risks.

**chief accountant** Accountant within a business who deals with all company accounting and the provision of financial information to managers and *directors*, in particular the financial director.

**child's deferred policy** Type of *life assurance* on a child that yields a sum when the child reaches a particular age (usually 18 years).

**Chinese Wall** Artificial barrier erected between the underwriting and brokering departments of a stockbroking company. The Chinese Wall has become necessary since the **Big Bang** changed the London Stock Exchange to a **dual capacity** system in 1986. The purpose of the Chinese Wall is to prevent *insider dealing*. *See also* **underwriter**.

**choice price**  On futures markets, refers to a situation which, when comparing different market-makers' bid-offer spreads, one finds identical bid and offer price. This price is known as the choice price. *See also* **backwardation**.

**choses-in-action**  Legal term for the right to assets such as property and money. Hence, a *debt* may be termed choses-in-action until the sum is repaid and then becomes *choses-in-possession*.

**choses-in-possession**  Legal term for property owned by a person.*See also choses-in action*.

**churning**  The practice of encouraging the buying and selling investments solely in order to generate higher *commission* income for the adviser.

**Cie**  Abbreviation of Compagnie (French for Company).

**CIF**  Abbreviation of *cost, insurance and freight* and **Common Investment Fund**

**CIMP**  Abbreviation of contracted-in money purchase pension scheme.

**CII**  Abbreviation of Chartered Insurance Institute.

**circuit breaker**  Method of limiting the overall movement (up or down) of share prices, used on the Tokyo Stock Exchange in an attempt to maintain stability.

**circulating capital**  Money used by a company to invest in *assets* for resale. When such assets have been sold, the capital raised returns to the company.

**City**  Name given to the financial district of London, situated in the City of London. It covers an area of roughly one square mile and for this reason is also known as the Square Mile.

**claim**  Request for payment to an insurance company in respect of loss or damage covered by an insurance policy, usually submitted by filling in a claim form.

**claim form**  Document filled in by somebody who is making a *claim* against an insurance policy.

**Claims Advice and Settlement System** (CASS)  System used by insurance brokers to issue loss advices to the claims office at *Lloyd's of London* and to *syndicates* (to authorize them).

**Claims and Underwriting Exchange** (CUE)  System established in 1994 to record claims made by insurance policyholders so that insurance companies can cross-check and detect fraudulent claims.

**claims expenses**  Direct costs incurred by an insurance company in the settlement of a claim.

**claims inspector**  Person who investigates insurance claims, often in consultation with the insurance company's solicitors. *See also loss adjustor.*

**claims made basis**  Insurance policy that is written on the basis that cover is for claims made during the period of insurance, regardless of when the loss actually occurred. Commonly used for liability policies particularly in the USA, it is becoming more popular in the UK for certain liability insurances, such as professional indemnity.

**Claims Management Scheme** (CLAMS)  System used by the *Institute of London Underwriters* to process loss advices and information of settlements.

**Claims Office Support System** (COSS)  System used by the claims office of *Lloyd's of London* to record claims information and pass it on to *syndicates*.

**claims outstanding**  Insurance claims that are currently being settled. Insurance companies keep a contingency fund (called a claims outstanding reserve) in respect of such claims.

**claims-made policy**  Insurance policy in which the insurer must meet only claims made during the time cover is provided (irrespective of when the loss occurred).

**CLAMS**  Abbreviation of *Claims Management Scheme.*

**clash cover**  Type of insurance cover that protects a *reinsurer* if one event (such as a major flood) gives rise to a variety of claims on different kinds of policy.

**class action**  Legal action in which a person sues while representing  a class of persons.

**clause**  Condition of an agreement, most often used in reference to a *contract* or *insurance policy.*

**clawback** Practice of demanding that a person or company return money paid by the Inland Revenue in the form of a tax **rebate**. A clawback most often occurs because of the changed status of the person or company involved.

**clean bill** *Bill of exchange* that has no documents or special conditions attached.

**clean float** Floating exchange rate that is completely uncontrolled by the central bank. *See also* **dirty float**.

**clean price** Price of **gilt-edged security** excluding any interest that has accumulated since the last payment of a dividend.

**clear** Term with three broad meanings:

1. To clear is to have something authorized.

*The goods cleared customs with no problems.*

2. It is to sell goods in order to make room for new **stock**.

*They are having a sale; everything is reduced to clear.*

3. It is a period of so many days, or a sum of money on which there is nothing to be paid.

*He was told that it would take three clear days before the sum was paid into his account.*

*This year the company made a clear profit.*

**clearance** Term with three meanings:

1. It is the receipt of money from a bill or cheque.

2. It is the completion of necessary formalities before goods can enter or leave the country (such as customs **duty**).

3. It is the completion of necessary formalities before an aircraft or ship may depart.

**clearing cycle** Process by which payments by cheque are transferred from the payer's account to the payee's account. It usually takes two or three days.

**clearing house** Institution that specializes in clearing debts between its members. The best known type of clearing house is a banker's clearing house, which clears cheques between the major banks

**Clearing House Automated Payment System** (CHAPS) Organization founded in 1985, a part of the Association for Payment Clearing Services (APACS), that provides a guaranteed same-day electronic transfer of sterling funds within the UK.

**Clearing House InterBank Payments System** (CHIPS) US organization founded in 1970 that provides on-line electronic transfer of funds in US dollars, mainly for international transactions.

**clerk** In the UK, person who deals with records of some kind, usually in an office. In the USA, the term is used in the more general sense of anyone dealing with customers, *e.g.* a salesperson in a retail store.

**client agreement** Document required to be given to the client under the Financial Services Act in all cases where advice is in relation to a non-packaged product, and is of a regular nature. It details the adviser's responsibilities to the client.

**CLMI** Abbreviation of *Commercial Lines Market Initiative.*

**close** Term with three meanings:
1. On a financial *futures* market, it is the thirty seconds before trading closes for the day.
2. It is sometimes used to refer to the *closing price.*
3. To close a *position* is to cover an open position on a futures or options market by making a further transaction.

**close company** Company whose shares are held privately, by a few individuals (usually not more than five people), and not traded on a stock exchange. The US alternative is closed company or closely-held company.

**closed** Something that is not open to such things as *risk* or the general public.

**closed company** US alternative term for *close company*

**closed economy** Economy that is self-sufficient in that it makes neither imports nor exports.

**closed-end fund** Alternative term for *investment trust.*

**closed indent** Order for goods placed with an agent abroad that specifies the supplier from whom the goods are to be obtained.

**closely-held company** US alternative term for *close company*.

**closing** Action that ends something, *e.g.* a day's trading or an auction.

**closing bid** Last bid at an *auction*, or more generally, the bid that is successful.

**closing price** Price of shares at the close of trading each day on a stock exchange.

**closing purchase** Purchase of an option that closes an open *position*.

**closing range** On a *financial futures* market the highest and lowest prices recorded during the close.

**closing rate** Rate at the close of business for the day for the foreign exchange of spot currency.

**closing sale** On an *options* market, transaction in which an option is sold in order to close a *position*.

**closing the sale** Persuading a customer or client to commit to a purchase.

**clustered policy** Unit-linked contract that splits into small clusters (often called "policies") within a plan. Each cluster or segment can be dealt with separately, allowing complete flexibility.

**CMI** Abbreviation of *Continuous Mortality Investigation.*

**CNAR** Abbreviation of *compound net annual rate.*

**Co** Abbreviation of *company.*

**c/o** Abbreviation of cash with order.

**COD** Abbreviation of *cash on delivery.*

**coemption** Legal term for *cornering the market.*

**coinsurance** Method of sharing insurance risk between several insurers. The policyholder will deal as a lead insurer who issues documents and collects premiums. The policy will detail the shares held by each company.

**cold call** Sales practice of approaching a potential customer, either by telephone or in person, without any prior introduction. It is also termed an unsolicited call.

**collar** A borrower or investor is protected against fluctuations in interest rates by a "cap and collar". The cap is the maximum rate, the collar is the minimum.

**collateral** Informal term for *security*, such as that put up against a loan.

**collecting friendly society** Mutual organization that specializes in *personal accident and sickness insurance* and *industrial life assurance. See also friendly society.*

**collective** Group of people working together towards a common aim.

**collective ownership** Ownership of *e.g.* a business or property with all the gains being equally divided among the members of the collective.

**collectivism**  Economic system in which all factors of production are owned by the community and controlled largely by the state. *See also communism.*

**combined household and contents insurance**  Type of insurance that covers both a property and its contents, often with contents cover set as a percentage of the household cover.

**come to market**  US term for a *new issue.*

**COMEX**  Abbreviation of Commodity Exchange of New York.

**commercial**  Describing a thing or person associated with business or commerce. The term has also come to mean a product that will sell well.

**commercial attaché**  Diplomat who specializes in representing the commercial interests of his or her country.

**commercial bill**  *Bill of exchange* that is not a *Treasury bill.*

**commercial code**  Code that is used by international traders in order to reduce the cost of sending faxes, telexes and cables.

**Commercial Lines Market Initiative** (CLMI)  Computerized system that allows insurance brokers to settle accounts and to trade claims, quotes and enquiries with *underwriters.*

**commercial motor insurance**  Type of *motor insurance* taken out by a company for non-privately owned vehicles, from cars and vans to heavy lorries.

**commercial paper**  Corporate debt in a tradeable form. It is a short-term, low-risk unsecured means of borrowing, the issuers being insurance companies, pension funds and other creditworthy institutions.

**commercials**  Shares in a commercial company, usually a seller of consumer goods. *See also industrials.*

**commercial undertaking**  Another name for a firm or business.

**commercial year**  Period (360 days) used by financial institutions to calculate discounts.

**commission**  Money paid to an *agent* or other intermediary, usually calculated as a percentage of the sum involved in the transaction.

*The salesman received 5% commission on each sale he made.*

*See also brokerage.*

**commission agent**  Agent who is paid a *commission*, usually calculated as a percentage of the value of sales.

**Commissioners of Insurance**  Persons appointed by US state governors to regulate and supervise the insurance industry in the USA.

**commitment fee**  Amount paid to a lender to keep a credit facility open.

**commitment window**  The amount of time an employee is prepared to spend in the service of one company.

**committee of inspection**  Committee made up of a bankrupt company's creditors to direct the company's *winding-up*, either in the hands of a receiver or a liquidator. *See* **liquidation; receivership.**

**Committee of Lloyd's**  Group of working members of the Council of *Lloyd's of London* which is responsible for the day-to-day running of the organization's affairs.

**commodity**  Term with two meanings:
1.  In economics, it is any tangible good that is traded.
2.  It is raw materials and foods, especially such goods as cocoa, coffee, jute, potatoes, tea, etc., which may also be traded.

**commodity broker**  Broker who deals in *commodities*, usually in a *commodity market*.

**commodity exchange**  *Commodity market* on which *actuals* and *futures* are traded.

**commodity market**  Market on which *commodities* are traded.

**common**  Describing something that happens very frequently, or that applies equally to a number of people, without exclusion or differentiation.

**common external tariff**  (CET)  Import tariff charged by all members of a trading community (*e.g.* the EU) on goods being imported from non-member countries.

**Common Investment Fund**  (CIF)  Investment fund for a charity with modest funds, run in a similar way to a *unit trust*.

**common pool**  Principle whereby individuals transfer a risk, in return for paying a small premium, to a pool which represents many other similar risks, and from which claims for insured risks are paid. In operating a common pool, the insurer benefits from the law of large numbers.

**communism** Political and economic system whereby all factors of production are owned and controlled by the state. *See also* **capitalism**.

**Community company** Insurance company that is based in a European Union (EU) country - formerly a European Community (EC) country - but with an underwriting branch in the UK.

**commutation** Exchange of a pension for a cash lump sum paid now, *e.g.*, a member of a pension scheme may commute part of his or her pension as a lump sum immediately on retirement and then accept smaller annual pension payments.

**commute** *See commutation.*

**commuted value** Cash lump sum paid from a pension plan.

**Compagnie des Agents de Chance** (CAC) Organization of which all French stockbrokers are members.

**Companies House** Office of the Registrar of Companies.

**company** Group of people that has been legally incorporated to produce certain goods or services, or to transact any other type of business.

**company doctor** Person who is brought into a company that is on the brink of liquidation, usually at board level. A company doctor often has powers to administer very strong medicine in order to put the company back on its feet.

**company pension** *See occupational pension scheme.*

**company representative** Employed or self-employed agent of a product provider, who may give advice only on that particular company's products (*see* **tied agent**). The term is also used to describe an employee of an appointed representative.

**company secretary** Someone who is responsible for ensuring that his or her company complies with company law.

**comparative advantage** State of being more efficient in one activity than in another, relative to a different country, *e.g.* a country is able to produce cars twice as efficiently as another, but produces aeroplanes ten times more efficiently. In a free market, this country would export aeroplanes and import cars and it is said that, in the production of aeroplanes, it has a comparative advantage over the other.

**compensation** Usually a sum of money paid in lieu of something lost.
*She received substantial compensation for the injuries she sustained in a road accident which prevented her from working for a full year.*

**competition** Effort directed towards doing better than someone else, especially that among rival companies in the same market.

*When they entered the market, Nutbrown Productions found themselves in direct competition with several much larger companies.*

**competition analysis** The process of gathering and assessing information about one's corporate competition.

**complements** Two goods that are related in such a way that when *demand* for one increases, demand for the other rises at the same time, *e.g.* cameras and photographic film are complements, as are cars and petrol.

**completion** The finish of something, such as a job or contract.

**compliance** In a financial institution, the activity that makes sure that the organization's operations comply with regulatory and statutory requirements, *i.e.*, within the law as it applies to such institutions. Many institutions have a compliance officer to check that this happens.

**compliance cost** Cost to a company of complying with a regulation, such as keeping records of *value added tax* (VAT) for the Customs and Excise.

**compliance officer** Required under the Financial Services Act, it is the person who monitors the *compliance* of a business and who is responsible for compliance arrangements and procedures.

**composite currency peg** Type of *exchange rate* system in which a country pegs its currency to a basket of currencies of its main trading partners.

**composite insurance company** Insurance company that provides all types of policies, such as accident, fire, life and pensions. Such companies form most of the UK market.

**composite rate tax** A rate of tax (3% below the basic rate) in the UK between 1951 and 1991 that banks and building societies deducted from the interest paid to investors. Taxpayers now have to pay the full basic rate of income tax on the interest, which is deducted by the bank or building society.

**compound** Term with two meanings:

1. It is to agree with creditors to settle a debt by paying only part of it.
*He compounded his debts with his creditors.*

2. It is to add something to a thing that is already there, *e.g.* compound

interest is calculated by adding each interest payment to the capital sum and taking this new total as the basis for the next reckoning.

**compound(ed) annual return** (CAR) Total return on a sum invested or lent over a period of a year, including the return on *interest* previously accrued. *See also compound net annual rate.*

**compound interest** Rate of interest calculated by adding interest previously paid to the capital sum plus previous interest payment. *See also simple interest.*

**compound net annual rate** (CNAR) Return, after deduction of tax at the basic rate, of interest from a deposit or investment that includes the return on interest previously accrued. *See also compound annual return.*

**compound reversionary bonus** For an *endowment policy*, a reversionary bonus that is calculated on both the basic sum assured and the annual revisionary bonuses already earned.

**comprehensive insurance** Type of *motor insurance* that provides more comprehensive cover than *third party insurance*. It normally includes protection for the driver, the vehicle and its contents, and third parties.

**COMPS** Abbreviation of contracted-out money purchase scheme.

**compulsory liquidation** Liquidation of a company that has become insolvent. In this case, the Official Receiver is initially in charge of the disposal of the company's assets. *See insolvency; receivership.*

**computer-assisted trading** (CAT) Method of trading in which brokers and traders use computers on, *e.g.*, the foreign exchange market or the stock exchange.

**concealment** In insurance, the deliberate withholding of information that is material to a policy. The person who does so is in breach of *utmost good faith* and, as a result, the insurance policy may be invalid.

**concern** Alternative term for a business or company.
*When he left the business, it was still a going concern.*

**concert party** Group of people who come together secretly to "act in concert", that is, to orchestrate a market in the group's favour, *e.g.* two or more people my form a concert party to buy shares in a company in order to effect a takeover. Such action is illegal.

**concession** Term with two broad meanings:
1. It is the right to use someone else's property as part of a business.

2. It is an allowance made to someone who would otherwise be charged.

**conditional** Something that is not certain but depends on an event or situation, such as a conditional bill of sale.

**conditional assignment** Assignment to a third party of a *life assurance* policy without all its rights and liabilities (*e.g.*, as when the policy is used as security for a loan).

**conditional bill of sale** *Bill of sale* by which the owner of the goods transferred retains the right to repossess them.

**conditional endorsement** Endorsement on which the endorser has added a condition, which has to be fulfilled before the endorser receives the proceeds of the bill.

**Confederation of British Industry** (CBI) Independent organization established in 1965 by combining the British Employers Confederation, the Federation of British Industry and the National Association of British Manufacturers. It represents industry in consultations with the government and promotes the activities of industry in the UK.

**conference line** Term with two meanings:

1. It is a service available to corporate telephone users, which allows several callers in different locations to talk to each other at the same time.
2. It is a group of shipping companies that have agreed on freight rates and passenger fares. Conference line shippers usually charge lower rates than non-conference lines.

**confidence** Feeling of certainty or security, *e.g.* confidence in a company's ability to produce goods is extremely important if it is to find *investment*.

**confirmation of renewal** Acknowledgement by an insurer that the insured has complied with the requirements of a *renewal notice*.

**conglomerate** Very large public company that is extremely diverse and probably international in its operations.

**consequential loss insurance** Insurance cover against losses that occur after a claim is made on another insurance policy (such as loss of revenue and costs accrued when a business cannot function after a fire, fire damage itself being covered by another policy). *See also business interruption insurance.*

**consideration**  In some forms of *contract*, the agreement is made binding by the payment of a sum of money from one party to the other. Such a payment is known as a consideration. The term is also used informally to mean any form of payment.

*If you want to buy a car, he'll find you the one you want for a consideration.*

**consignment**  Shipment of goods sent to someone (*e.g.* an agent), usually so that he or she may sell them for the consignor.

**consistency concept**  In *accounting*, a concept whereby accounts for one period are constructed on the same principles as for another.

**Consol**  Abbreviation of Consolidated Stock or Consolidated Loan, a form of fixed-interest government security that has no *redemption date*.

**consolidated accounts**  If a company has subsidiary companies, each *subsidiary company* has its own set of profit and loss accounts, but these must also be consolidated to form accounts for the whole group. These are known as consolidated accounts. *See also profit-and-loss account.*

**consolidation**  Term with three meanings:
1. In shipping, it is the practice of putting together goods for shipping to the same destination.
2. In *accounting*, it is the practice of putting together the accounts of *subsidiary companies* of a group, to calculate overall results for the group as a whole.
3. In share dealings, it is the practice of combining a number of low-priced shares, to produce a realistically marketable *lot*. *See also split.*

**consortium**  Group of companies that come together to bid for a certain project. It is usually dissolved after that one project is complete. It is similar to a *syndicate*, only more short-term.

**constitution**  Set of rules and details of aims, laid down by a society or club. Constitution (with a capital C) is a list of members of a *Lloyd's of London syndicate*.

**consumable**  Describing something that is used up (*e.g.* computer printer ink, degreasing solvents, welding rods) in a business or industry, as opposed to things (*e.g.* raw materials) that are incorporated into a product.

**consumer durable**  Consumer goods of some technological sophistication that yield utility over a period of time, *e.g.* clothing, cars, washing machines, etc.

**consumer goods**  Goods that are consumed in use, either over a short period (*e.g.* foodstuffs), or over a longer period, such as motor vehicle tyres (or even the motor vehicles themselves). *See also* **consumer durable.**

**consumer price index**  US term for *retail price index.*

**consumption**  Act of consuming, *i.e.* using goods or services that are thereby damaged or used up and cannot therefore be re-sold.

**conspicuous consumption**  Consumer trend that involves the consumer buying goods (usually status symbols, such as sports cars, etc.), deriving satisfaction, not from consumption of the goods themselves, but from being seen by other people to own them.

**contango**  Former stock exchange term for a delayed settlement of a bargain from one account to the next. A *premium* is payable. The term is also used more frequently in futures trading to mean the opposite of *backwardation.*

**contemptuous damages**  Damages awarded if the court agrees that the defendant was at fault, but believes that the loss or injury caused was so minor that the case should not have been brought.

**contents insurance**  Insurance that gives cover the loss of or damage to personal possessions kept in the home. It may be included with *household insurance* in a combined household and contents insurance.

**contingency**  Something that is liable, but not certain, to happen at some time in the future. *See also* **contingent.**

**contingency insurance**  Type of insurance that covers financial losses that could result from some specified event, such as rain spoiling an outdoor event (*see* **weather insurance**) or the birth of twins.

**contingent**  Something that depends on an uncertain event taking place. *The company's willingness to insure the building is contingent upon our re-pointing the brickwork on the gable end.*

**contingent annuity**  Annuity that is paid to the annuitant only in the event of a certain set of circumstances arising, *e.g.*, a wife may take out a contingent annuity for her husband which becomes payable only in the event of her death.

**continuation**  Option in a life assurance policy that allows insurance to continue/be extended without underwriting. It is available in some group life schemes should a member leave employment.

**C**

**Continuous Mortality Investigation** (CMI) Ongoing study of mortality, resulting in the production of mortality tables, by the Institute and Faculty of Actuaries.

**contra** Latin for the "opposite side". *See also per contra.*

**contract** Term with two meanings:

1. It is a legally binding agreement between two or more parties.
2. It is to form such an agreement.

**contract bond** Alternative term for *performance bond.*

**contracted-out** Describing employees who have opted out of the *State Earnings-Related Pension Scheme* (SERPS) through an appropriate personal pension or a contracted-out occupational scheme.

**contracted-out final salary scheme** *See contracted-out salary-related scheme.*

**contracted-out money purchase scheme** (COMPS) Money purchase occupational pension scheme which has contracted out of the *State Earnings-Related Pension Scheme* (SERPS). Both employer and employee pay lower National Insurance contributions. The employer guarantees to pay a minimum contribution to the protected rights part of the plan.

**contracted-out salary-related scheme** (COSR) Final salary occupational pension scheme that has contracted out of the *State Earnings-Related Pension Scheme* (SERPS). Both employer and employee pay lower National Insurance contributions. The scheme provides a *guaranteed minimum pension* for pre-April 1997 benefits. After 1997, such a scheme is subject to a reference test, which is a test of the overall quality of the scheme.

**contract guarantee insurance** Type of insurance that guarantees the solvency of a contractor during the life of a contract. If the contractor goes out of business with the contract unfinished, the insurance company pays the insurer the contract price (in order to employ another contractor to complete the work).

**contract in** In general, to make an agreement to join some scheme (and participate in its benefits). In particular, it is the decision of a company to make contributions towards the *state pension* scheme for its employees. If a company does contract in in this way, it is also able to provide extra pensions by using private schemes. *See also **contract out**.*

**contractor's all risks** Type of insurance that provides compensation to a contractor in the event of damage to construction works (*e.g.* a motorway bridge) from a wide range of perils.

**contract out** In general, to make an agreement to forego some activity (and its possible benefits). In particular, the term refers to opting out of the *State Earnings-Related Pension Scheme* (SERPS). This can be done via a personal pension or an occupational scheme.

**contract size** Size (*i.e.* weight) of a futures contract, so as to ascertain its value. Contract sizes are all fixed, *e.g.* COMEX gold is 100 oz.

**contra entry** In double-entry *book-keeping* an item that is entered to balance out another. Its purpose is to negate the original item, often because that entry was made in error.

**contra proferentem rule** Nickname for the following Latin maxim: *verba chartarum fortuis accipiuntur contra proferentem* – the words of the contract are construed more strictly against the person proclaiming them. In effect, the contra proferentem rule means that if a contract is ambiguous, it will be construed in a way that is the least advantageous to the party that drew up the contract.

**contrarian** Informal term for a speculator in *stocks* and *shares* who goes against short-term trends, *e.g.* a contrarian may decide on a buying policy in a *bear market.*

**contribution** Term with two meanings:

1.  It is money paid as an addition to another sum.
2.  It is a term in insurance in which a risk has been insured twice over, and each insurance company shares the costs of a claim payment.

**contributory negligence** Lack of care in looking after something that reduces the value of damages or an insurance payment in the event of a claim being made.

**contributory pension** Pension for which an employee makes contributions during his or her working life. The contribution is usually a percentage of the employee's gross salary, deducted at source and added to the employer's contribution.

**controlled economy** Economy in which the government tries to control elements of economic activity by legislating for key areas rather than taking direct charge of the factors of production. *See also planned economy.*

**controlling interest** Sufficient holding of voting shares in a company (more than 50%) to give a single shareholder control of the company. Legally, a director has a controlling interest if he or she owns more than 20% of the voting shares.

**conventional option** Alternative term for *traditional option*.

**conversion** Term with two meanings:

1. It is the changing of one thing into another that is equivalent.
2. In a legal context, it is interference with the property of someone else, so as to deprive him or her of the right of ownership.

**convertible** Describing something that is easily capable of *conversion*. The term has the more specific meaning of loan stock, bonds and debentures that are easily converted into ordinary shares. These are known as convertibles, or, in the USA, converts.

**convertible bond** Also known as convertible loan stock or convertible, a bond that is offered at a fixed, low rate of interest with an option to convert the bond into an equity share.

**convertible currency** Currency that is easily exchangeable for another currency.

**convertible term insurance** Type of *term assurance* that can be converted into an *endowment assurance* policy or a *whole-life insurance* without the need for a medical examination within the policy term.

**conveyance** Transfer of ownership of land or other property.

**cooling-off period** Period of 14 days (in the UK) during which a person who has agreed to a certain form of contract may withdraw from that agreement and have his or her money repaid. Such a period exists in order to minimize the effects of hard selling that some companies or their agents undertake. A cooling-off period is a statutory requirement for most life and pension contracts.

**co-operative** Group of people who come together to produce goods or services and who share all profits.

**co-operative society** Society of consumers and producers (or retailers) who share the profits of their co-operation.

**copyhold** Alternative term for *freehold*.

**copyright** Legal term for the right of ownership of an author over his or her own work. Copyright extends for a term of 70 years after the author's death.

**corpocracy** If a company is involved in several mergers, its management is at risk of becoming cumbersome and confused. The resulting corporation thus labours under a large and inefficient bureaucracy and is known informally as a corpocracy.

**Corn Exchange** London commodities exchange that deals in such commodities as cereals and animal foodstuffs.

**corner the market** To build a virtual *monopoly* in particular goods or services, so that the monopolist is able to dictate *price*.

**corp** Abbreviation of *corporation*.

**corporate** To do with a *corporation*.

**corporate bond** Bond issued by a company which represents a commercial loan.

**corporate bond PEP** *See personal equity plan.*

**corporate culture** Culture that grows up within a company, among its employees. Corporate culture embodies such factors as dress, its employees' attitudes towards working and their expectations, and the style of working relationships.

**corporate identity** Identity of a company as displayed in the visual images it uses, *e.g.* its logos and colours.

**corporate image** Image that a company presents to the general public. Some large companies now spend large sums in an attempt to improve their corporate image.

**corporate name** Limited liability company that becomes a name at Lloyd's. *See Lloyd's of London.*

**corporate planning** Activity undertaken to plan the future aims of a company, covering such subject areas as new products, sales targets and production targets.

**corporate raider** Someone who buys enough shares of *target company* to take it over or to sufficiently influence the management to make changes that improve the share value of the company. The raider can then sell the shares at a profit.

**corporate veil** Protection against liability that is afforded to multiple shareholders in a company as opposed to one single owner. *See also limited liability.*

**corporate venturing** Practice of a company providing *venture capital* for another. Corporate venturing is usually undertaken to give the investing company a potential foothold in a new (or related) market or field, or to lay the foundations for a possible *takeover* at some future date.

**corporation**  Large *company*, usually with several *subsidiary companies*. In the USA, it is a company that has been incorporated under US law. Therefore, the term is a virtual synonym for company. It is often abbreviated to corp.

**corporation tax**  (CT)  Tax levied on a company's profits. *See also advance corporation tax.*

**COSR**  Abbreviation of *contracted-out salary-related scheme.*

**cost**  Amount of money that has to be expended to acquire something, in most cases its price.

**cost accountant**  Accountant who specializes in reckoning the *cost* of manufacturing a unit of a product, taking into account such variables as cost of raw materials and *labour*, and thereby making a *projection* of probable cost at the planning stage of a project. This in turn enables the manufacturer to *tender* a price to a prospective buyer.

**cost accounting**  Work undertaken by a *cost accountant.*

**cost analysis**  Examination of the *cost* of producing a particular product, normally undertaken before the project is begun.

**cost and freight**  (CF, or C & F)  When exporting goods, a contract in which it is agreed that the exporter pays all costs up to the delivery point except for insurance (which is paid for by the buyer). *See also cost, insurance and freight; cost, insurance, freight and interest.*

**cost centre**  For *accounting* purposes, location (*e.g.* a geographical area or department) or piece of equipment that can be isolated, with a view to ascribing specific costs to it. *See also overheads; unit cost.*

**cost-effective**  Something that gives value for money. It is often used as a relative term.

**cost, insurance and freight**  (CIF)  Foreign trade contract stipulating that the exporter pays all costs up to the point of delivery, including insurance of goods in transit. *See also cost and freight; cost, insurance, freight and interest.*

**cost, insurance, freight and interest**  (CIFI)  Export contract, by which the exporter is bound to pay all costs to delivery, along with insurance on goods in transit and interest on the value of the goods. *See also* **cost and freight**; *cost, insurance and freight.*

**cost minimization** Practice of seeking the minimum cost at which a company is able to produce the output it requires.

**cost of living** In national terms, the amount of money each person has to spend in order to buy food and accommodation. *See also* **retail price index.**

**cost-plus** System of charges whereby the buyer pays the cost of the item plus a commission to the seller.
*Peter decided to charge for the goods on a cost-plus basis.*

**cost-push inflation** Theory that inflation is caused by increases in the costs of the manufacturing process, thus pushing overall prices to the consumer up. *See* **demand-pull inflation.**

**costs** Term with two meanings:
1. It refers to expenses incurred during a court case.
*Bill was fined £200 and ordered to pay costs.*
2. It is the sum of the cost of each item used during production of goods or services.

**cost unit** One article, to which a cost may be ascribed for *accounting* purposes. Cost units may include simple articles such as raw materials (*e.g.* a plank of wood), or articles in production (although these are more complicated in that they require the accounting to take into account direct and indirect costs). *See also* **cost centre.**

**costing** Practice of working out how much a product will cost to produce, taking into account costs such as raw materials, labour, overheads, etc. A frequent alternative term is costing-out.

**costing-out** *See costing.*

**Council of Lloyd's** Group of members of **Lloyd's of London** who are in overall charge of the organization's affairs, including disciplinary matters and the making of rules.

**counter** Term with two meanings:
1. It is a (figurative) table across which goods are bought and sold.
2. It is a prefix meaning against (as in, *e.g.*, counterinflationary).

**counterbid** Bid that is made (*e.g.* during a takeover battle or an auction) against a previous bid, going one better.

**counterclaim**  Claim for damages made by a defendant against a plaintiff, in the hopes that the counterclaim will offset any *damages* payable to the plaintiff in the first action. *See also* **set-off**.

**counterfoil**  Document kept as a record of a transaction, often attached to (and then detached from) a bond, certificate or cheque.

**countermove**  Tactical action taken in response to moves made by an opponent, *e.g.* during *takeover* battle.

**counter-offer**  Offer (*e.g.* of a price on a property) made in response to a previous offer.

*Both companies wanted the premises so badly that counter-offer after counter-offer was made, until the final price was astronomical.*

**countersign**  To sign a document that has already been signed by someone else.

*Please would you ask Mary to countersign this contract before I return it.*

**countervailing credit**  Alternative term for *back-to-back credit*.

**coupon**  Term with two meanings:

1. It is a document attached to a bond, that must be detached and sent to the paying party in order for the bond holder to receive *interest* payments. Each payment is detailed on the coupon for each payment period.
2. It is an alternative term for interest that is payable on a *fixed-interest security* (such as *gilt-edged security*). *See also* **cum coupon**; **ex coupon**.

**coupon bond**  Alternative term for *bearer bond*.

**covenant**  Term with two meanings:

1. It is broadly any form of *agreement*.
2. More specifically, it is an agreement taken out between two parties, stating that one party agrees to pay the other a series of fixed sums over a certain period of time. If the covenant covers a period longer than six years, then the payer is entitled to *tax relief* on the payments.

**cover**  Term with several meanings:

1. It is any form of *security* (*i.e.* collateral).
2. It is used in financial futures markets to the buying of contracts to offset a short position.

**C**

3. It describes the number of times a company could pay its dividends to shareholders from its earnings.

*This year's annual report shows that C & F White plc are three times covered.*

4. It is to make enough money in selling products or services to pay for their production.

*I am pleased to say that last year we more than covered our costs.*

5. It is the amount of money an insured person stands to receive from an insurer should he or she make a claim (*see* **insurance cover**).

*Tim has £600,000 insurance cover for his small art collection.*

6. It is the constituent amount put up as **margin** per unit of quotation on a futures contract, which combined will dictate the margin.

**covered bear** Dealer who sell **shares** or **commodities** he owns, hoping to buy them back later at a lower price (*i.e.* he or she is not taking the risk of **short selling**). He or she is also known as a protected bear.

**covered interest arbitrage** System in which money borrowed in one currency is converted into another and then invested, before selling it for a future delivery against the first currency. *See also* **arbitrage**.

**coverholder** Agent who receives authority from an **underwriter** to accept and deal with insurance business on his or her behalf (usually within certain specified limits).

**cover note** Document issued by an insurance company giving cover for a short time, often one month, while a complete policy (and, possibly, an insurance certificate) is drawn up and issued.

**CPA** Abbreviation of certified public accountant.

**CPP** Abbreviation of *current purchasing power (accounting)*.

**crash** Term with two meanings:
1. It is an informal term for a very severe drop in prices on securities, financial and commodities markets. The most famous was the Wall Street Crash of 1929, which led to the 1930s depression; the largest in recent years was the worldwide drop in share prices on 15 October 1987.
2. It is an informal term for a computer failure. In the USA, this is also known as a brownout.

**crawling peg** Form of fixed *exchange rate*, in which the rate is allowed to fluctuate according to supply and demand, but within certain specified minimum and maximum limits. It is also known as a sliding peg. *See also adjustable peg.*

**creative accountancy** *See number fudging.*

**credit** Term with several meanings:

1. It is a loan of money.

*Andrew found it difficult to obtain credit from any bank.*

2. It is to add a sum to an *account*.

*My building society credits my account with interest automatically.*

3. In book-keeping, it is a *balance* that shows a profit.

*When he had rationalized his extremely complicated personal finances, he found that he was in credit after all.*

4. It is the financial standing of a person or company.

*Their credit is very good, so you may feel confident about lending them money.*

**credit agency** (US **credit bureau**) Company that gathers information on the credit-worthiness of individuals and companies, and distributes this information to those providing credit facilities. *See also* **credit rating**.

**credit balance** In accounting, balance showing that more money has been received than is owed and so the account is in *credit*.

**credit bureau** Alternative term for *credit agency*.

**credit control** System that ensures repayment of outstanding debts within an organization.

**credit crunch** Situation in which *short credit* becomes scarce and thus more expensive than *long credit*.

**credit entry** Item of *credit* recorded in a *ledger* for accounting purposes.

**credit freeze** Action by banks to restrict the extension of credit to customers. It is also known as credit squeeze.

**credit guarantee** Type of insurance that gives cover against default by somebody who has obtained credit.

**credit insurance** Insurance against the risk of non-payment of a commercial debt (possibly because of insolvency).

**credit limit** The maximum sum that a person is prepared to lend to another.

*At Christmas I spent right up to my credit limit.*

**credit line** Extent of credit available to a borrower under a credit agreement.

**credit note** Document, often printed in red, issued to confirm the transfer of credit from one account to another.

**creditor** Person or company to whom money is owed.

**credit rating** Rating assigned to a person or company in order to indicate creditworthiness.

**credit scoring** Method of assessing a company's or person's ability to make loans.

**credit squeeze** Alternative term for *credit freeze*.

**credit union** Non-profit making mutual organization that offers facilities for savings, makes small loans, and may provide basic personal insurance within a local area.

**creditworthy** Describing a person who, from his or her record, is deemed willing and able to pay back credit. Thus, a creditworthy person finds it easier to borrow (and to borrow larger sums) than someone who is deemed to be a credit risk.

**creeping takeover** Gradual increase in a shareholding through open purchase on the stock exchange with the aim of accumulating enough shares to make a *takeover bid*.

**CREST** Electronic (and therefore paperlesss) system introduced by the Bank of England for processing shares for the securities market. It includes registration, purchases, sales and the payment of dividends as they become due.

**critical illness insurance** Type of insurance that provides a lump sum on diagnosis of one of the specified critical illnesses in the policy (*e.g.* cancer, heart attack, stroke).

**critical yield** Yield required under a pensions transfer plan which is needed to match the preserved benefits. It is calculated using a *transfer value analysis* system.

**CRT** Abbreviation of *composite rate tax*.

**cross** Practice of buying and selling the same block of *shares* or *futures* contracts simultaneously by the same broker.

**cross-border accord**  Agreement made between two neighbouring countries, often with regard to trading.

**cross-firing**  Fraud that involves opening two or more accounts at different banks. Money withdrawn from the first bank is backed by a cheque drawn on the second bank, and so on.

**cross guarantee**  Guarantee required by a bank from a a parent company when making a loan to one of its subsidiary companies.

**cross rate**  Rate at which one currency may be exchanged for a second, expressed in terms of a third currency.

**crowd**  The people who wish to trade in a particular option or future, so named because to do so, they must gather around the relevant *pitch*.

**crown jewel tactic**  Strategy undertaken by a company that is threatened by *takeover*, in which it sells, or offers to sell, the best part of its business to someone other than the *raider* (*e.g.* a *white knight*), in order to make the target seem less desirable.

**CT**  Abbreviation of *corporation tax*.

**CTT**  Abbreviation of *capital transfer tax*.

**CUE**  Abbreviation of *Claims and Underwriting Exchange*.

**cum coupon**  *Security* that is passed from one holder to another with *coupon* (enabling the holder to claim *interest* payments) attached. *See also* *ex coupon*.

**cum dividend**  Shares that are sold with the right of the new holder to claim the next *dividend* payment. It is sometimes abbreviated to cum div. *See also* *ex dividend*.

**cum new**  Shares that are sold with the right to claim participation in a scrip or rights issue. *See also* *ex new*; *scrip issue*.

**cumulative preference share**  Kind of *preference share* whose holder can claim any dividends not paid in earlier years, as long as the company has funds to pay them. Even then, eventual payment is guaranteed before payment to holders of ordinary shares.

**currency bond**  *Bond* issued in a foreign country. It is repaid in the appropriate foreign currency.

**currency contract period**  Following the devaluation of a currency, the time during which contracts negotiated before the devaluation become due.

**currency exposure**  Risk of holding assets in a foreign currency. The risk is incurred because its value, relative to that of the host nation's currency, may be unstable. It is possible to hedge against currency exposure by selling foreign currency on the *forward* markets. *See* **hedging**.

**currency gyration**  *See floating exchange rate.*

**currency inconvertibility**  Situation that arises when a company cannot change *local currency* into a *convertible currency* in order to transfer funds out of the country.

**currency option contract**  Contract that allows the purchaser of the option the right (if he or she wishes) to trade in a foreign currency at a pre-set exchange rate within a specified time period.

**currency swap**  Transaction where one currency is exchanged for another at a fixed rate.

**current**  Describing a continuing state of affairs that is occurring or relevant now, and is expected to remain so in the near future.

**current account**  Part of the balance of payments, which refers to national income and expenditure, including visible trade and *invisible trade.*

**current asset**  Asset that is used by a company in its day-to-day operations, *e.g.* raw materials, etc.

**current assets ratio**  Slightly different to the *acid-test ratio*, the current assets ratio is the ratio of a company's assets including its stock-in-trade, to its current liabilities.

**current cost accounting**  (CCA)  Also known as inflation accounting, a method of accounting that takes changes in prices due to *inflation* into account, adjusting values of assets, costs, etc.

**current expenditure**  Expenditure on assets for resale, such as raw materials rather than on fixed assets. It is also known as above-the-line expenditure. *See fixed asset.*

**current liabilities**  Money owed (by a company or individual) that should be paid within a year of the date on the balance sheet. *See also long-term liabilities.*

**current purchasing power accounting**  (CPP)  Method of accounting that has been advocated since the 1970s, and which involves stating all accounts in terms of a unit of purchasing power, calculated from a price *index*. Current purchasing power accounting has not yet become a common method.

**current ratio** Test of *liquidity* made by dividing a company's *current assets* by its *current liabilities*. It is also called current assets ratio or working-capital ratio.

**current year basis** Basis of assessment for UK tax in which tax is charged on profits from the accounting year ending in that tax year. Therefore, an accounting year that ends on 31 August 1998 will be charged to tax in the 1998/99 tax year.

**current yield** *Dividend* calculated as a percentage of the price paid for each share.

**curriculum vitae** Latin for the "course of life". It is a document that relates (most usually in tabular form) the education, qualifications, and career of a person. It is known in the USA as a resumé.

**Customs and Excise** UK Government department charged with levying indirect taxes, including *value-added tax* (VAT) and *customs duty* on goods imported into the UK or produced in the UK for home consumption (*excise*). It full name is Board of Customs and Excise.

**customs barrier** High level of customs duty that makes trade difficult. It is also known as a tariff barrier.

**customs duty** Duty levied on imports by the *Customs and Excise*, either as a protectionist measure, or simply to raise revenue.

**cut a deal** To agree on the basic principles of an agreement. Negotiation or finalization of details usually follows.

**CWO** Abbreviation of cash with order.

**cyclical unemployment** Unemployment caused by movements in the trade cycle, *e.g.* during a *recession*.

**cyclicals** Shares in companies that are involved in basic industries, such as the provision of raw materials, metals, etc. They are so called because their prices on the stock market tend to rise and fall with the business cycle.

# D

**DA** Abbreviation of *deposit account* and *discretionary accounts.*

**D/A** Abbreviation of *documents against acceptance.*

**daisy chain** Buying and selling the same *stocks* or *shares* several times, usually to make it appear that there is more activity in their trading than there really is.

**damages** Civil court award of monetary compensation for loss or injury.

**dangling debit** Method by which a firm creates a goodwill account by writing off goodwill to reserves. Funds in a goodwill account are excluded from shareholders' funds.

**data** Items of information, particularly in computer applications.

**data acquisition** Purchase of data, computing software, etc.

**database** Data organized to allow easy access to the most up-to-date information and its collation with older data. The term is generally applied to electronic storage devices (*i.e.* computers), which can store, organize and search for data more rapidly than was hitherto possible.

**data processing** Sorting and organization of data in order to produce the desired information, generally according to standard procedures.

**Data Protection Act** Act of Parliament in the UK of 1984, which is intended to protect the consumer against misuse of personal information about him or her stored in a computer system.

**data security** Protection of data from electronic criminals. Data security generally entails the production of programs intended to deny unauthorized persons access to a database by means of passwords and other identification procedures. Maximum security is obtained by encryption, in which information is held in a coded form. *See electronic crime.*

**date** The day, month and year. In the UK these are usually recorded numerically in that order (*i.e.* 1:2:98 is 1st February 1998). However in Europe and the USA they are recorded in the order month, day, year (*i.e.* 1:2:98. is January 2nd 1998). The potential for confusion is vast.

**D**

**dated stock** Stock that has a fixed maturity date, as opposed to undated stock.

**dawn raid** Buying of a significant number of a target company's shares at the start of the day's trading, or before the market becomes aware of what is happening, often at a price higher than normal. The purpose of a dawn raid is to give the buyer a strategic stake in the *target* company, from which the buyer may launch a *takeover* bid.

**day book** Ledger in which transactions are listed on a daily basis prior to transfer to ledgers that deal with transactions on a subject basis. It is usual to keep separate purchase and sales day books.

**day-one-scheme** Type of index-linked property insurance.

**day order** Order given by an investor to a *stockbroker* which is valid only on the day it was given. A day order also specifies a price limit on the transaction envisaged. If not completed on the day in question, the transaction is automatically cancelled.

**days of grace** Term with two meanings:

1. It is a period of time, either 14 or 30 days, allowed for payment of an insurance premium after the due date.

2. It is a period of three days still allowed in the UK for the payment of any *bill of exchange* except for *bills of sight*.

**day-to-day money** Alternative term for overnight loan or day-to-day loan, borrowed particularly by a financial institution that is temporarily illiquid. The money is lent to companies wishing to be paid *interest* on money earned in the previous day's trading.

**DCF** Abbreviation of *discounted cash flow*.

**dead cat bounce** Brief rise in the stock *index* of a falling market. The term refers to the supposed ability of a cat always to land on its feet: if a falling cat bounces, it must be dead. *See also* **bottoming out**.

**dead security** Security backed by an exhaustible industry (such as mining), which is thus a poor risk for a long-term loan.

**deadweight** *Debt* that is not covered by or incurred in exchange for real assets, *e.g.* the part of the National Debt taken on to pay for war is a deadweight debt.

**deal** Agreement or transaction; in particular, any bargain made on a stock market.

**dealer** Anyone who is engaged in trading on a financial market.

**dealing** Activity of dealers.

**dear money** Money is said to be dear when it is difficult to find investment or loans and the interest rate for borrowing is consequently high.

**death benefit** Amount payable on the death of a *life assurance* policyholder.

**death future** Purchase of a terminally ill person's life insurance policy by a company that pays the person a lump sum, and collects on the policy when he or she dies. *See also **viatical company**.*

**death valley curve** Period of time during which a start-up company uses venture capital at an extremely fast rate, to the point where it is using equity capital to fund overheads, an unhealthy state of affairs.

**death valley days** Nickname for "dry" periods on the financial markets, days on which little trading takes place. *See also **valium picnic**.*

**debenture** Long-term loan to a company made at a fixed rate of interest and usually with a specified *maturity date*, generally between 10 and 40 years. Debenture holders are numbered with the company's creditors, and in the event of *liquidation* have preferential claims on the firm. Debentures may be treated as tradable *securities*.

**debenture capital** That part of a company's capital that is issued in the form of *debentures*.

**debenture issue** Issue of *debentures*, whether secured or unsecured, by a company wishing to raise loan capital. The debenture-holders become the company's principal *creditors* and have the right to preferential repayment of their loans in the event that the firm encounters financial difficulties. *See also **loan capital**.*

**debenture stock** *Debentures* may be divided into units and traded on the exchange. These securities are known as debenture stocks.

**debit** A sum owed by or a charge made on a person.

**debit balance** In accounting, balance that shows a *debit*.

**debit card** Plastic card issued by banks and building societies that allows the account holder to use the card at retail outlets to debit a current account immediately. It is also called a payment card.

**D**

**debit entry** Item of *debit* recorded in a ledger for accounting purposes.

**debit note** In *accounting*, notification sent to a customer that the *supplier* is about to debit the client's account with a certain sum. Debit notes are normally issued in unusual situations, *e.g.* when a client has been charged too little for goods received.

**debit side**   In *accounting*, the side of a *ledger* on which debits are listed. Hence, in informal use, it is the negative points in an argument.

**debt**   Sum of money, or value of goods or services, owed by one person, group or company to another. Debt arises because the seller allows the purchaser *credit*. Assignable debts may be transferred in whole from one person to another; such debts therefore become *negotiable instruments*. In commerce, the term is also used to describe the whole of a company's borrowings.

**debt bomb**   Financial repercussions envisaged if a major international debtor were to default.

*There was general concern on the money markets as the economy of two of the debt bomb nations showed a marked deterioration.*

**debt collection agency**   Firm that charges a *commission* for collecting its clients' outstanding debts.

**debt discounting**   Purchasing a debt at a discount, usually from a trader such as an exporter.

**debt factoring**   Purchasing of a company's debts (at a discount) by a factor. *See debt discounting; factoring.*

**debt-for-equity**   Proportion of a company's debt that is covered by its *share capital*.

**debt forgiveness**   In international finance, writing off part of a nation's debt, or selling the debt to a third party for a large discount.

**debtor**   (Dr)   Person or company that owes money, goods or services to another.

**debt rescheduling**   When a debtor has difficulties making repayments, a method by which the lender defers interest or repayments, extends the loan period, or agrees to a completely new loan.

**debt servicing**   Payment of *interest* on a debt.

**debt-to-equity ratio**   A company may finance itself through borrowing or through shareholder investment, depending on current interest rates. The proportion of each is known as debt-to-equity ratio, or *gearing*.

**debut** Arrival on the stock market of the shares of a new company and the first day's trading in that company's stock.

**deceased partner** Normally a partnership is dissolved when one of the partners dies. But the partnership agreement may allow for the business to continue trading and the value of the deceased person's share is passed to his or her nominee. If a partnership's bank account is overdrawn when one partner dies, the account is closed and another opened in the names of the surviving partners, so that the deceased person's estate remains liable for part of the debt.

**decentralization** Distribution of the constituent parts of a company or government to a variety of geographical locations. The advantages include the availability of cheaper labour (that is likely to be initially offset by the cost of relocating key personnel), increased efficiency and, in the case of government, the provision of incentives to industry to consider non-metropolitan locations.

**declaration** Signed statement made by somebody seeking insurance that the information provided is accurate and complete. It usually forms part of the *proposal.*

**declaration policy** Type of insurance policy in which the insured declares details of the subject matter and sum insured under a policy at regular intervals.

**decreasing term assurance** Life assurance for a specified term in which the sum assured decreases by level amounts over the duration of the policy. *See also* **inter vivos policy**; **mortgage protection policy.**

**declaration of solvency** Formal statement by a company's directors that it is seeking voluntary liquidation but that it expects to pay its creditors within at least 12 months.

**de-diversification** Shedding of interests and companies acquired by a corporation in the process of *diversification*, so as to reduce the variety of business in which the company engages.

**deductible** Initial amount of loss paid by the insured in commercial property insurance. It is a large *excess.*

**deduction** Money legally deducted from wages and salaries at source and allotted to pay taxes and (in the UK) National Insurance contributions. Payments for a *contributory pension* are also legal deductions.

 **deductions at source** *Income tax* deducted by an employer from an employee's pay before he or she receives it, or the deduction of income tax from interest earned by, *e.g.*, a building society account. The sum deducted is then paid by the company to the Inland Revenue. Deduction at source helps to prevent *tax evasion*.

**deed**   Document that records a transaction and bearing the seals of the parties concerned to testify to its validity.

**deed of covenant**   Document that formalizes the transfer of income from one person to another or to an institution in order to reduce income tax payable. It is often done to make donations to a charity; the donor deducts basic rate tax (often then getting tax relief) and the charity reclaims the tax deducted.

**deed of partnership**   Agreement that forms the basis of a partnership between two or more people.

**deed of transfer**   Legal document that gives authority to registrars of securities to transfer them from the seller to the buyer.

**deep discount**   Loan stock that is issued at a discount exceeding 15%, or $\frac{1}{2}$% per complete year between issue and redemption if less.

**deep market**   Financial market where many transactions can occur without affecting the price of the underlying financial instrument.

**deep-pocket view**   Theory that some *subsidiary companies* may have access to more funds than an independent firm of similar size. The deep-pocket view argues that the subsidiary may call upon the greater resources of its parent company to engage in competition with independents in its sector.

**de facto**   By virtue of existence, rather than any legal right, *e.g.* the de facto owner of a property may be the person in occupation, whether or not he or she has legal title to the land.

**default**   Failure to comply with the terms set out in a *contract* (such as the repayment of a loan). Legal proceedings generally follow if the matter cannot be settled amicably.

**default notice**   Notice issued by a lender to a borrower who is in default on a loan subject to the 1974 Consumer Credit Act. If the notice is not complied with, the lender can seek an *enforcement order*.

**defeasance**   Condition built into the wording of a deed that renders the deed void if the condition is complied with. The term is also used  for any annulment or act that renders something null and void.

**defence bond** Bond issued by the UK government to cover spending during and immediately after World War II. Defence bonds were first issued in 1939 and discontinued in 1964.

**defensive stock** Shares in companies that are not affected by economic cycles, because they produce necessities, *e.g.* food.

**defensive tactics** The strategy used when a "player" feels threatened by aggression. Thus the subject of a hostile *takeover* bid sometimes arranges defensive tactics with the aim of making the takeover more difficult, *e.g.* by pushing up its own share price. Examples of defensive tactics are the *Lady Macbeth strategy* and the *poison pill*.

**deferment** Postponement, *e.g.* of a payment.

**deferred annuity** *Annuity* for which payments commence at a later specified date, possibly when the policyholder attains a specific age.

**deferred asset** Expense incurred that does not match the income it will provide in the same accounting period. It is also termed a deferred debit.

**deferred coupon note** Type of *bond* on which interest is due after a specified date.

**deferred credit** Income received before it is earned in a given accounting period, such as a government grant. It is also termed a deferred liability.

**deferred futures** Futures contracts that are farthest away from their *maturity date. See also nearby futures.*

**deferred liability** Liability that does not fall due until after a period of a year.

**deferred ordinary shares** Category of shares, usually issued to a company's founders, entitling them to special dividend rights.

**deferred pension** *Occupational pension* that is paid to an employee some time after retirement from employment.

**deferred period** Length of time that is agreed in advance for permanent health insurance. It represents the period from the start of an illness to when the claim payment starts. It is used to eliminate small or minor illnesses, and ranges from 4 weeks to 104 weeks depending on what the insured requires, or can afford.

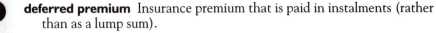

**deferred premium** Insurance premium that is paid in instalments (rather than as a lump sum).

**deferred taxation** Tax for which a person or company is liable, but which has not yet been considered or demanded by the Inland Revenue.

**deficit** Excess of *expenditure* over *income*, or *liabilities* over *assets*.

**defined benefit scheme** Type of *occupational pension* in which the pension provision is defined (and guaranteed; the employer has to make up the difference if the scheme fails to perform as well as expected). It is also known as *final salary pension scheme*, *e.g.* a company may provide a defined benefits pension scheme offering 1/60 of final salary for each year of service with the company.

**defined contribution scheme** Type of *occupational pension* that has a fixed contribution rate. It is also known as a *money-purchase pension scheme*.

**definition of disability** Term used in permanent health insurancee to define exactly when a claim payment is made. There are three standard definitions used by insurers:
1. To be unable to follow one's own occupation.
2. To be unable to follow own occupation or any other to which one is suited.
3. To be unable to follow any occupation.

**deflation** Persistent decrease in prices, generally caused by a fall in the level of economic activity within a country. Deflation should not be confused with *disinflation*.

**deflationary gap** The difference between the actual level of *investment* and the level necessary to restore full employment.

**defray** To settle an *account* or to lay out money in payment for goods or services.

**defunct** Describing a company or organization that no longer functions as such.

**degearing** Reduction of *risk* or *leverage*. Examples include cutting *borrowing* and reducing *exposure* to forces which a company or *dealer* cannot control. *See also* **hedging**.

**dehoarding** Putting back into circulation money (or goods) that have been unavailable for business or commercial use.

**de-industrialization** Decline in the relative importance of manufacturing to the economy.

**delayed payment surcharge** Extra payment (in addition to interest) that is charged while a debt is outstanding.

**del credere (agent)** Person who accepts goods on consignment from exporters, agreeing (in return for an additional *commission*) to pay for them in the event that the original purchaser defaults.

**del credere risks** Risk of debt arising from default of a debtor or insolvency.

**delegation** Term with two meanings:
1. It is a body of accredited representatives to a gathering (*e.g.* a conference).
2. It is to cede responsibility to other, usually junior, members of staff.

**delegatus non potest delegare** Latin for "a delegate cannot delegate", a principle that disallows subcontracting if the client feels it vital to deal directly and exclusively with the principal agent.

**delivered pricing** Practice of calculating a price of goods for sale that includes the cost of delivery.

**delivery** Handing over of *property* or monetary *assets*. In the City the term has two more specific meanings: it describes a transfer of *securities*, and the receipt of the financial instrument or cash payment specified in a financial *futures* contract. *See also* **cash on delivery**; *delivery note*.

**delivery note** Broadly, a note advising a recipient of the intended delivery of goods. In the *securities* market, however, a delivery note requests the delivery of a security.

**delivery of bill** Transfer of possession of a bill (or a cheque) from one person to another or his or her agent.

**delta** Stock exchange classification of shares that are traded on the Alternative Investment Market. They are generally relatively inactive and stable shares in small companies. *See also* **alpha**; **beta**; **gamma**.

**demand** Term with two meanings:
1. It is the desire for possession of a particular good or service at a specific price expressed by those able and willing to purchase it.
2. It is a request, such as a request for payment of a *debt*.

**demand bill** *Bill of exchange* to be paid on demand, also called a demand draft. Examples include a cheque and a draft drawn by a bank on itself or its head office.

**demand deposit** Deposit with a bank, building society or other financial institution that may be withdrawn at a moment's notice. It is also called a sight deposit.

**demand draft** *See demand bill.*

**demand-pull inflation** Theory that inflation is caused by excess of demand over supply, thus pulling prices up. *See cost-push inflation.*

**demerger** Spltting up of a large company or group of companies into smaller independent ones, or the selling off of a group's subsidiaries. It is usually done to improve the value of the company's shares.

**demurrage** Damages due to a shipowner if loading or unloading of a cargo is delayed beyond the date contracted.

**demutualization** Process of changing a *mutual* into a *public limited company*. A minimum agreement of members is required before this is possible.

**denationalization** The *privatization* of a previously nationalized industry by floating the company involved on the stock exchange and selling shares to members of the public or institutions. In the UK, denationalized industries include British Telecom, British Gas, British Airways and British Rail. A change in government may subsequently lead to the renationalization of a denationalized industry.

**denomination** The face value of something, *e.g.* the unitary classification of coinage, or the nominal value of *bills* and *bonds*.
*The US government issues Treasury bonds in denominations of $10,000.*

**Department of Trade and Industry** (DTI) Government department in the UK that advises on and controls business and finance.

**depauperization** Relief of poverty (generally through economic growth).

**dependant** Term with two meanings:
1. It is somebody who is financially dependent on somebody else.
2. It is a subsidiary of an insurance company.

**deposit** Term with several meanings:
1. It is goods or money placed with a bank, building society or other financial institution.
2. It is an initial payment made on an item to reserve it.
3. It is an initial payment for something being bought on *hire purchase* or by means of a *credit sale* agreement.

4. In insurance, it is payment of part of a *premium* before a contract is finalized.

5. It is an amount an insurance company has to pay to the government before being authorized to do insurance business.

**deposit account** (DA) Bank account that pays interest, but sometimes notice has to be given before funds may be withdrawn.

**deposit account administration plan** Secure *pension plan* in which contributions are paid into a low-risk deposit account. Annual dividends, interest or profits accrue to build up the pension rights.

**depositor** Person who makes a *deposit*.

**deposit premium** In insurance, part of the premium paid at the proposal stage.

**deposit receipt** *See deposit slip.*

**deposit slip** Document that records the time and place of a deposit and its value. It is also termed a deposit receipt.

**depository** Secure place where money or goods are stored (deposited). Depositories may be distinguished from banks in that they do not transact other financial business and do not necessarily offer ready access to the assets stored. *See also deposit.*

**depreciation** Progressive decline in real value of an *asset* because of use or *obsolescence*. The concept of depreciation is widely used in *accounting* for the process of writing off the cost of an asset against profit over an extended period, irrespective of the real value of the asset. *See also historical cost accounting.*

**depreciation rate** Rate at which *depreciation* occurs.

**depression** Major and persistent downswing of a trade cycle, characterized by high *unemployment* and the under-utilization of other factors of production. A less severe downswing is known as a slump or recession.

**deregulation** Removal of controls and abandonment of state supervision of private enterprise. The most notable recent instance of deregulation is that of the London Stock Exchange (commonly termed the **Big Bang**).

**derivative** Transferable high-risk security such as a *future* or an *option.*

**D**

**derivative-based funds** Types of unit trust linked to the performance of *derivatives* (futures or options), and therefore regarded as high-risk investments.

**designated market maker** Market maker who undertakes to be present on the trading floor of the stock exchange and to maintain up-to-date two-way prices in return for certain concessions.

**detinue** Legal term meaning action to recover something that has been detained.

**devaluation** Reduction in the relative value of a *currency*. The devaluation may be relative to an absolute value (*e.g.* the *gold standard*) or to other relative values (*e.g.* other currencies). *See also revaluation*.

**develop** To begin to realize the potential of, *e.g.*, a product or company.

**developing country** Country that is beginning to industrialize, but which is still too poor to do so without *foreign aid*. Developing countries are characterized by improving standards of health, wealth (standard of living), education, capital investment and productivity, and by a broadening of the economic base.

**development aid** Financial and material aid to a *developing country*.

**development area** Economically depressed area suitable for reindustrialization. Development areas are designated by the state and incentives are provided to help to attract new businesses to the area, to encourage the relocation of existing businesses, and to enhance the prospects for employment.

**development capital** Funds made available (to *venture capital* companies and other specialists) through investment in equities and *loan capital*.

**development expenditure** Money spent by a company on *research and development*. Development expenditure may be tax deductible.

**dies non** Day that is not counted for some purpose, *e.g.* Saturday and Sunday are not counted as days of the working week. *See also non-business days*.

**differential** The difference between two values, *e.g.* prices or salaries.

**dilution** Term with two meanings:

1. It is the reduction in the skill of a workforce overall, as comparatively unskilled workers are recruited in response to a rise in *demand*.

2. It is a deliberate increase in the number of shares on the market that has the effect of reducing the price of each individual share.

**dilution of equity** Reduction of individual stakes in a company by the issue of further shares. See *dilution of shareholding*.

**dilution of shareholding** Reduction in the relative value of a share in the event of a new issue. For example, if a company has a capital of £1,000 in £10 shares, each share represents 1% of the total capital. If a new issue of 5,000 £10 shares is made, a shareholding of £10 represents only 0.16% of the firm's capital. Thus the relative power of each existing shareholder to influence corporate affairs is reduced. See also *rights issue*.

**diminishing** Describing something that is declining or falling.

**diminishing balance (method)** Method of calculating *depreciation* by writing off a fixed proportion of the total residual value of an asset each year.

**diminishing marginal product** Alternative term for *diminishing returns*.

**diminishing returns** Concept that suggests that as additional units of one factor of production are added, the relative increase in output will eventually begin to decline, *e.g.* a factory can increase its output by employing more labour, but unless the other factors of production (*e.g.* machinery) are also increased each additional employee will be working with a smaller proportion of the other, fixed, resources available.

**Diplock principle** Definition of reasonable care as it applies to insurance. In essence it maintains that reasonable care has *not* been taken if the insured acts recklessly, not caring about a risk because it is insured against. A much-quoted example is leaving a car unlocked with the keys in the ignition.

**direct** Immediate or unobstructed.

**direct action** Attempt to take control of a company by purchasing a controlling interest of shares, rather than by negotiation with the company itself. See also *dawn raid*.

**direct arbitrage** Foreign exchange dealings that are restricted to one centre.

**direct business** In insurance, business carried out directly with the public without the intervention of a broker.

**D**

**direct chain of events** In insurance, if a series of events are linked, the initial *peril* insured against is deemed to be the cause of the subsequent loss. *See proximate cause.*

**direct costs** Costs of materials, items or activities that are directly involved in the production of goods, and without which those goods could not be produced in the short run.

**direct dealing** Method by which some *syndicates* at Lloyd's of London deal in *motor insurance* directly with non-Lloyd's brokers.

**direct expenses** Expenses that may be attributed to one or another factor of production. *See also* **indirect expenses.**

**direct insurer** Insurance company that accepts the *risk* defined in a policy (as opposed to a *reinsurer*). Recently it is a term also used to describe insurers who sell direct to the public rather than via intermediaries.

**directive** European Union (EU) legislation that states what has to be done within a timescale, and which is binding on member states. However, member states decide for themselves exactly how the legislation is enacted.

**direct mail** Form of advertising and selling. Individual potential customers receive promotional material and information through the post, and order goods that are delivered by post or courier.

**director** One of the principals of a company, in a *public limited company* (plc) appointed by its shareholders. Most companies have a group of directors (the *board of directors*) who act collectively as the senior management of the company, being responsible to the shareholders for its efficient running and future development. The duties and legal responsibilities of a director are defined in the Companies Acts. They include the compilation of an *annual report* and the recommendation of an annual *dividend* on shares.

**directorate** Alternative term for a *board of directors.*

**Director of Savings** Official responsible for running the National Savings Bank and its various accounts, bonds and certificates.

**directors' and officers' (D & O) liability insurance** Type of insurance that provides a company's directors and officers with cover against losses incurred through misleading statements or negligence.

**directors' interests** Interests in a company's debentures, shares and share options held by the directors of the company, which must in law be disclosed.

**directors' valuation** In *accounting*, the right of a board of directors to estimate the value of a firm's shareholding in an unquoted company. The directors' valuation is called for only if the value of the shares concerned has changed since they were purchased. *See also unquoted company.*

**direct placement** Selling of shares directly to the public without using an *underwriter.*

**direct sale** In insurance, a sale made directly to an insured, without an intermediary.

**direct taxation** System of taxation whereby companies and individuals pay tax on income directly to the Inland Revenue (or through an employer), as opposed to *indirect taxation*, in which tax is added to the price of goods and services.

**dirty float** Partly-managed floating *exchange rate*, in which the central bank continues to intervene in the market for its own currency. *See also clean float.*

**dirty money** Money obtained illegally, generally through unlawful international business activities. *See also black money.*

**disability insurance** *See loan protection insurance; permanent health insurance; personal accident and sickness insurance.*

**disability pension** State pension paid in the UK to a person who is disabled in some way. There are also private disability pensions, some of them payable from a company pension scheme if the disability was caused at work.

**disbursement** Payment made on behalf of a client by a banker, solicitor, or other professional person. It is ultimately charged to the client's account.

**discharge** Term with three meanings:

1. It is to dismiss a member of staff from one's employment.
2. It is to pay a debt such as a *bill of exchange.*
3. It is a signed declaration by somebody who has made an insurance claim stating that no further claims will be made in regard of the same event.

**discharged bankrupt** Person discharged from bankruptcy (*see discharged in bankruptcy*). The debts of the person concerned are considered to be settled and, if solvent, he or she can begin again.

**discharged bill** *Bill of exchange* that has been paid by the drawer or drawee, or is being held by an *acceptor*. If a holder renounces rights to the debt against an acceptor, the bill is also deemed to be discharged.

**discharge in bankruptcy** Occurs when the bankrupt is released from bankruptcy by the court after his or her debts have been paid, or it has been seen that all reasonable efforts have been made to do so.

**disclaimer** Clause in a *contract* that states that one of the parties does not take responsibility for some occurrence, *e.g.* the owners of many car parks advise drivers that they disclaim any responsibility for loss or damage to cars or anything contained in them.

**disclosure** Revealing of relevant information. The term has two major uses:

1. It is the requirement that a limited company must disclose its financial dealings and position by the publication of accounts, and deposit at Companies House lists of directors and shareholders in the company.

2. It is the requirement that parties to any contract should disclose relevant information, *e.g.* a person holding a life assurance policy must notify the assurers of his or her medical history.

**discount** In commerce and insurance, term with several specialized meanings:

1. It refers to the amount by which a new share issue stands below its par value. *See parity.*

2. It refers to the price of a share whose *price/earnings ratio* is below the market average.

3. It refers to the amount by which a currency is below par on the foreign exchanges.

4. It is to make a reduction in the face value of an article (or the price being charged for it), generally in order to make a purchase more attractive to a customer.

5. On financial markets it is the charge made for cashing an immature *bill of exchange*, the discount being proportional to the unexpired portion of the bill.

6. In insurance, it is a reduction in a *premium*, *e.g.*, given to a motorist in regard of no previous claims (*see no-claims bonus*), to non-smokers seeking *life assurance*, or to a person seeking *household insurance* whose property is fitted with special locks and alarms.

**discounted cash flow** (DCF) Method of assessing a company's investments according to when they are due to yield their expected returns, in order to indicate the present worth of the future sum. In this way it is possible to determine preference for one of a number of alternative investments.

**discounted value** If a share price falls below its par value, then the lower price is known as its discounted value.

**discount house** Company whose main activity is the *discounting* of *bills of exchange*.

**discounting** Act of making a *discount*. More specifically, it is the practice of selling a debt at a discount to an institution.

**discounting bank** Bank that specializes in discounting *bills of exchange*.

**discount market** That part of the London money markets that involves the buying and selling of short-term *debt* between the commercial banks, the *discount houses* and the Bank of England, which acts as the lender of the last resort.

**discount rate** Rate at which a *bill of exchange* is discounted. *See discounting.*

**discretionary** Something that is not compulsory, but is left to the discretion of the person or authority involved, such as a *discretionary grant*. It is the opposite of mandatory.

**discretionary account** (DA) Account into which *discretionary funds* are placed.

**discretionary approval** Basis of Inland Revenue approval for most occupational pension schemes. It relies on the discretion of the Inland Revenue.

**discretionary client** Person on behalf of whom a stockbroker makes investment decisions. *See also advisery client.*

**discretionary fund** Sum of money left with a stockbroker, to be invested at his or her discretion. *See also discretionary personal equity plan; managed fund; unit trust.*

**discretionary grant** Grant that is not automatically paid, but is made at the discretion of the authority concerned. *See also mandatory grant.*

**discretionary investment management agreement** Document required to be given under the 1986 Financial Services Act which details the limits of an adviser's discretion over an investment portfolio, as well as his or her duties and responsibilities.

**discretionary personal equity plan** *Personal equity plan* (PEP) in which the funds of several investors are pooled and managed at the discretion of the *fund manager*. *See managed fund.*

**discretionary share portfolio personal equity plan** *Personal equity plan* (PEP) that uses direct investments in *stocks* and *shares*. The fund is managed, *i.e.* investment decisions are made, by a *fund manager* or *stockbroker*.

**discriminating monopoly** Monopoly in which the monopolist sells its goods or services at two different prices to two or more different sectors, *e.g.* the electricity industry may sell electricity at a cheaper rate to industrial users than to domestic users, in an attempt to prevent the larger industrial users from changing to cheaper alternative forms of power.

**disguised unemployment** Also known as concealed unemployment, unemployment of those who are not earning and not searching for work, *e.g.* during times of high unemployment, a housewife may wish to work but decide it is not worth trying to find a suitable job. This form of unemployment is "disguised" by the method of calculating unemployment figures in the UK. It can be said not to exist in the USA, where calculation methods enable the authorities to take such cases into account.

**dishonour** To refuse to accept or discharge a *bill of exchange* when it falls due for payment. *See also acceptance for honour.*

**disinflation** The curbing of *inflation* by the adoption of mild economic measures such as the restriction of *expenditure*. Other measures include increasing *interest rates* and the deliberate creation of a budget surplus. Disinflation is a mild form of *deflation*, which by contrast indicates an uncontrolled fall in prices.

**disintermediation** Withdrawal of a financial intermediary from a negotiation. The term may also be applied to the flow of funds from lenders to borrowers "off balance sheet" without the intervention of an intermediary (*e.g.* a mortgage broker).

**disinvestment** Withdrawal or sale of an investment. Governments and companies sometimes decide to disinvest from nations whose economic or political complexion offends them.

**disposable income** That part of a person's income that he or she may dispose of in any way, *i.e.* what is left after such necessities as accommodation and food have been paid for.

**disposables** Non-durable goods; those that are consumed during their use. Food, drink, and fuel are all disposables.

**disqualification notice** Order from the *Securities and Investment Board* (SIB) that prohibits a person from giving investment advice.

**dissaving** Preference for spending rather than saving.

**dissident shareholder** One of a group of shareholders who have expressed their discontent with present management performance, and are determined to replace current managers.

**dissolution** *Winding up* of a company, usually by the legal process of *liquidation*. In the case of a *partnership*, dissolution may be occasioned by the death or retirement of one or more partners (*see death of a partner*), by *bankruptcy* or by the expiry of a specified time period, without recourse to law.

**distraint** The legally-authorized seizure of *assets* to compel a debtor to pay a *debt*. If the debt remains outstanding, goods obtained by distraint may be sold on order that the *creditor* may obtain satisfaction.

**distress borrowing** Situation in which a company or person is forced to borrow money even when interest rates are high.

**distress merchandise** Goods and assets made available for sale by a company facing or already consigned to *bankruptcy*. Most distress merchandise is placed on the market on the orders of an official *receiver* in order to provide liquid sums for the payment of creditors. *See also receivership.*

**distributable profits** Company profits that can be distributed to shareholders as dividends. For a public company, such distribution must not reduce the net assets to less than the sum of the undistributable reserves and the called-up share capital.

**distributable reserves** Retained company profits that can be distributed to shareholders as dividends.

**distribution** Term with four meanings:
1. It is the transport, allocation and placement of raw materials or goods to and from the factory to warehouses and shops.
2. It refers to payments made by a company from its profits (e.g. dividends).
3. It is the apportioning of a *scrip* or *rights issue* of shares.

**4.** It is the division of property according to the law, *e.g.* the distribution of a deceased person's estate.

**distribution bond** Bond, resembling a *unit trust*, that is sold by a company dealing in *life assurance*.

**distribution slip** Document that describes the goods that have been distributed, their location and eventual destination.

**distributor** Wholesaler; a person or company that acts as an agent in the distribution of goods to *retail* outlets.

**diversification** Extension of the range of goods or services offered into new areas, either material or geographical. By extension the term may also be applied to attempts by local authorities or central government to attract a variety of industries to an area heavily dependent upon a single industry, particularly one in decline.

**divestment** Sale or *liquidation* of parts of a company, generally in an attempt to improve efficiency by cutting loss-making businesses and/or concentrating on one product or industry. Divestment is therefore the opposite process to *merger*.

**divestiture** Act of *divestment*.

*RCF plc today announced the divestiture of its unprofitable subsidiary, MG Ltd.*

**dividend** A share in the profits of a limited company, usually paid annually. Dividends are usually expressed as a percentage of the nominal value of a single ordinary share. Thus a payment of 10p on each £1 share would be termed a dividend of 10%. Dividends are determined by the *directors* of a company and are announced at the end of the *annual general meeting* (AGM) of the company. *See nominal value; ordinary share.*

**dividend cover** Degree to which a dividend payment on ordinary shares is covered by profits earned. Thus a company that declares after-tax profits of £10m and makes a total dividend payment of £2m on ordinary shares is said to be "covered five times". An uncovered dividend, on the other hand, is a payment made at least partly from reserves rather than current profits. *See also after-tax profit.*

**dividend equalization account** *See dividend equalization reserve.*

**dividend equalization reserve** Also known as the dividend equalization account, a *reserve* from which a company may make a dividend payment during periods of low profit or trading loss. The firm pays profits into the reserve during years of significant *profit*. The purpose is to maintain shareholders' confidence in the company.

**dividend limitation** Government instructions to companies to limit increases in their dividend payments as part of a prices and incomes policy. Dividend limitation curbs the *income* of the shareholders and the management in the same way that wage restraints limit increases in the salaries paid to workers. *See also* **dividend restraint.**

**dividend mandate** Mandate signed by a shareholder and delivered to a company, instructing it to pay dividends directly to a third party (generally into a bank account).

**dividend per share (in pence)** Expression of a dividend in pence per share rather than as a percentage of the total value of a share. Thus a 10% dividend on a share worth £1 would be termed a "10p per share dividend".

**dividend policy** Company policy, agreed by the board of directors, regarding the allocation of profits between shareholders (in the form of dividends) and *reserves*.

**dividend restraint** Policy of minimizing increases in dividend payments, generally implemented by a company wishing to build its reserves for investment and corporate growth.

**dividend stripping** Method of *tax avoidance* that makes it unnecessary for a person or company to receive dividend payments (on which tax is payable). Also called bond washing, the technique involves buying gilt-edged securities *ex dividend* and selling them *cum dividend* before the next dividend falls due.

**dividend tax** Form of income tax on share *dividends*. When in operation, dividend tax is deducted by the company at source.

**dividend warrant** Order to a company's bankers to pay a specified dividend to a shareholder.

**dividend yield** Yield calculated in relation to the current market price of the investment: the dividend divided by the share price. *See nominal value.*

**documents against acceptance** (D/A) Way of paying for exported goods in which the exporter sends a bill of exchange with the shipping documents which is held, on arrival, by an agent or bank which releases the goods when the bill has been accepted.

**dole** Informal term for any variety of social security payments, but particularly unemployment benefit.

**dolphin** Informal term for a person who buys shares in new issues and then sells for high profit as soon as trading opens. *See also flip*.

**domestic** Concerning the internal economy of a nation.

**domestic credit expansion** (DCE) Measurement of the growth of a nation's *money supply* which allows for changes in the *balance of payments* by deducting net foreign currency reserves from the figure for money supply itself. It is thus a measure of domestic *liquidity*.

**domestic economy** Internal economy of a nation.

**domestic insurer** In the UK, an insurance company that is domiciled in the UK. In the USA, it is an insurance company that is domiciled in a specific state (as opposed to a foreign insurer, domiciled in another state, or an alien insurer, domiciled outside the USA).

**domestic market** Market for goods and services that exists within a country, as opposed to the international market that is reached by *exports*.

**domestic mortgage indemnity** (DMI) Type of insurance taken out by a mortgagee against the risk of non-payment by the mortgagor (particularly on mortgages with a high rate of interest). The mortgagor pays the premiums. It is also termed mortgage indemnity insurance (MIG) and mortgage indemnity guarantee .

**domestic production** Total production of a particular good or goods within a nation.

**domestic sales** Goods sold within the country of origin, as opposed to foreign sales, which are goods sold as *exports*.

**domicile** A person's place of residence for legal and tax purposes. A person domiciled in the UK is liable to pay British taxes and is subject to British law.

**donation** Money or other asset given by a person or organization to another person or organization (such as a charity or political party).

**donee** Person in receipt of a *donation*.

**donor** Person who gives a *donation*.

**double bottom** In the analysis of share market trends, a term that describes a price that hits a low point equal to the last low point. The prediction is that once two similar low points have been reached, the price will tend to go up. *See also double top.*

**double-entry book-keeping** Process of recording financial transactions under two parallel headings, *debits* and *credits*. *See balance.*

**double-figure inflation** Inflation that has reached the rate of more than 10 per cent.

**double insurance** Insurance cover against the same risk with two different insurers. In practice, it is impossible to receive more than the value of the cover, and in many cases one insurer would require a *contribution* to the claim from the other insurer.

**double option** Option to either buy or sell shares at a fixed price on a particular date. *See option.*

**double or quits** Terms offered in a wager or *speculation*; the losing speculator offers another wager on the same terms as before, but for twice the money. As a result, the winning speculator either doubles the sum earned or is left in the same position as before. Offering and acceptance of such terms implies that each of the two possibilities has an equal chance of occurring.

**double pricing** Practice of displaying two prices on goods, usually to show the prospective customer that the price has (apparently) been reduced.

**double time** Rate of overtime payments to workers that is double the normal hourly rate.

*It doesn't worry me that I sometimes have to work on Sundays and Bank Holidays, because I am paid double time.*

**double top** In the analysis of share market trends, a price that rises twice to similar high points. The prediction is that after the double top, the price will tend to fall. *See also double bottom.*

**Dow Jones Industrial Average** Often called simply the Dow Jones, a security price index used on the New York Stock Exchange and issued by the US firm of Dow Jones & Co.

**down and dirty** Describing the practice of arranging, for a company in financial difficulties, a refinancing package that would severely dilute the holdings of minor shareholders were they not to participate. *See also dilution.*

**D**

**downgrade** To reduce the status of someone or something, *e.g.* a person downgrades his or her shareholding by selling part of it.

**down-market** Describing something that is of poor quality and often low-priced.

**downside** The amount a person stands to lose when taking a risk, *e.g.* the amount by which a share price may fall, or the amount a person is liable to lose by making a speculative investment.

**downside risk** Risk that the actual outcome (*e.g.* of an investment) will be worse than some fixed level.

**downsize** To reduce the size of a company's workforce (*i.e.* making employees redundant), usually to make financial savings.

**downstream** Describing an economic activity in or close to the *retail* sector, *i.e.* one involving the distribution and selling of goods and services. The term is frequently applied to the oil industry, in which context the petrol station is downstream and the oil rig is *upstream*.

**downtick** Describing a transaction concluded at a lower price than a similar previous transaction. It is also a small and temporary fall in the price of a share. *See also* **uptick**.

**downturn** Point at which something begins to fall; *e.g.* a share price that has been rising and begins to fall, or productivity that is beginning to decline.

**DPS** Abbreviation of *dividend per share (in pence)*.

**Dr** Abbreviation of *debtor*.

**draft** Written *order* from a customer to a financial institution, requesting that money is paid from the customer's account to a third party. To draft is to draw up any document, especially a *contract*.

**dragon** Informal term for a newly industrialized eastern country (such as Indonesia, Malaysia and Thailand).

**draw** To write a bill of exchange, cheque or promissory note. The person who does so is the drawer.

**drawback** Repayment of customs and excise *duty* on certain goods to an exporter who has already paid duty on imported raw materials, *e.g.* drawback may be claimed on tobacco imported to make cigarettes when the cigarettes are then exported. *See also* **re-export**.

**drawdown** Sum of money borrowed or taken against a credit facility.
*The drawdown on that project was £100,000.*
*See also* **income drawdown**.

**drawee** Person or company to whom a *bill of exchange* is addressed, *e.g.* the bank *account* on which a *cheque* is drawn, or the *acceptor* of a *bill of exchange*.

**drawer** Person who draws a *bill of exchange*, *i.e.* orders payment (from the drawee).

**dread disease** *See critical illness insurance.*

**drip-feed** Steady payment of money at regular intervals. It is usually a pejorative term that implies that the recipient is dependent on the payments. It is often applied to *foreign aid* to underdeveloped countries. The term is also used by venture capitalists for *venture capital* payments made to a start-up company in stages.

**drive** Concerted effort.

**drop-dead date** Date on which it is expected that a troubled company will run out of funds.

**drop-dead fee** Payment offered to a bidder by the *target* of a (usually *takeover*) bid in an effort to induce the bidder to withdraw the bid.

**drop-dead rate** Amount demanded by a would-be corporate *raider* to withdraw the bid.

**drop lock** Loan stock issued when a specific *interest rate* is reached. The purpose is to convert short-term borrowing into long-term loans. *See loan stock.*

**DTI** Abbreviation of *Department of Trade and Industry.*

**dual capacity** Stock exchange system that makes no distinction between the functions of *stockbrokers* and *jobbers*. One person (a *market maker*) may therefore both buy and sells *stocks* and *shares* on the *exchange*. The London Stock Exchange was converted to dual capacity in October 1986. *See Big Bang; single capacity.*

**dual control** Situation in which two people are required to fulfil a single function. In a business, *e.g.*, two officers may hold keys, both of which are needed to open a safe.

**dud** Informal term for something that is worthless or forged.
*She was very angry to find that she had accepted a dud £10 note.*

**due** Something that is owed to someone, or something that belongs to someone by right.
*Last Friday, my rent for next month became due.*

**D**

*Each year she paid her dues to the trade union.*
*See also due date.*

**due date** Date on which a *bill of exchange* is due to be paid. Instruments not payable on demand, on sight or on presentation are allowed three *days of grace.*

**dull market** Market on which little activity is taking place. *See also valium picnic.*

**dummy** Something that is false and has no substance.
*I discovered that it was a dummy company.*

**duopoly** *Market* in which there are only two competing companies. Because competition between duopolists is particularly fierce and destructive, there tends to be some form of implicit or explicit agreement to share the market, *e.g.* on a regional basis. *See also monopoly.*

**duopsony** *Market* in which there are only two purchasers of a type of goods or services, but a number of competing suppliers. *See also duopoly; monopsony.*

**durable** Describing goods that are not consumed by their use but which endure for a reasonable period of time. Some manufacturers of durables incorporate some form of *obsolescence* to ensure a continuity of demand. *See also disposables.*

**Dutch auction** Type of auction in which the seller begins by proposing a high price and gradually begins to lower it until someone agrees to buy.

**duty** Broadly, any *tax* levied by a public authority, particularly that imposed on imports, exports and manufactured goods. *See also Customs and Excise.*

**duty-free** Describing goods on which no *duty* is charged. In the UK, the term is most usually applied to goods which, although sold elsewhere in the UK, are available (from duty-free shops and ports) to those about to enter or leave the country. It is a condition that the goods are for consumption overseas or for personal consumption. The EU intends to end the practice.

**duty of disclosure** Positive duty to disclose material facts in an insurance proposal. *See utmost good faith.*

**duty-paid** Authenticated statement attached to goods on which duty has been paid, to facilitate their passage through customs.

**D**

**dynamic risk** Any insurance risk resulting from a human decision.

**dynamics** Analysis of the behaviour of variable elements.

*There have been changes in the dynamics of stock exchange trading since Big Bang.*

**dynamization** Term with two meanings:

1. Giving new dynamism (drive) to a company, generally by importing a new management team.

2. In pensions it describes an increase in salary granted a number of years before retirement compared to its "real" value. This enables a highly-paid employee or director to maximise his or her pension entitlement under Inland Revenue rules.

**D**

# E

**E & O** Abbreviation of *errors and omissions insurance.*

**E & OE** Abbreviation of *errors and omissions excepted.*

**early bargain** Deal struck on the stock exchange after the exchange has closed and considered to be among the first transactions of the following day. Early bargains are also known as after-hours dealings.

**early stage investment** Funds, usually provided by a *venture capital* company, that finance the start-up of a new business.

**early surrender** Cashing in a *life assurance* policy before its *maturity date*, often yielding less than the amount already paid in (because of loss of bonuses, etc.).

**early withdrawal penalty** Penalty charged for withdrawal of funds from a fixed-term investment before the investment matures.

**earmarking** Term with two meanings:
1. It is making up the shortfall between assets and liabilities of a member of **Lloyd's of London** from the *central fund*.
2. In pensions, it refers to the nominal setting aside of pension scheme assets for another person. Since the 1995 Pensions Act, this is common in divorce situations.

**earned income** Income received in exchange for labour, rather than derived from investments (the definition does, however, include some pension and social security payments.)

**earned premium** For an insurance policy, the part of the *premium* that relates to an expired period of cover.

**earnest money** Either part payment (*deposit*) made on goods or services, showing that the buyer is serious about buying; or the *margin* on a futures market.

**earning** Act of generating *income.*

**earning capacity** Value of an employee's services to a company, *e.g.* the earning capacity of an advertising sales executive is equivalent to the *revenue* he or she brings in. The term is also applied more colloquially to describe the maximum wage that can be earned in a specific job.

**earning potential** Net present value of a person's expected future earnings. Earning potential is as a key determinant of *creditworthiness*.

**earning power** Value of a person's services at a specified time and in a free market. Earning power is indicated by the salary that could be commanded if the person were to change jobs.

**earnings** Return, monetary or otherwise, for human effort. Broadly earnings may be defined as wages plus any bonuses (*e.g.* for overtime worked). The term is also used to describe the income of a company.

**earnings before interest and tax** (EBIT) Company's profit before deductions are made for tax and any interest owed.

**earnings cap** Limit on earnings introduced in the 1989 Finance Act for pension purposes. It represents the maximum earnings that can be pensioned. It does not apply to scheme members under approval basis before 1989 or to retirement annuities.

**earnings per share (in pence)** (EPS) Method of expressing the *income* of a company, arrived at by dividing the annual net income attributable to the shareholders by the number of shares. Earnings per share can then be used to calculate the *price/earnings ratio* of a company.

**earnings yield** Hypothetical figure that provides a reliable measurement of the worth of an investment. It is reached by relating a company's divisible net earnings to the market price of the investment. Sometimes, with reference to fixed interest *securities*, the term is used interchangeably with *flat yield*.

**earn-out** Employee incentive scheme whereby the employee is offered *share* options that give him or her an interest in the company for which he or she works.

**EAS** Abbreviation for *Enterprise Allowance Scheme*.

**easement** Legal term that refers to the right of a landowner to take or use something from a neighbouring piece of land. Right of way is an example of easement.

**easy market** Market in which there are few buyers; prices are therefore low.

**easy money** Money borrowed at a low rate of *interest*, usually consisting of funds made available by authorities wishing to encourage economic activity. It is also known as cheap money. *See also* **tight money**.

**E**

**EBIT** Abbreviation of *earnings before interest and tax.*

**echelon** Level in the hierarchy of a company.
*He rose very quickly to the higher echelons.*

**EC** Abbreviation of *European Commission* and of *European Community*, now replaced by the *European Union* (EU).

**ECA** Abbreviation of *Electronic Closing and Accounting Service.*

**ECG** Abbreviation of *Environmental Claims Group.*

**ECGD** Abbreviation of *Export Credits Guarantee Department.*

**ECI** Abbreviation of equity capital for industry.

**econometrics** Branch of statistics that uses mathematical models to test economic hypotheses, describe economic relationships, and forecast economic trends. Econometrics is employed to produce correlated quantitative data rather than to prove economic causation.

**economic** Term with two meanings:
1. It is something that concerns the study of economics.
2. It is something that is cost-effective.

**economic cost** Total expense involved in undertaking a certain activity. Economic cost includes *accounting cost* and *opportunity cost.*

**economic development** Per capita increase in national income. Broadly, the rate of economic development is a way of expressing the growth of an economy and can be used to determine the relative growth of a number of competing or allied economies. The rate of economic development is often used as a simple guide to the health of an economy.

**economic indicator** One of several measurable variables used to study change in an economy. In addition to the variables mentioned above, economists study production indexes, unemployment trends, the amount of overtime worked and levels of *taxation.*

**economic profit** Profit calculated in *accounting* as the difference between *income* and *cost.* In economics, however, economic profit also takes into account *opportunity cost.*

**economic refugee** Person who leaves his or her country for economic (rather than political) reasons. The term embraces both *tax exiles* and those who leave a country in which employment prospects are bleak.

Irish emigrants to the USA and (in the post-war period) British emigrants to Australia were economic refugees.

**economy** Term with two meanings:

1. It is the financial and productive apparatus of a nation.
2. It is (the exercise of) frugality.

**economy drive** Effort to improve the efficiency of a company by cutting unnecessary *expenditure* and costs and making better use of resources.

**economy of scale** Reduction in the average cost of production made possible by the large size of a firm or industry. Internal economies of scale are defined as those enjoyed by a single large company or organization and are, broadly, made possible by the distribution of indirect costs and improvements in technology, which increase the optimum level of output.

External economies of scale are those associated with an industry or location, *e.g.*, a concentration of shipbuilding companies on a river leads to the creation of a large pool of skilled labour which can be drawn on if one company wishes to expand.

**econospeak** Economic jargon.

**ECU** Abbreviation of *European Currency Unit*.

**ECU Treasury Bill** *Treasury Bill* whose denomination is in *ECUs*.

**EDP** Abbreviation of *electronic data processing*.

**educational insurance** Type of *endowment assurance* (usually on the life of parents) taken out on behalf of a child to contribute to the cost of his or her education.

**EEC** Abbreviation of *European Economic Community*, now replaced by the *European Union* (EU).

**effective** Actual, real or capable of producing a desired outcome.

**effective date** Date on which a *contract* becomes effective.

**effective demand** The quantity of an article or service actually purchased at a particular price. *See also* **pure demand**.

**effective exchange rate** Average of a country's exchange rate and those of its important trading partners. The currency rates are weighted to take into account the relative levels of trade.

**E**

**effective yield** Yield calculated as a percentage of the price of an investment.

**efficiency** Measure of the use of resources. High efficiency is achieved by getting the most output from the least input.

**EFTA** Abbreviation of *European Free Trade Association*.

**EGM** Abbreviation of extraordinary general meeting, any meeting of company shareholders except the *annual general meeting* (AGM).

**EIL** *See environmental impairment liability insurance.*

**ejusdem generis** Latin for "of the same kind"; it is a rule of statutory interpretation.

**EL** Abbreviation of *employer's liability insurance*.

**ELASS** Abbreviation of *Electronic Loss Advice and Settlement System*.

**Electronic Closing and Accounting Service** (ECA) Computerized system by means of which brokers send closing information for insurance risks to be dealt with by the *Lloyd's Policy Signing Office*.

**electronic cottage** Popular US term for the home of someone who makes use of computer communications to enable him or her to dispense with travelling to an office.

**electronic crime** Criminal activities conducted with the help of computers. It generally involves breaking into other computer systems (hacking) via a *modem*, often by using special programs to run combinations of letters and numbers until a password is discovered. Expert users can then manipulate records and data to their own advantage.

**electronic data interchange** (EDI) Method by which companies or people communicate with their banks, clients and suppliers using computers. Insurance companies may be *on-line* to each other; other users may employ *modems* and telephone lines.

**electronic data processing** Collection, interpretation and transmission of data by electronic means. Most electronic data processing is performed by computers, which receive information inputs from their own keyboards or from other computers, interpret it using computer programs and transmit it electronically via cables (*on-line*) or telephone lines (using a *modem*).

**Electronic Loss Advice and Settlement System** (ELASS) Computerized processing system for members of the *London Insurance and Reinsurance Market Association* (LIMRA).

**electronic mail** (e-mail) Service provided by a number of organizations (notably Prestel in the UK and Internet worldwide) that allows two computer users linked by *modem* to deposit messages on each other's machines.

**Electronic Placing Support** (EPS) Computerized system that allows the placing of insurance risks in the London market.

**electronic transfer of funds** (ETF) Movement of funds using a computerized system.

**elephant** Informal term for a large corporate entity that is slow but dominant and displays a tendency towards the creation of monopolies. *See monopoly.*

**Elves of Wall Street** US banking and stockbroking community centred on *Wall Street*. The term is an Americanization of Harold Wilson's description of the Swiss banking community as the *gnomes* of Zurich.

**e-mail** Abbreviation of *electronic mail.*

**embargo** Prohibition of the import or export of specified goods from or to a particular country or bloc, generally for political reasons.

**embedded value** (EV) Value of in-force business of an insurance company plus the value of its net assets, a method of valuing the company.

**embezzlement** Theft by an employee of money belonging to his or her employer.

**emolument** *Salary*, particularly that paid to the holder of high office.

**employee** Someone under a contract of service with an *employer*.

**employee buy-out** *Takeover* of a company by employees who have purchased a majority of its shares.

**employee share ownership plan** (ESOP) Scheme by which employees can purchase shares in the company for which they work. *See also earn-out.*

**E**

**employer** Person or company that employs a workforce (employees) in exchange for wages and salaries.

**employer's liability insurance** (EL insurance) Compulsory insurance for employers which requires them to insure against liability for death, injury or disease sustained to employees while in the course of employment. A certificate of insurance must be issued.

**employment** The act of employing somebody, the provision of work, or the state of having a job.

**employment bureau** Business that acts as an intermediary between employers and employees, supplying labour in exchange for a *commission* payment by the employer.

**emptor** Purchaser.

**encryption** *See data security.*

**endorse** To sign one's name on a *bill of exchange* to certify its validity.

**endorsee** Person who signs an *endorsement.*

**endorsement** Term (which in banking may be spelled *indorsement*) with three meanings:
1. It is a signature or explanatory statement on a document.
2. It is a confirmatory statement.
3. It is a note attached to an insurance policy detailing an alteration in the original terms.

**endowment assurance** Type of assurance policy that pays the sum assured on survival to the end of the specified term (*maturity date*) or on death, whichever is earlier. A *with-profits* endowment provides bonuses in addition to the basic sum assured. *See also flexidowment; low-cost endowment; unit-linked endowment.*

**endowment mortgage** Interest-only *mortgage* that uses an *endowment* as the vehicle for repayment of the loan at the end of the term. *See mortgages.*

**enduring power of attorney** Type of *power of attorney* that cannot be revoked except by order of the Court of Protection.

**enforcement order** Court order dealing with default on a loan subject to the 1974 Consumer Credit Act. *See also default notice.*

**engineering insurance** Type of industrial insurance, often combined with property insurance, that covers such things as boilers, electrical plant, computers and engines.

**E**

**enterprise** Any undertaking, but particularly a bold or remarkable one, or the quality of boldness and imagination in an undertaking.
*He showed great enterprise in developing an entirely new market.*

**Enterprise Allowance Scheme** (EAS) UK government scheme set up to encourage the establishment of new businesses by the unemployed by offering, among other incentives, grants and tax concessions.

**Enterprise Investment Scheme** (EIS) UK government scheme since 1994 that allows relief when shares in a company (not quoted on the Stock Exchange) are issued on subscription. It replaced the former Business Expansion Scheme (BES).

**EIS** *See Enterprise Investment Scheme.*

**enterprise zone** Geographical area in which economic activity is promoted by the government. Small businesses are encouraged, and the relocation of firms and industries to enterprise zones is helped by the provision of *incentives*. *See also Enterprise Allowance Scheme.*

**entertainment allowance** Amount an executive is allowed to spend on the entertainment of clients or prospective clients during the course of his or her business.

**entertainment expenses** The expense of entertaining business associates and potential clients, *e.g.* the cost of meals in restaurants.

**entrepreneur** Person who controls a commercial enterprise – the risk-taker and profit-maker – the person who assembles the factors of production and supervises their combination. The term also has the connotation of someone who has a brilliant idea and then finds the money to back it.

**entrepreneurial veteran** Entrepreneur with extensive experience of business. Often, it is someone who has taken many risks.

**entrepreneurial virgin** Entrepreneur with little experience.

**entry** Term with two meanings:
1. It is the appearance of a company on a certain market.
2. It is an item of information entered onto a record, *e.g.* in double-entry *book-keeping*.

**entry and exit** Term that refers to the appearance of companies in an industry and the disappearance of other companies, as new companies are established and others diversify, go into *liquidation*, or merely cease to trade. *See barrier to entry.*

**entry charge** Cost of entry into a building, market, etc. Stock exchanges levy entry charges on firms applying for a listing.

**environmental audit** Assessment of the risks and impact to the environment through the activities of an organization.

**Environmental Claims Group** (ECG) Group that represents insurers and Lloyd's of London *syndicates* that issue policies relating to claims for onshore pollution in the USA.

**environmental impairment liability insurance** (EIL insurance) Insurance contract that covers the liability for costs of pollution damage and clean-up costs.

**EPP** Abbreviation of *executive pension plan.*

**EPS** Abbreviation of *earnings per share (in pence)* and *Electronic Placing Support.*

**equalization** Return on *capital* invested in a *unit trust.* All investors in a trust receive an equal sum per unit held, although some may only have invested in the period since the last *distribution.* The distribution paid on the latter's stock therefore comprises the *dividend* and an equalization that brings the return up to par. *See parity.*

**equalization of estates** Equal distribution of an *estate* among two or more parties. Equalization of estates normally results from a court case in which a beneficiary applies unsuccessfully for a greater share of the estate, the court ruling that all beneficiaries have equal rights.

**equalization reserve** Buffer fund maintained by an insurance company to prevent large swings in costs caused by claims arising out of catastrophes.

**Equitas** *Lloyd's of London* company that services liabilities for insurance policies issued before 1993.

**equitable lien** Lien that arises from a dispute over *equity.*

**equities** Alternative term for *ordinary shares.* Equities entitle their holder to share in the issuing company's profits. Ordinary shareholders bear the ultimate risk, in that they have no entitlements in the event of *liquidation.*

**equity** Term with five meanings:
  **1.** It refers to the ordinary share capital (risk capital) of a company. *See equities.*

**E**

2. It is the residual value of the *variation margins* and *initial margins* of a liquidated *future*.
3. It is the residual value of common *stock* over the debit balance of a margin account.
4. It is the difference between the market value of a property and the mortgage still owed on it.
5. It is used to describe the concept of fairness, of central importance to a branch of law distinct from common law, and as such it has a significant effect on all kinds of contracts, dealings and trusts.

**equity capital** Capital of a company that belongs to the owners of the company (in many cases, holders of ordinary shares), rather than capital provided by owners of *fixed-interest securities*. *See equity*.

**equity dilution** Reduction in the unit value of *ordinary shares* effected by a *bonus issue*.

**equity gearing** Ratio of a company's borrowings to is *equity*.

**equity-linked policy** Type of *life assurance* policy whose value is linked to fluctuations in the stock market. Some pension schemes and savings plans are also linked to equities in this way.

**equity play** Any investment strategy operated on the stock market.

**equity-release loan** Method of borrowing used by a home owner whose property is worth more than the outstanding mortgage on it (*i.e.*, there is positive *equity* in the property). It is a type of equity withdrawal.

**equity sharing** Method of buying a property by repaying a mortgage on a percentage of the *equity* (usually 25% initially) and paying rent on the remainder. As further shares in the equity are purchased (a process termed staircasing), the mortgage repayments increase and the rent decreases.

**equity withdrawal** *See equity-release loan*.

**ergonomics** Study of workers and the choices that confront them in ordinary working situations. Ergonomics has as its goal an increase in the efficiency of the workforce and therefore in productivity. *See also time and motion*.

**ERM** Abbreviation of *Exchange Rate Mechanism*.

**errors and omissions excepted** (E&OE) Denial of responsibility for clerical errors and omissions, often included in invoices and other documents as a safeguard.

**errors and omissions insurance** (E & O insurance) Insurance that covers liability for errors and omissions, such as incorrect records or accounting.

**escalator clause** Term with two meanings:

1. Also known as an escalation clause, condition of a long-term contract that sets out the agreement concerning rising costs, *e.g.* of raw materials and labour.

2. In insurance, it is a clause in a fire policy that allows the sum insured on a property policy to rise throughout the year.

**escape clause** In a contract, clause that allows one or other party to withdraw from the contract should certain events take place, *e.g.* in a *lease*, it is possible to have a clause that allows the *lessee* to withdraw should the *lessor* increase the *rent*.

**escheat** Confiscation of a property. Escheat is a legal doctrine that states that property or titles revert to the crown in the event that the owner or holder dies intestate and without heirs. *See also* **intestacy**.

**escrow** Document held in *trust* by a third party, *e.g.* deeds and titles may be held in escrow until a person reaches the age of majority, or until some specified condition has been met.

**ESCB** Abbreviation of European System of Central Banks. *See* **central bank**.

**ESOP** Abbreviation of *Employee Share Ownership Plan*.

**establishment business** Overseas insurance business written by a local branch, office or subsidiary of a UK company.

**estate** Term with two meanings:

1. It is the residual possessions of someone who has died.

2. It is land, most especially a large area of land owned by one person.

**estate protection reinsurance** *Lloyd's of London* insurance cover for a member's outstanding underwriting liabilities.

**estimate** Approximate valuation of an uncertain quantity. It may be an approximate price quoted by a company before it undertakes work. In making such an estimate, the firm binds itself to complete the work at that price unless there is a change in the price of some key variable. An estimate therefore differs from a contractually-binding *quotation*, *e.g.* a printer's estimate could be revised if an increase occurred in the cost of paper.

The term also refers to UK government documents setting out proposed *expenditure* that accompany requests to Parliament for funds (*e.g.* the naval estimates).

**estimated maximum loss** (EML) Used in fire, explosion and material damage insurance policies, it is an estimate of the monetary loss that could be sustained on a single risk as a result of a single peril, which is considered by the underwriter to be possible.

**estoppel** Legal restrictions on a person's actions. The law insists that a person must bear liability for previous actions. Estoppel is generally used to prevent a denial of responsibility, *e.g.* the parties to a *contract* cannot subsequently claim that they were unaware of its conditions.

**ETF** Abbreviation of *electronic transfer of funds.*

**ethical** Describing an action that conforms to the moral constraints of an industry or society. "Professional ethics" restrict a number of undesirable practices that are not strictly legal, *e.g.* it is unethical but not illegal for a *stockbroker* to advise his or her clients to buy a *share* when the stockbroker fully intends to sell his or her own holding.

**EU** Abbreviation of *European Union.*

**euro** Standard currency unit of the European Monetary Union (*see European Monetary System*).

**euroaussie** Popular term for an Australian government bond traded *offshore*, but not necessarily in Europe.

**eurobond** Medium- or long-term bearer bond denominated in a *eurocurrency*. Eurobonds are issued by governments or multinational companies. The eurobond market developed in the 1960s and is independent of the stock market. *See bearer bond.*

**eurocheque** Cheque drawn on a European bank.

**Euroclear** Clearing house for *eurobonds*, set up in Brussels in 1968.

**eurocredit** Loan made in a *eurocurrency*.

**eurocurrency** Currency of any nation held *offshore* in a European country, such as eurodollars. The eurocurrency markets deal in very large-scale loans and deposits rather than the purchase or sale of *foreign exchange*.

**eurodollars** US dollars held outside the USA, particularly those circulating in Europe. The post-war economic ascendancy of the USA has made the eurodollar an international currency medium. *See also eurocurrency.*

**euromarket** *Market* in which *eurocurrency* is traded.

**European Commission** (EC)  Major institution of the EU, established in 1967, responsible for implementing the Treaty of Rome. It introduces EU legislation and reconciles disagreements between members.

**European Community** (EC)  Short form of European Economic Community (EEC), now called the *European Union* (EU).

**European Currency Unit** (ECU)  Unit of account in use by the European Economic Community (EEC) from 1979 and now by the *European Union* (EU). The value of the ECU is calculated by taking a weighted average of the current value of EU member-states' own currencies. It exists only on paper, but is used to settle intra-Union debts and in the calculation of Union budgets. Because it is an inherently stable currency, the ECU is increasingly favoured in the international money markets and as a medium for international trade.

**European Economic Area** (EEA)  Organization formed in 1992 between members of **EFTA** and the **EU** (with the exception of Switzerland).

**European Economic Community** (EEC)  Association of some twelve European nations that were joined by a customs union and committed to the promotion of free trade within the boundaries of the community, now renamed the *European Union* (EU). It was often abbreviated to European Community (EC) and was originally known as the Common Market.

**European Exchange Rate Mechanism** *See Exchange Rate Mechanism* (ERM).

**European Free Trade Association** (EFTA)  Trade association, established in 1960 between several west European countries, some of whom left when they joined the European Union.

**European Monetary System** (EMS)  System established in 1979 for stabilizing exchange rates between EU member states (*see Exchange Rate Mechanism*). It can also be seen as a step towards the European Central Bank (ECB)  and a single currency as part of European Monetary Union.

**European Monetary Union** (EMU)  *See European Monetary System.*

**E**

**European Settlements Office** (ESO) Settlement system for ECU bills of exchange founded by the Bank of England in 1993. Its members have terminals *on-line* to the ESO, enabling same-day real-time settlements.

**European Union** (EU) Association of European nations formerly known as the European Economy Community (EEC) or European Community (EC), and before that the Common Market. It is intended that in the long run all the factors of production may be moved within the community at will, and remaining customs barriers are expected to be removed some time in the near future. The EU operates a protectionist policy by maintaining common tariffs on imports, and generates a substantial portion of its income from import duties and value added tax. In finance, its committed aims include a *European Monetary System*, and all that it entails.

**eurosclerosis** Popular term for a "seizure" (breakdown) in the *euromarkets* caused by *illiquidity* or some other financial panic.

**EV** Abbreviation of *embedded vaule*.

**event of default** In a loan agreement, a clause that if breached requires repayment of the loan immediately.

**ex ante** Latin for "from before": what is expected to be the position after some future event. *See also ex post.*

**exception** In insurance, a *peril* that is specifically excluded from the cover provided by a policy.

**exceptional items** Below-the-line *costs* and *revenues* that arise outside the normal business activities of a quoted company. The sale or purchase of new buildings or plant are examples of exceptional items.

**excess** Sum that a policyholder has (by agreement) to contribute to an insurance claim, *e.g.*, on a *motor insurance* the policyholder may have to pay the first £50 or £100 (the excess) on any claim. It may be compulsory or voluntary. *See also franchise policy.*

**excess capacity** Capacity to produce goods over and above the current rate. Excess capacity is more strictly used to denote the increase in production necessary to bring the average cost to a minimum.

**excess of loss** In reinsurance, an agreement that requires the reinsurer to bear any loss over a certain stated amount.

**E**

**excess profits tax** Tax paid on a company's profit over and above a level that is thought to be normal.

**exchange** Term with two meanings:

1. It is to give one thing and take an equivalent in return.
2. It is any place where goods or stocks are traded.

**exchange control** Control of foreign exchange dealings by the government, either by means of restrictions on trade or by direct intervention in the market. Exchange controls help a government to exert some influence over the international value of its own currency. In the UK, exchange controls were abolished in 1979.

**exchange dealings** Trading of *stocks*, *shares* and other financial instruments on an exchange.

**exchange exposure** Extent of the risk that results from quoting assets or liabilities in a foreign currency, because variations in the *exchange rate* can affect the values.

**exchanger** Person who exchanges one currency for another.

**exchange gain** Profit made by an importer if there is a favourable change in the *exchange rate*.

**exchange loss** Loss made by an importer if there is an unfavourable change in the *exchange rate*.

**exchange permit** Document needed by an importer's government that allows the importer to exchange his or her own country's currency into another currency (to pay the seller abroad).

**exchange rate** The price at which one currency may be exchanged for another. Such transactions may be carried out on either the spot or forward markets, and are usually conducted either to permit investment abroad or to pay for imports. There is, in addition, considerable speculation on the exchange rates. *See forward market; spot market*.

**Exchange Rate Mechanism** (ERM) EU regulation that limits variations in the exchange rates of its member states to within closely defined limits. It is a vital feature of the *European Monetary System* (EMS). Britain (and Italy) left the ERM in 1992.

**exchange rate spread** Difference between the price paid for foreign currency and what it is sold for.

**exchange restrictions** *Exchange control* that enables a government to limit the sale or purchase of foreign or domestic currency, usually in order to maintain the *exchange rate* for its own currency at an artificial level.

**Exchange, The** Computerized system that provides *independent financial advisers* with information on prices from about 50 insurance companies.

**Exchequer** Broadly, the central depository of government funds. As the department charged with the supervision of the nation's economic affairs, the Treasury is responsible for ensuring that all monies due to the government are paid into the Exchequer, and all spending approved by parliament is paid for from Exchequer funds.

**excise duty** Duty levied on home-produced goods, either to control consumption and thus influence spending, or to raise revenue. Goods that currently attract excise duty in the UK are alcohol, petrol and tobacco.

**excluded claim** Insurance claim specifically not covered by an insurance policy.

**excluded peril** Peril that is specifically excluded from an insurance policy cover. *See exclusion.*

**exclusion** In insurance, a declared risk that the insurance company will not pay a claim on (e.g., on a *life assurance* policy, an exclusion may be death resulting from suicide).

**exclusive agreement** Agreement whereby an agent is authorized to act as sole agent in representing a particular company or product.

**ex coupon** Stock that does not give the purchaser the right to the next interest payment due to be paid on it.

**ex dividend** (ex div) Stock that does not give the purchaser the right to the next *dividend* payment, or to any dividend payment due within a specified period, generally the next calendar month. However, he or she does have the right to receive subsequent dividends.

**execution only** Describing a service where no advice is given or received.

**executive** Person charged with decision-making, specifically a member of the management of a company.

**executive director** Also called a working director, a company director who is an employee of the company and therefore involved in the day-to-day management of the company.

**executive pension plan** (EPP) *Money-purchase pension scheme* set up for, usually, directors and key employees of a company. The company usually makes substantial contributions to the plan; the employee may, or may not, contribute in addition.

**executive share option** Allocation of shares to a company's executives or rights to buy shares at less than market price, used as an incentive or reward to senior employees.

**executor** Person appointed by a will to see that the terms of the will or bequest are carried out.

**exemplary damages** Punitive damages awarded in an attempt to compensate for damage to an intangible thing (such as feelings or reputation) or to deter others from repeating the action that resulted in the award.

**exempt** Not chargeable, usually in relation to tax.

**exempt approval** Type of approval by the Pension Schemes Office of the Inland Revenue granted to pension schemes. Full tax concessions are given when a scheme is "exempt approved".

**exempt approved scheme** Pension scheme that has exempt approval from the Pension Scheme Office of the Inland Revenue. It receives maximum tax concessions.

**exempt supplies** Supplies of goods and services that are exempt from *value-added tax* (VAT). The category includes insurance, postal services and education.

**exempt transfers** Transfers that are not chargeable to income tax. It includes transfers between spouses, certain marriage gifts and gifts to charities.

**exercise** To make use of a right or option.

**exercise date** Date on which the holder of a traded *option* can implement it.

**exercise notice** Formal notification that a *call option* is to be taken up. The price paid is known as the exercise price or *striking price*.

**exercise price** Alternative term for *striking price*.

**ex gratia** Describing a payment made in thanks, *e.g.* a tip, or *golden handshake* payment to a retiring worker. *See ex gratia payment.*

**ex gratia payment** In insurance, a payment made to settle an issue (such as an insurance claim) but without admitting liability.

**ex-growth** Euphemism for decline.

**exhaustive events** Set of possible events that collectively cover every possible occurrence in a given context. It is a useful concept in corporate planning.

**exit** To leave a *market* by selling all relevant *stocks* and *shares*, or to cease production.

**exit charge** Charge made to an investor in some *unit trusts* when he or she liquidates the investment.

**ex new** Alternative term for *ex rights*.

**ex officio** By virtue of office.

**expansion** Development or growth of a business, either by *takeover* or *merger*, or by an increase in sales, production or investment by a firm.

**expectation of life** Statistical assessment made by an *actuary* of the likely length of someone's life (for *life assurance* purposes).

**expectations** Prospects; that which is anticipated. Expectations of future business activity are one of the most significant influences on *investment* and thus have a significant effect on the level of unemployment.

**expenditure** Money spent on attaining some object.

**expense account** Sum of money that an employee can spend on personal expenses (such as travel and entertainment) in order to do his or her job.

**expenses** Costs incurred by a business or individual in the course of normal activities.

**expenses loading** Element of an insurance premium that is designed to cover the insurer's administrative costs.

**experience rating** Method of calculating insurance premiums based on previous claims experience.

**expiry date** Date on which an agreement lapses. In insurance, it is the date on which a *term assurance* ends.

**exploding warrant** Warrant introduced in order to dilute the shareholding of a company *raider* during a *takeover* bid. It is also known as a springing warrant.

**export** To sell goods and services outside the country of origin, or the good or services themselves. *See also* **import.**

**Export Credits Guarantee Department** (ECGD) UK government department, established in 1991 and partly privatized, that makes available export credit insurance and guarantees to repay banks that give credit (over two years or more) to exporters. *See also* **buyer credit.**

**export declaration** Statement provided to the Customs and Excise detailing the cost, price, destination and nature of goods leaving the country.

**export duty** Tax levied on exports. Because export duties tend to discourage export and adversely affect the *balance of payments*, they are seldom raised.

**export house** Company that assists other companies involved in the export trade, either by providing short- or medium-term credit (*e.g.* an export finance house) or by acting as an overseas agent for companies that do not maintain their own representatives in the countries to which they export.

**export incentive** Government incentives to promote exports. They include direct-tax incentives, subsidies, favourable terms for insurance and the provision of cheap credit.

**export insurance** Type of insurance taken out by exporters. It may give cover against failure to pay (perhaps because of insolvency of the buyer) and inconvertibility of currency (perhaps because of political factors).

**export leasing** Practice of selling goods for export to a leasing company in the country of origin. The leasing company ships them overseas and leases them to a foreign customer.

**export restitution** EU term for subsidies paid to member food exporters.

**ex post** Describing the position that arises after a certain event has taken place. *See also* **ex ante.**

**exposure** Extent of *risk.*

**exposure to loss** Extent to which a loss can arise in insurance.

**exposure unit** Measure of loss potential in insurance.

**expression of wish** Pension scheme member's nomination as to whom he wishes the death benefits to be paid. The nomination does not bind the trustees but is normally used as the basis for their decision.

**expropriation** Dispossession; the confiscation of, *e.g.*, an *estate* or *property*.

**expropriation insurance** Type of insurance that provides cover against seizure of assets by a foreign country.

**ex quay** Describing goods that are sold for collection after they have been unloaded from a ship. The seller therefore pays freightage and the cost of unloading.

**ex rights** Also known as ex new, a stock exchange term for shares that are sold minus the right to take up *bonus issues*.

**ex ship** Describing goods sold to a purchaser who must pay the cost of unloading. The seller therefore pays only the cost of freightage.

**extended** Prolonged or offered.

**extended credit** Credit that is to be repaid over a very long period of time. *See also long credit*.

**external** Something that is outside, such as external trade.

**external audit** Audit carried out by an independent external auditor.

**external company** In insurance, a company with headquarters outside the European Union (EU) but with an agency or branch in the UK.

**external member** Person (a "name") who invests in *Lloyd's of London* without any control over the activities of the *underwriters*.

**external trade** Trade with countries other than one's own.

**extractive industry** Companies and people involved in primary production, *e.g.* fishing, farming and mining. *See also primary production*.

**extraordinary** Describing additional items, expenditure, etc., acquired or incurred in addition to normal business.

**extraordinary items** Non-recurrent material items below the line on a *balance sheet*, such as the sale or purchase of premises.

**extrinsic value** Constituent part of the value of a traded *option* not calculated by difference in market price to exercise price. Extrinsic value is governed by such factors as time left to run and the volatility of the market concerned.

# F

**face value** Alternative term for *nominal value*.

**factfind** Document used by insurance companies and advisers to satisfy the "know your customer" rules under the Financial Services Act. It allows the adviser to complete a pre-agreed form when giving advice to a client.

**facsimile transmission** *See fax*.

**factor** Company that undertakes *factoring* or, in Scotland, the manager of an estate of land.

**factoring** Activity of managing the *trade debts* of another firm. Commonly, a company sells due debts to a factor at a discount. The factor then makes a profit by recovering the debts at a price nearer the face value. Factoring relieves companies of the burden of administering debts and gives them access to ready cash before payment is due. *See also nominal value*.

**factor of production** Collective term for those things necessary for production to take place. Factors of production are most usually divided into the following categories: capital, labour and land.

**facultative** Type of reinsurance in which risks are coded on an individual basis. The coding company can choose whether or not to reinsure and the reinsurer can decide to accept or reject the business.

**facultative endorsement** Special endorsement to a *bill of exchange* that waives a duty toward the endorser. *See waiver*.

**facultative-obligatory reinsurance** (fac-ob) Type of treaty agreement whereby the insurer can choose whether or not to reinsure a risk, but once ceded, the reinsurer must accept.

**failure investment** Practice of buying shares in companies that are doing badly, in the hope that their performance will improve.

**fair copy** Copy of a document, including any alterations and revisions. Also known as final copy.

**fair price provisions (US fair price amendments)** Clause in a corporate charter whereby a buyer of the company's shares must pay the same amount or make the same consideration for all shares purchased. It is used as a defensive tactic against **bootstrapping**.

Fair-price provisions are also price controls, generally instituted by a government, that guarantee fair prices to the consumer by ensuring that the manufacturer and retailer make reasonable rather than excessive profits.

**fallen angel** Company, or shares in a company, whose *rating* has recently fallen significantly.

**family company** Company founded by and owned almost exclusively by members of one family.

**family income benefit** Form of term life assurance that pays out the sum assured in yearly (or monthly) instalments. These are paid from the date of death until the end of the policy term.

**fan club** Group of investors in the same shares, but who do not cooperate as a *concert party*.

**FAPA** Abbreviation of Fellow of the Association of Authorized Public Accountants.

**FAS** Abbreviation of *free alongside ship*.

**FASB** Abbreviation of *Financial Accounting Standards Board.*

**fate** Decision whether or not to accept a negotiable instrument when it is presented for payment. *See also* **advise fate**.

**fax** Sort for facsimile transmission, a document transmitted via telephone lines to a computer or fax machine.

**FAVC** Abbreviation of *free-standing additional voluntary contribution.*

**FCA** Abbreviation of Fellow of the Institute of Chartered Accountants. *See* **chartered accountant**.

**FCCA** Abbreviation of Fellow of the Chartered Association of Certified Accountants. *See* **certified accountant**.

**FCCI** Abbreviation of Fellow of the *Chartered Insurance Institute.*

**FCIA** Abbreviation of *Foreign Credit and Insurance Association.*

**FDIC** Abbreviation of *Federal Deposit Insurance Corporation.*

**F**

**FECDBA** Abbreviation of *Foreign Exchange and Currency Deposit Brokers Association.*

**Federal Deposit Insurance Corporation** (FDIC) Organization that makes available *deposit insurance* for US banks. It is part of the Federal Reserve System, employing the US Bank Insurance Fund.

**Federation of Insurance Brokers** Former trade association of insurance brokers, replaced in 1977 by the British Insurance Brokers Association.

**fee** Amount charged for a service performed, *e.g.*, a stockbroker charges a fee for buying and selling shares for clients, and accountants charge fees for carrying out company audits.

**fee simple** Property held in fee simple may be bequeathed and inherited without limitation. Effectively the highest form of land ownership for any citizen, ending only if the owner dies *intestate*, without heirs, in which case the property passes to the crown.

**feemail** Popular term describing the exorbitant fees charged by lawyers who handle *greenmail* cases.

**FIA** Abbreviation of Fellow of the *Institute of Actuaries*.

**fictitious assets** Assets that do not exist but are entered onto a company's *balance sheet* to balance the books, *e.g.* a *trading loss* may be one example of a fictitious asset for tax purposes.

**fictitious payee** Non-existent person named as the payee on a *bill of exchange*; the bill is treated as if it were made payable to bearer.

**fidelity guarantee** Guarantee of the trustworthiness of a person for employment purposes.

**fidelity guarantee insurance** Commercial insurance that covers misappropriation of funds or other wrongdoing by an employee. It is also called fidelity insurance.

**fidelity insurance** See *fidelity guarantee insurance*.

**fiduciary** Person or body acting in trust. Anyone holding, say, cash in trust for another is said to be acting in a fiduciary capacity.

**FIFO** Abbreviation of *first in first out*.

**fight the tape** Practice of selling when prices are rising and buying when prices are falling. The tape is the ticker tape that once relayed prices to brokers.

**figures book** Summary of insurance claims, premiums and reinsurances processed by the *Policy Signing Office* of Lloyd's of London.

**fill or kill** On a *futures* market, an order to trade that must be either fulfilled immediately or cancelled.

**FIMBRA** Abbreviation of *Financial Intermediaries and Brokers Regulatory Authority*, a former self-regulatory organization (SRO).

**final accounts** Normally, the *annual accounts*. However, the term may also refer to the final report submitted by a liquidator at the end of *liquidation*.

**final dividend** Last share *dividend* paid by a company during a trading year.

**final salary pension scheme** *Occupational pension scheme* in which the benefit at retirement is defined and guaranteed. The benefits are defined in terms of an accural rate (*e.g.* 1/60 or 1/80) per year of pensionable service. This fraction is then applied to the member's final salary as defined by the scheme.

**finance** Term with two meanings:

1. It is a noun, meaning resources of money and their management.

*He is trying to raise the finance to float another company.*

2. It is a verb, meaning to supply money for a certain purpose.

*He finally found a backer who would finance the whole operation.*

**Finance Act** Annual legislation enforcing the measures set out in the UK government's *budget*.

**finance house** Also known as a finance company or an industrial bank, a company that provides finance (credit), *e.g.* to operate **hire purchase** transactions on behalf of retailers of consumer goods such as cars and electronic and electrical equipment.

**financial accountant** Accountant who is concerned with the movement of cash, rather than with money that is involved in production (*see cost accountant*). The financial accountant is responsible for overseeing the level of cash available for paying debts and for investment, and for managing and recording all financial transactions.

**Financial Accounting Standards Board** (FASB) Private regulatory body that sets the accounting standards for US public companies. *See also Securities and Exchange Commission* (SEC).

**financial adviser** Person (or institution) who gives advice on raising, lending or managing money, or on particular transactions, usually for a fee.

**financial futures** Contracts for the delivery of financial instruments (*i.e.* a currency) on a future date. Financial futures are used to *hedge* against the rise and fall of interest and exchange rates.

**financial institution** Bank, building society, finance house or other institution that collects, invests and lends funds.

**financial instrument** *Bond, certificate of deposit, treasury bill* or any other method of financing.

**Financial Intermediaries, Managers and Brokers Regulatory Association** (FIMBRA) Former organization (a *self-regulatory organization*, or SRO) that regulated financial advisers and firms selling and managing securities and unit trusts. In 1995 its functions were taken over by the *Personal Investment Authority* (PIA). *See also financial intermediary.*

**financial intermediary** Insurance company, finance house, bank, building society, or other business that collects funds (from members, or lenders) to use for making loans (to borrowers). Any person or organization that sells insurance (but is not an employee of an insurance company) is also regarded as a financial intermediary.

**financial planning** Making short- and long-term plans to arrange an individual or company's financial affairs in a tax efficient manner, with regard to both security and liquidity of investments.

**Financial Planning Certificate** (FPC) Qualification obtained by *financial advisers* who pass the compliance examinations of the *Chartered Insurance Institute*. There is also an Advanced Financial Planning Certificate.

**financial risk** Risk of loss that can be measured in monetary terms.

**financial risk control** Plans and provisions to ensure that money is available to meet any losses that occur. It can include risk retention and risk transfer.

**financial services** Broad term that covers services offered by banks, building societies, insurance companies and advisers. It includes money transmission services, mortgages and lending, life assurance, pensions and investments. The term is more strictly defined in the Financial Services Act as "investment business".

**Financial Services Act** (FSA) Act of Parliament in the UK of 1986, introduced to prevent abuse of the de-regulated stock exchange system, principally by placing all people or institutions involved in financial services under the authority of a *self-regulatory organization* (SRO).

**Financial Services Authority** (FSA) Authority established in 1998 that will take over regulation under the Financial Services Act of all those doing "investment business". The FSA will absorb the work of the three self-regulatory organizations – *Personal Investment Authority* (PIA), *Investment Management Regulatory Organization* (IMRO) and *Securities and Futures Authority* (SFA) – as well as the *Securities and Investment Board* in 1998 and 1999. It will also be responsible for regulating banks and Lloyd's of London.

**financial statement** Document summarizing a company's activities, assests and liabilities, including the *balance sheet* and *profit-and-loss account.*

**financial supermarket** Financial institution that provides more than one type of financial service. A significant number sprang up after *deregulation.* A financial supermarket may also be known as a *boutique. See also Big Bang; Chinese wall.*

**Financial Times Stock Exchange 100 Index** (FTSE, or FOOTSIE) Index of shares of the 100 largest companies, a weighted average which is updated every minute during the working day. The index value of 1000 was set on the base date of 3 January 1984.

**Financial Times 30 Index** (FT Index, or FT-30 Index) Index of changes in prices of 30 major industrial and commercial ordinary shares on the London Stock Exchange, updated hourly during the working day. The index value of 100 was set on the base date of 1 July 1935.

**financial year** Period of twelve months, beginning anywhere in the calendar year, used for company accounting purposes. The financial year is the period of twelve months beginning on 1 April to which *corporation tax* rates apply. *See also fiscal year.*

**fine bill** *Bill of exchange* for which the backer is extremely creditworthy and so there is little or no risk.

**fine price** Price of a security on a market in which the difference between the buying and selling prices is very small.

**fine rate** Best rate of interest that can be obtained in a given situation.

**fire insurance** Insurance against damage or loss to property caused by fire. In general, fire insurance only covers cases in which actual ignition took place and in which the insured was not culpable. Most policies also provide limited cover in the event of damage caused by lightning or explosion.

**firm** Commonly, any company or business. Strictly, a firm is a partnership of professionally qualified people, such as lawyers, accountants, surveyors or civil engineers. In this case, firms are legally distinct from companies and so do not, for instance, issue shares. Also, the *liability* of individual partners is not (and legally cannot be) limited. *See also incorporation.*

**firm bid** (or **offer**) Bid (or offer) that has no conditions. *See subject bid* (or *offer*).

**firm market** Market in which prices are steady.

**firm price** Guaranteed price, usually offered only if the cost of providing goods or service can be assessed accurately.

**first class paper** *Bills* issued by financial institutions of high standing, *e.g.* the *Treasury*.

**first in first out** (FIFO) Accountancy principle whereby *stock-in-trade* is assumed to be issued to customers in the order that it is received. Thus, stock currently held may be valued at current prices. *See also last in first out.*

**first loss insurance** Type of *fire insurance* or *theft insurance* in which the full value of the insured item is declared, but a lower sum is insured (at a consequently lower premium).

**first mortgage debenture** *Debenture* giving the holder first charge over a company's property.

**fiscal year** Period of twelve months for the purposes of tax calculation. In the UK the fiscal year runs from 6 April to the following 5 April. *See also financial year.*

**fixed** Unchanging, not subject to movement. The term is commonly found in phrases such as *fixed assets, fixed charge, fixed costs, fixed deposit, fixed exchange rate, fixed-interest securities, fixed trust.*

**fixed assets** Sometimes also known as *capital assets*, assets used in the furtherance of a company's business, *e.g.* machinery or property.

**fixed capital** Alternative term for *fixed assets.*

**fixed charge** Asset against which a *mortgage* is secured. It is also used as an alternative term for *fixed costs.*

**fixed costs** Costs that do not vary with short-term changes in the level of output (such as heating costs or rates).

**fixed deposit** Money placed in a *deposit account, i.e.* an account from which it cannot be withdrawn without suitable notice being given. The US equivalent is time deposit.

**fixed exchange rate** *Exchange rate* that the government attempts to control and fix in the short term by instructing the Bank of England to buy or sell foreign exchange reserves, or by introducing *tariffs*.

**fixed expenses** Expenses that are incurred regardless of the level of other activities. *See overheads.*

**fixed-interest securities** Securities for which the income is fixed and does not vary. They include *bonds, debentures* and *gilt-edged securities.*

**fixed penalty notice** Document (issued by the police) advising a driver that he or she has incurred a fixed penalty for a motoring offence. Although it may lead to an endorsement of the driver's licence, it does not constitute a conviction (as defined by most kinds of *motor insurance*).

**fixed rate** Describing a charge or interest that does not change. *See also floating rate.*

**fixed-rate mortgage** Mortgage with an interest rate determined at the beginning of the loan period and fixed for at least the first few years.

**fixed trust** Unit trust in which investors' money is invested in a set portfolio.

**fixed yield** Return that remains the same.

**fixture** Any *chattel* attached or annexed to land, in which case it becomes part of the property.

**fixtures and fittings** In *household insurance*, fixtures to a property are permanently fitted and are covered by insurance of the building. Fittings that are removable (even if sold with the property) are normally covered by contents insurance.

**flat rate** Comprehensive charge applied to a group of items, as opposed to a differential rate, which varies depending on the individual items. The term is most often used with regard to insurance *premiums*.

**flat yield** Yield on a fixed interest security shown by relating the income from the security to the present market price. It is also known as the *running yield.*

**fleet insurance** Motor insurance policy that covers a group of vehicles from one organization.

**flexible insurance plan** (FLIP) Insurance that involves a lump-sum payment into a savings account, which provides funds to pay the interest on a loan.

**flexible trust** Unit trust in which investors' money is not invested in a set portfolio, but moved from one investment to another in order to increase earnings.

**flexidowment** Endowment policy that can be encashed at any time after ten years in force.

**flight capital** Capital that is removed from a country that seems to be politically (or economically) unstable, and taken to a more stable environment.

**flip** Practice of buying then selling shares (usually in the manner of a *stag)* at high speed in order to make a fast profit.

**FLIP** Abbreviation of *flexible insurance plan.*

**float** Term with two broad meanings:
1. It is cash or funds used either to give change to customers or to pay for expenses.
2. To float is to sell shares in order to raise share *capital* and obtain listing on the stock exchange. It is also now more frequently used to mean to start a new company.

**floater** Security owned by the bearer, the person who holds it. More formally it is termed a bearer security.

**floating asset** Alternative term for *current asset.*

**floating charge** Charge made on the varying assets of a company (such as raw material stock and finished goods in store) by a lender in order that the company may secure a loan. The charge becomes fixed (*i.e.,* it crystallizes) if the company goes into liquidation or defaults on the loan.

**floating contract** Insurance policy that covers all shipments of exports.

**floating debt** Short-term government borrowing, *e.g. Treasury bills.*

**floating exchange rate** Also known as a free exchange rate, an exchange rate that is not in any way manipulated by a central bank, but which moves according to *supply and demand.*

**floating money** Money for which no profitable investment can be found quickly, usually at a time of high liquidity.

**floating policy** Insurance that covers goods of different values and at different locations. In marine insurance, it covers a ship's cargoes for a stated number of voyages (during a specified period).

**floating rate** Charge or rate of interest for a loan (such as a mortgage) that may change during the period of the loan.

**floating rate note** Security issued by a borrower on the *Eurobonds* market that has a variable rate of interest.

**floating warranty** Guarantee given by one party that induces a second to enter into a contract with a third party.

*Before using the mortgage broker, the home buyer sought a floating warranty from the estate agent.*

**floor** Usually refers to the trading area of an exchange. *See also floor trader.*

**floor trader** Someone who is authorized to trade on the floor of a stock or commodities exchange.

**flotation** Act of selling shares in a company to raise capital and be listed on the stock exchange.

**fluctuation** Movement of prices up or down on a market. Downward fluctuation is also known as slippage.

**FOB** Abbreviation of *free on board*.

**FOOTSIE** Abbreviation of *Financial Times Stock Exchange 100 Index*.

**for declaration only** Describing an insurance policy with no specified cover or premium. A premium is assessed later, based on the history of claims.

**foreclosure** If a property has been mortgaged, *i.e.* stands as security against a loan, the lender may take possession of the property if the borrower fails to pay off the loan. Such an act of possession is known as foreclosure and requires a foreclosure order issued by the court.

**foreclosure order** *See foreclosure.*

**foreign aid** Aid, most often in the form of loans or investment, to developing and Third World countries.

**foreign bill** *Bill of exchange* that is drawn in a foreign country. *See also inland bill.*

**F**

**Foreign Credit and Insurance Association** (FCIA) US organization that offers exporters short-term cover against commercial and political risks, such as default on export credit.

**foreign currency translation** Accounting procedure in which sums stated in a foreign currency are converted into sterling, either at the current exchange rate or at the rate that prevailed at the time of the entry.

**foreign draft** *Bill of exchange* that is payable abroad, or a bankers' draft drawn on a foreign branch, usually in the foreign currency.

**foreign exchange** (FOREX, or FX) Currency of a foreign country, and the buying and selling of such currencies.

**Foreign Exchange and Currency Deposit Brokers Association** (FECDBA) Professional organization that represents the interests of brokers who deal in foreign exchange and foreign currency deposits.

**foreign-exchange broker** *Broker* who deals in foreign currencies on the *foreign exchange market*, usually on behalf of commercial banks.

**foreign exchange market** Market where foreign currencies are traded by foreign-exchange brokers (intermediaries) and foreign-exchange dealers (bank employees). *Options* and *futures* on forward exchange rates are also traded.

**foreign exchange risk** Risk taken in buying or selling foreign currency (because the exchange rate could change unfavourably between buying and selling).

**foreign insurer** In the USA, an insurance company that is domiciled in another state, as opposed to a domestic insurer (in the same state) and an alien insurer (domiciled abroad).

**foreign investment** Acquisition of another country's *assets* through any form of investment. It serves to stimulate economic growth in the investing nation and helps to maintain a favourable *balance of payments*.

**FOREX** Abbreviation of *foreign exchange*.

**forged share transfer** If a bank accepts a share certificate with a forged stock transfer form, the bank is liable to the company that issued the shares.

**forgery** The offence of making a false instrument so that it can be accepted as genuine.

**fortuitous event** To be insurable, the happening of an event must be

**F**

fortuitous as far as the insured is concerned. This means that the event must be unexpected. It would not be possible to insure against an event which would definitely occur, such as damage inflicted by the insured on purpose.

**forward** To send something on to someone (*e.g.* to a new address) or something (*e.g.* a *futures* contract) to be completed some time in the future, or an adjective describing something (such as a transaction) in the future.

**forward dating** Practice of dating documents in advance, *e.g.* an invoice or a cheque may be dated some time in the future. It is also known as postdating.

**forwardation** Situation in which spot goods are bought by a dealer (usually on a *commodities* market) and carried forward to deliver against a forward contract (because the spot goods are cheaper than goods for forward delivery). *See also* **backwardation.**

**forward dealing** Accepting or awarding a contract (most usually on a *commodities* market) for settlement or delivery by a pre-arranged future date. *See also* *futures.*

**forward exchange contract** Agreement to buy foreign exchange at some future date at an agreed rate of exchange.

**forward integration** Taking on by a company of activities at a subsequent stage of production or distribution (which are carried out by another company), *e.g.* an oil production company undertakes forward integration when it invests in refineries, tankers and petrol stations.

**forward market** Market in (contracts or options for) goods that are to be delivered at a future date. *See also* **buy forward**; *futures*; *spot market.*

**forward price** Price quoted for goods not immediately available or not yet manufactured. The forward price is usually lower than the eventual retail price because it takes into account only the estimated costs of manufacture at some future date. More specifically, it is the price quoted in a *futures* deal.

**forward purchase** Buying of *securities* or *commodities* in advance of delivery. *See* *futures.*

**forward rate** Exchange rate quoted on a *forward exchange contract.*

**founder's shares** Alternative term for *deferred ordinary shares.*

**FPC** Abbreviation of *Financial Planning Certificate.*

**F**

**franchise** Term with two meanings:

1. It is a licence bought by a retailer or supplier of services that entitles him or her to sell the goods of a particular manufacturer under a particular trading name. This system enables the manufacturer to have direct control over who sells the goods, and often gives the seller exclusive rights to sell those goods in his or her area.

2. In insurance, a franchise is an agreed figure below which an insurance company does not have to meet a claim. A loss above the franchise figure is paid in full. *See also* ***excess***.

**franchise policy** Insurance policy under which the insured makes no claims for loss or damage up to a specified sum, known as the franchise. Claims for sums exceeding the franchise are met in full by the insurer. The purpose of such a policy is to eliminate the insurer's obligation to deal with small but time-consuming claims. In motor insurance, a similar principle is incorporated in the *excess*.

**franked investment income** Dividends and other distributions from UK companies that are received by other companies. The dividends have already had tax levied upon them, and therefore they can pass through other companies without being liable for any further corporation tax.

**franked payment** Dividend or distribution from a UK company plus any advance corporation tax attributable to it.

**fraternal insurance** Cover provided in the USA by mutual assistance or *friendly societies*. It is an old-established type of pension or unemployment insurance, founded in the 1800s.

**fraud** Illegal practice of obtaining money from people under false pretences, *e.g.* fraud is committed if facts pertaining to a contract are purposefully misrepresented. Fraudulently diverting one's company's or employer's money for one's own use is *embezzlement*.

**free alongside ship** (FAS) An exporter who sells goods FAS pays for their carriage up to the point when they are standing on the dockside waiting to be loaded. *See also* ***free on board***.

**free asset ratio** In insurance, the ratio of an insurer's free assets (at market value) to its liabilities.

**free capital** *Working capital* of a bank or other financial institution.

**free competition** Situation in which rival companies are allowed to compete freely with each other for a share of the market. In a free competition or free market economy, the laws of *supply and demand* regulate prices. *See also perfect competition.*

**free cover** Level of life cover provided by a group life assurance scheme without the necessity for medical evidence.

**free depreciation** In accounting, depreciation of an *asset* over any time period the company thinks fit.

**free enterprise** Economic system under which individuals or groups may own the factors of production and exploit them for their own benefit within the limits of the law.

**freehold** Land or buildings that are owned freehold are owned absolutely by the freeholder. *See also leasehold.*

**free limits** Geographical limits under a permanent health insurance policy within which a claim will be paid. It usually includes the UK, Europe, the USA, Canada and Australasia.

**free lunch** Non-existent benefit ("There's no such thing as a free lunch"; someone always pays for it).

**free market** Term with two meanings:
1. It is a market that operates essentially by the laws of *supply and demand.*
2. On the stock market, it is a situation in which a particular *security* is freely available and in reasonably large quantities.

**free market economy** Economy in which the allocation of resources is determined by the level of *supply and demand* without intervention by the state. No pure free-market economy exists.

**free on board** (FOB) An exporter who sells goods FOB pays for the carriage up to the point where they are loaded aboard ship. *See also free alongside ship.*

**free reserve** Term with two meanings:
1. It is the excess of reserves held by a bank or insurance company over the minimum laid down by the regulator.
2. It is the total reserves held by a building society less its fixed assets.

**free resources** For an insurance company, its assets less its liabilities.

**free-standing additional voluntary contribution** (FSAVC) Additional sum paid to an independantly administered "top up" plan with an insurance company.

**free trade** Concept of international trading in which there are no tariff barriers between countries.

**freeze** Broadly, act of stopping something (*e.g.* wages or prices) from moving.

*The Government has decided to freeze wage levels of certain public-sector employees for the next twelve months.*

**freeze-out** Situation in which a company successfully out-competes its competitors, causing a new ice-age for them and thus freezing them out of the market.

**freight** Expenses incurred in transporting cargo.

**frictional unemployment** Unemployment caused by the movement of people between jobs. Thus, there may be enough jobs to go round, but some people may experience periods of unemployment between the finish date of one job and the start date of the next.

**friendly** Used more and more frequently to mean something that is sympathetic to the needs of a particular person or group.

**friendly society** Society (first coming into existence in the 17th century, to help provide working people with some form of security) that provides mutual benefits to its members, such as *life assurance* and pensions in return for a yearly subscription. There are various kinds of friendly society, including:

*accumulative society*, which operates by keeping a float to cover claims.

*affiliated society*, which has centralized administration.

*collecting society*, so-called after the method of collecting subscriptions house-to-house.

*deposit society*, which adds part of the funds remaining (after claims have been met) to members' accounts, thus providing them not only with a form of insurance cover but also a method of saving.

*dividing society*, which periodically divides the funds remaining after all claims have been met between its members.

**friendly takeover** Purchase of control of a company that is welcomed by the *target* company's board and shareholders.

**fringe benefit** Items that are given to employees as part of their payment but apart from their wages or salary, *e.g.* a company car, health insurance, or goods at a discount.

**fringes** Popular US abbreviation for *fringe benefits*.

**from the ground up** Term used in insurance to show that all claims in a stated type of insurance have been considered in an analysis, despite high claims having been reinsured.

**front company** Company established to conceal its true ownership or the true activities of its owners.

**front door** Popular term for the Bank of England's practice of lending money to discount houses in order to inject cash into the money market.

**front-end** The marketing (rather than the manufacturing) side of a company.

**front-end fee** Initial fee charged when a financial product is bought.

**front-end loading** Initial charges made in a life assurance policy or investment plan which are levied on the plan within a short period of commencement, *e.g.* one or two years.

**fronting** In insurance, selling certain products with the intention of passing them on to another company.

**front loading** Administration charge (usually 5%) added to a loan which is paid off first, before actual loan repayments begin.

**front money** Alternative term for *seed money*.

**frozen assets** In contrast to *liquid assets*, frozen assets are those that may not be converted into ready money without incurring a loss of some kind, or which may not be converted because someone has a claim on them or there is an order that they may not be transferred. The latter is also called a frozen fund.

**frozen fund** *See frozen assets.*

**FSA** Abbreviation of *Financial Services Act* and *Financial Services Authority.*

**FT Index** *See Financial Times 30 Index.*

**FTSE 100** *See Financial Times Stock Exchange 100 Index.*

**full basic pension** In the UK, a basic *state pension* payable if the pensioner has paid *National Insurance contributions* for at least 90% of his or her working life. Fewer National Insurance contributions result in a reduced pension.

**full coverage** Describing an insurance policy that, in the event of a claim, pays the full value of what is insured, without any deduction for an *excess*. *See also* **all-risks policy**; **franchise policy**.

**fully-insured scheme** Pension scheme for which an independent insurance company insures the benefits totally.

**fully-paid shares** Shares that have been fully paid for by the shareholder. A company may not *call* upon holders of such shares to make any further contribution to *share capital*. Most shares are traded in this fully-paid form. The major exception is that of large new issues, in which trading sometimes begins while they are still partly-paid. *See* **partly-paid shares**.

**functional currency** For a company that does business in several countries, the currency of the country in which most business is done (which it is required to use).

**fund** As a verb, to make finance available.

*He was unable to raise sufficient capital to fund the project.*

As a noun, money set aside for a specific purpose (e.g. from which to pay pensions or insurance claims), or lent to an institution or government. More specifically, it is the money the UK government borrows from institutions and the public by issuing various forms of **government bonds**.

**fundamental analysis** Analysis of the *value* of a company's *stock*, in order to predict movements in its share prices.

**fundamentalist** *See* **fundamental market analyst**.

**fundamental market analyst** In contrast to the modus operandi of the technical market analyst, the fundamental market analyst (fundamentalist) takes the performance of the company in question as the basis for prediction of share-price movements.

**fundamental risk** In insurance, a risk that is outside anybody's control, such as earthquakes, floods and other natural disasters. It is widespread in its effect. *See also* **particular risk**.

**funded debts** Broadly, any short-term debt that has been converted into a long-term debt.

**funded pension** Type of pension that is paid for by contributions paid in advance. These are invested in a range of financial products (a "fund").

**funding** Practice of providing money for a specific purpose. *See* **fund**; **tranche funding**.

**fund manager** Person who manages the investment fund of an institution such as an insurance company or pension scheme. He or she makes investment decisions on behalf of investors, and is also sometimes called an investment manager.

**fund of funds** *Unit trust*, organized and managed by an institution to invest in other of its own unit trusts.

**fungible** Stock market term for *securities* that are in hand, *i.e.* that have not yet been settled.

**futures** Contracts that are made for delivery of *e.g.* currencies or *commodities* on a future date. Futures markets provide an opportunity for *speculation*, in that contracts may be bought and sold (with no intention on the part of the traders to take delivery of the goods) before the delivery date arrives, and their prices may rise and fall in that time.

*Following reports that bad weather in Brazil had seriously damaged the coffee crop, coffee futures rose sharply today.*

**future value** Value that a sum of money invested at compound interest will have in the future.

**FX** Abbreviation of *foreign exchange.*

**FY** Abbreviation of *fiscal year.*

# G

**G5** *See* *Group of Five.*

**G7** *See* *Group of Seven.*

**G10** *See* *Group of Ten.*

**GAAP** Abbreviation of generally accepted accounting principles, a code of practice set out by the US *Financial Accounting Standards Board* (FASB).

**gadfly** Shareholder who appears at shareholders' meetings and asks awkward questions.

**gain** Alternative term for *profit.*

**gainsharing** Alternative term for *profit sharing.*

**gain to redemption** Difference between the amount realized by selling stock now and keeping it to *maturity date.*

**galloping inflation** *See* *hyperinflation.*

**gambling** Applied figuratively to the commitment of money on any venture with a high degree of *risk.* Gambling on a stock market is similar to *speculation* in that it is shorter-term, riskier and less serious-minded than *investment. See also* **bet the ranch.**

**gamma share** Share that is traded infrequently and in small quantities.

**G & A** Abbreviation of *general and administrative expenses.*

**garnishee** Person to whom a *garnishee order* is addressed.

**garnishee order** In bankruptcy, an order may be made by the court to holders of a bankrupt's funds (third parties such as banks etc.) that no payments are to made to the bankrupt until the court authorizes them. The third party is known as the garnishee and the court order is known as a garnishee order (an order from a County Court is called a garnishee summons). The purpose of the order is to protect the interests of the bankrupt's creditors. *See also* **bankrupt.**

**garnishee summons** *See* *garnishee order.*

**G**

**GATT** Abbreviation of *General Agreement on Tariffs and Trade.*

**gazetted** Refers to items published in the *London Gazette* (in Scotland, the *Edinburgh Gazette*), a weekly publication that includes the details of appointments, bankruptcy orders, notices of winding-up, changes in company constitutions, etc. If information is gazetted, it is assumed that everybody in the nation has been notified, even if they have never seen or heard of the publication.

**gazump** To raise the asking price of a property after an offer has been agreed verbally or in writing and before the exchange of contracts, in order to take advantage of rising prices.

**gazunder** To reduce the price offered for a property after an offer price has been agreed verbally or in writing and before exchange of contracts, in order to tale advantage of falling prices.

**GDP** Abbreviation of *gross domestic product.*

**geared investment** Investment trust that borrows money, causing shares to rise faster in rising markets and fall more quickly in falling markets.

**gearing** The proportion of long-term debt to equity finance on the balance sheet of a company. More specifically, it is the ratio of borrowed capital against total capital employed, expressed as a percentage. It is sometimes known as leverage.

**gearing effect** Way in which the gearing of a company affects share dividends.

**GEMM** Abbreviation of *gilt-edged market maker.*

**general agent** Agent with authority to represent the principal in all matters concerning a particular activity.
*The sales representative acted as general agent for the company.*

**General Agreement on Tariffs and Trade** (GATT) An international organization with more than eighty members countries, whose object is to negotiate on matters of trade policy, notably the reduction of *tariffs* and other barriers to free trade. *See also **most-favoured nation clause**; **trade barrier.***

**general and administrative expenses** (G & A) Administrative expenses plus *operating costs.*

**general average** In insurance, a situation in which a loss, resulting from a deliberate act of sacrifice to save other goods, is shared by the insurers concerned (such as the insurer of a vessel and the insurer of its cargo where part of the cargo has been jettisoned – and lost – to save the ship). *See also* **average**.

**general expenses** Non-specific expenses incurred in the day-to-day running of a company or firm.

**general insurance** Broad classification of insurance business which covers transportation insurance, *property insurance, pecuniary insurance* and *liability insurance*. Usually contracts are of one year's duration, with a new contract negotiated at "renewal". *Personal accident and sickness insurance* and *private medical insurance* are also general insurance contracts. It is also known as general business.

**general lien** The right to take possession of *assets* at will after default.

**general offer** Offer made to the general public, *e.g.* a person may offer to pay a certain amount for a piece of information, and members of the public accept the offer by sending the information.

**general partner** *Partner* whose liability for the debts of the partnership is unlimited.

**general partnership** Formal *partnership* in which each partner shares equally in the running of the firm and accepts liability for an equal share of its debts, although his or her share of the profits is usually proportional to the capital that he or she has invested.

**general personal equity plan** *Personal equity plan* (PEP) with a *fund* based on a range of investments (as opposed to a *single-company* personal equity plan).

**general policy** Insurance taken out by an exporter to cover all the goods that will be handled in a year. Each individual cargo is certificated and an additional premium paid for its insurance as its is shipped.

**general power of attorney** *Power of attorney* for which there is no limitation on the powers of the donee (who holds the power).

**general reserves** Sometimes also known as revenue reserves, profits not distributed to a company's shareholders.

**gentleman's agreement** Verbal agreement between two parties who trust each other and have a strong sense of honour.

**geographical diversification** Diversification into new geographical areas, *e.g.* a company that owns a chain of stores in Scotland may diversify by acquiring similar shops in Wales and England.

**geographical rating** In insurance, the practice of basing *premiums* on the geographical location of the risk insured, often based on the post code. It is applied particularly to motor vehicle insurance and property insurance.

***Gesellschaft*** German equivalent of **limited company** (Ltd). *See also* ***Aktiengesellschaft*** *(AG);Gesellschaft mit beschrankter Haftun (GmbH)*

***Gesellschaft mit beschrankter Haftun (GmbH)*** German equivalent of a UK *private limited company* (plc). *See also* ***Aktiengesellschaft*** *(AG)*.

**GIGO** Acronym for garbage in, garbage out, a precept in the world of computing, meaning that the data delivered by a computer is only as good as the data supplied to it.

**Giffen good** Good that violates the law of demand. When the price of a Giffen good increases (such as a cosmetic), demand increases, instead of falling off as would normally be expected.

**gilt** Common term for *gilt-edged security*.

**gilt-edged market maker** (GEMM) Person who is authorized by the Bank of England to deal in *gilt-edged securities* (gilts) on the stock exchange.

**gilt-edged security** *Security* that carries little or no *risk*; in particular, British government-issued stocks, commonly known as a gilts for short. Gilts are one of the safest investments because the government is unlikely not to pay either the interest (coupon) or redemption value. There is a wide range of gilts on offer, including shorts (redeemable in less than five years), mediums (5-15 years) and longs (not redeemable for 15 years or more). Irredeemable (or undated) stock has no redemption date.

In the United States gilt-edged refers to bonds issued by companies with a good reputation for **dividend** payment and with a good profit record. *See also* **Consol**.

**gilt fund** *Unit trust* or other collective investment in a range of *gilt-edged securities* (gilts).

**gilt switching** Process of selling one *gilt-edged security* and investing the entire proceeds in another. One reason for gilt switching may be to take advantage of changes in *interest rates*, when a long-dated gilt may be switched for a short-dated gilt, or vice versa.

**glass insurance** Insurance that provides compensation for accidental breakage of plate glass in windows and doors. Shops often extend the policy to cover goods on display in a shop window.

**global custody** Service, usually for *fund managers*, for settling cross-border transactions, offered by major investment banks.

**global equities market** Worldwide market in *equities*, still in its infancy, involving principally the stock exchanges in London, New York and Tokyo.
*Global equities have been hailed for several years now as the new era in securities markets.*

**globalization** Increasing internationalization of all markets, industries and commerce.

**global village** Term coined by Marshall McLuhan to describe a world closely interconnected by modern telecommunications, especially television, which greatly reduces the intellectual, cultural and trading isolation formerly caused by geographical separation.

**GM** Abbreviation of *gross margin.*

**GmbH** Abbreviation of *Gesellschaft mit beschrankter Haftu.*

**GMP** Abbreviation of *guaranteed minimum pension.*

**gnome** Rhetorical term for a remote and detached financial operator, as in the "Gnomes of Zurich" blamed by UK Prime Minister Harold Wilson for the fall in the international value of the pound sterling during the Labour Government of 1966 to 1971.

**Gnomes of Zurich** *See gnome.*

**GNP** Abbreviation of *gross national product.*

**godfather offer** An offer that cannot be refused. In a *takeover* situation, a godfather offer for the company's shares is made at such a good price that the management and shareholders of the target company can only accept it.

**gogo (fund)** Investment fund that is being actively traded, producing high capital gains and high market prices.

**going private** Removing a company from stock exchange listing, a process achieved by the company purchasing its own shares. Going private is usually the result of a decision by the principal shareholders that they require more direct control of the company. Its primary purpose is to reduce interference by outside investors and to render the company considerably less vulnerable to takeover bids.

**going public** To offer shares in a company to financial institutions and the general public, and thereby receive a listing on the stock exchange.

**gold and dollar reserves** Stock of gold and US national currency held by the US government or central bank.

**gold and foreign exchange reserves** As *gold and dollar reserves*, with national currencies other than the US dollar included in the stock.

**gold bug** Investor who uses gold *reserves* as a cushion against *inflation*.

**golden handcuffs** Contractual arrangement between a company and its employee whereby the employee has a very strong financial incentive (other than loss of normal salary) to remain with the company, such as a low-interest mortgage or share options that expire if the employee resigns.

**golden handshake** Gratuitous payment made by a company to an employee who is leaving, or has recently left. Such a payment may be made out of goodwill, or to maintain good relations with the employee, or to induce the employee to resign where there are no grounds, or dubious grounds, for statutory dismissal or redundancy.

**golden hello** Payment other than normal salary paid to an employee on joining a company in order to induce him or her to do so.

**golden parachute** Term in a contract of employment whereby the employer is bound to pay the employee a substantial sum of money in the event of dismissal or redundancy.

**gold fixing** Activity that occurs twice a day when the five dealers of gold bullion on the London exchange meet to determine the price of gold.

**gold (or golden) share** Single share in a company that has special voting rights such that it can outvote all other shares in certain circumstances.

**gold standard** Historical arrangement whereby the comparative values of national currencies such as the pound sterling or US dollar were determined by a fixed price for gold.

**good faith** *See bona fide.*

**G**

**good money** Federal funds in the USA that are available immediately.

**goods** Physical items manufactured, sold or exchanged; contrasted with *services*, where no physical items are transferred.

**goods in transit insurance** Insurance that provides compensation to the owner of goods if they are lost or damaged while in transit.

**goodwill** Value of a business over and above the book value of its identifiable or physical assets. Or the amount paid on acquisition of a business over its current stock market valuation. It can refer *e.g.* to the literal good will of the established customers of a retail business (shop or restaurant) whose benevolent habit (or custom) of using it cannot be shown in the accounts.

**goodwill account** See *dangling debit*.

**government actuary** Officer of the government whose team uses population trends to forecast future government spending on such things as pensions and social security benefits.

**government bond** Fixed-interest security issued by a government agent such as the Treasury. It is also known as a *Treasury bond*.

**government broker** Firm of brokers used by the UK government to transact its business in *gilt-edged securities* and to provide the Treasury with advice.

**government securities** Alternative term for *gilt-edged securities*.

**graduated pension scheme** Form of state pension operated in the UK between April 1961 and April 1975. People earning more than £9 per week paid additional contributions which entitled them to a graduated pension in addition to the basic state pension, the amount due being proportional to contributions and, therefore, to their income during that period.

**grant** Funds provided by a government, government body or other institution (*e.g.* the Leverhulme Trust or the Nuffield Foundation).
*The theatre company received a smaller grant from the Arts Council this year than last.*

**grantee** In *life assurance*, the person whose life is assured; the policyholder.

**grant of probate** See *probate*.

**gratuity** Payment made voluntarily in excess of statutory or contractual obligation, *e.g.* a tip in a restaurant or a bonus payment on retirement.

**green baize door**  Alternative term for *Chinese Wall*.

**green book**  Informal name for the former *Unlisted Securities Market*, published by the London Stock Exchange, setting out requirements for entry into the *Unlisted Securities Market* (USM) and regulations.

**green card**  International Motor Insurance card; a document issued to a holder of motor insurance certifying that the cover provided is at least the statutory minimum required by the foreign country or countries named.

**green currency**  Currency of an EU country (based on the European Currency Unit, ECU) that uses an artificial rate of exchange to protect farm prices from fluctuations in the real rates of exchange.

**greenmail**  Procedure whereby a person with a sufficient shareholding in a company seeks a sum of money, or the repurchase by the company of his or her shares at an unreasonably high price, in order to induce him or her to refrain from making a *takeover bid*.

**green pound**  Notional unit of currency used in the administration of the Common Agricultural Policy of the European Union to determine the relative prices (and hence subsidies) of farm produce from the different countries of the EU.

**green shoe**  When a company goes public it may grant its underwriting firm an option on extra quantities of shares. This prevents the underwriter making a loss should the issue be undersubscribed and the underwriter have to buy shares on the open market to cover a short position.

**grey (US gray)**  Normally describing something that is ambiguous, shady or too far off to identify.

**grey knight**  In a *takeover* situation, a third party, acting as a counterbidder, whose intentions towards the target company are not at all clear. Grey knights are normally unwelcome to both the *target* and the original *raider*. *See also* **white knight**.

**grey market**  Any semi-legal market; one that keeps within the letter but not the spirit of the law. The term is most usually applied to the market dealing in any stock or share whose issue has been announced but which has not yet taken place. Traders therefore gamble on the eventual selling price of the issue when it comes onto the market.

**grey wave**  Normally used in venture capital circles to describe a company or new industry that shows potential but whose realization is, however, a long way in the future. *See also* ***venture capital.***

**gross** Term with two meanings:

1. It is twelve dozen (144) units.

2. It is an amount calculated before the deduction of certain items, the items being conventionally specified according to context, *e.g.* a salary or interest paid "gross of tax" is paid before deduction of tax, in contrast to "net of tax", where the tax is deducted before payment.

**gross claims incurred** In insurance, the total claims incurred without deduction for payment by reinsurers.

**gross domestic product** (GDP) Measure of the value of goods and services produced within a country, normally in one year. GDP does not take into account the value of goods and services generated overseas. It is sometimes also known as gross value added. *See also* ***gross national product*** (GNP).

**gross earnings** Earnings before *tax* has been deducted.

**grossing up** Calculation of a gross amount from the net amount by adding back the amount deducted.

**gross interest** *Interest* on an investment before deduction of income tax. After tax deduction it is known as net interest.

**gross mark-up** Amount by which a seller increases the purchase price of a product in order to sell it at a profit, usually expressed as a percentage of its purchase price.

**gross margin** (GM) Similar to *gross mark-up*, but expressed as a percentage of the selling price. It is also sometimes used instead of *gross profit*.

**gross premium** Insurance *premium* before deduction of commission and any reinsurance.

**gross profit** Profit on a transaction or series of transactions before deduction of *indirect expenses*, interest or taxation. *I.e.* the sales revenue or fees minus only those costs directly incurred in the purchase, manufacture and delivery of the item concerned.

**gross margin** Difference between the selling price of an article and the direct cost of the materials and components used in its manufacture.

**gross national product** (GNP) Measure of the value of all goods and services produced by a country, including those produced overseas, usually in one year. *See also* **gross domestic product.**

**gross retention** Total unit of liability accepted by one insurer on any one risk. It is also known as "gross line".

**gross yield** Return on an investment calculated before tax is deducted.

**ground rent** Payment made, normally annually, by the occupier of a building to the owner of the land on which the building stands (the freeholder). Ground rent is paid only if the building is occupied **leasehold.** If it is not paid, the property owner has the right to terminate the lease.

**ground rent receipt** Proof that *ground rent* has been paid, required by a bank that makes a loan secured by a **leasehold** property.

**group** Another name for a *conglomerate.*

*The A & G Group plc now has 10 subsidiary companies.*

**group accounts** Alternative term for *consolidated accounts.*

**group insurance** Type of insurance policy taken out by a group of people sharing an activity, such as members of an orchestra. *See also* **group life assurance.**

**group life assurance** Life policy that covers several people, such as a company's employees or the members of an association. Premiums can be deducted from salaries or membership fees and underwriting is more lenient than for individual life assurance.

**Group of Five** (G5) Five leading industrial nations (France, Japan, Germany, the UK and the USA), which meet from time to time to discuss common economic problems.

**Group of Seven** (G7) Seven leading non-communist industrial nations consisting of the *Group of Five* countries, Canada and Italy.

*The G7 countries managed to keep exchange rates close to the targets set out in the Louvre Accord.*

**Group of Ten** (G10) Also known as the Paris Club, the ten countries Belgium, Canada, France, Germany, Italy, Japan, the Netherlands, Sweden, the UK, and the USA. These countries signed an agreement in 1962 to increase the funds available to the **International Monetary Fund** (IMF) and to aid those member countries with **balance of payments** difficulties.

**group personal pension** An arrangement for employees that is usually set up by an employer and is funded, in part, by employer contributions. It is a collection of individual *personal pension* arrangements under the umbrella of one plan, and therefore giving the advantage of reduced charges. It is subject to the usual personal pension rules.

**growth** Process of increase in an entity, activity or quantity.

*Strong demand from our customers has led to growth in sales.*

Growth may also be the speed or rate of increase in any entity, activity or quantity.

*The growth in GDP forecast for the current year is 2%.*

**growth bond** Bond that provides capital growth rather than income.

**growth funds** Long-term investments that concentrate on capital growth (at a higher risk than a slower-growing but safer investment).

**growth option** With a *guaranteed income bond*, an option to reinvest the annual income from the bond to increase the overall return.

**growth stocks** *Stocks* or *shares* that are expected to provide the investor with a larger proportion of capital growth (*i.e.* growth in the value of the stock or share) to income (in the form of dividends) than other shares.

**growth recession** Situation in which the **GNP** and unemployment are both increasing slowly.

**guarantee** Term with two meanings:

1. It is a document stating that goods or services are of good (merchandizable) quality.

*The washing machine came with a five-year guarantee.*

2. It is a promise to pay the debt of someone else in the event that the debtor defaults. A guarantee is not to be confused with *indemnity*.

**guaranteed acceptance** Feature of some *life assurance* policies that allows the policyholder to top up the policy without again having to provide medical evidence. It also refers to a scheme that guarantees acceptance of all life policies which fall within the specified limits.

**guaranteed equity bond** Performance-related lump-sum investment that guarantees the capital and a minimum return, as well as retaining potential for income from the stock market.

**guaranteed income bond** *Life-assurance* company bond that guarantees a fixed income and the return of the capital at the end of a fixed term or on the death of the purchaser.

**guaranteed minimum pension** (GMP)  The minimum pension that an *occupational pension* or *personal pension plan* (PEP) taken out before April 1997 must guarantee a person who has contracted out of the *State Earnings-Related Pension Scheme* (SERPS). After April 1997 new schemes were subjected to a different test of quality.

**guarantee fund**  Fund set up with a financial organization to meet losses through misappropriation by an employee.

**guarantor**  Person who guarantees, if necessary, to pay someone else's debt.

*Her father agreed to act as guarantor for her bank loan.*

**guaranty bond**  Type of surety that protects against loss resulting from the failure of someone (specified) to do something (also specified).

**gyration**  Fluctuation on the financial markets.

*The deregulation of the London Stock Exchange has helped to cushion the London market against the recent wild gyration in trading.*

# H

**haggle** To persistently discuss a price or the terms of an agreement in an attempt to reduce or improve them.

**haircut** Normally, a *discount* on the market value of a *bond*. It may also be any discount or deduction from the normal value, or a cutting of the budget for a particular project or operation without harming the budget itself.

**half a bar** Half a million pounds sterling.

**half-commission man** Person whose business is to introduce new clients to a *stockbroking* firm, receiving in return a share of the *commission* received from those clients.

**hammering** Stock Exchange term that refers to the announcement of the inability of a member to pay his or her debts.

**hammer out** To enter into extended negotiations and to discuss the details of an agreement at length.
*We managed to hammer out an agreement, but it took us several months of negotiations.*

**Hang Seng Index** Index of share prices on the Hong Kong Stock Exchange.

**Hancock annuity** *Annuity* taken out by a company to provide an income for an employee during his or her retirement. The capital used by the company in this way is deductible as an allowance against *corporation tax*.

**hard** Reliable or tangible, as in *hard currency*.

**hard copy** Text typed or printed on paper of a document that has been written or stored on a computer disk or on microfilm.

**hard currency** Currency, used in international trade, from a country with a stable and prosperous economy. It is thus in high demand and preferred to less stable or legally restricted currencies.

**hard dollars** Dollars traded on the foreign exchange markets, for which demand is persistently high because of a US trade surplus. The value of hard dollars tends to rise.

*See also **dollar gap**.*

**hard goods** Consumer durables, *e.g.* furniture and household appliances.

**hard numbers** Financial projection that can be relied upon.

**haulage** Charge made for transporting goods by road. It does not normally include a charge for loading and unloading.

**hazard** In insurance, factor that could increase the size or possibility of a loss occuring. *See **moral hazard**; **physical hazard**.*

**headhunter** Person or agency that finds suitable (usually high-grade) staff for posts that companies have vacant, taking a commission from the company involved in relation to the "head's" salary.

**heading** In insurance, the name and address of the insurer at the top of a policy.

**heavy shares** Shares that command a relatively high price on the stock market.

**hedging** Method of protecting oneself from price fluctuations. Hedging happens commonly on the commodities *futures* market.

**Heinrich triangle** Illustration that shows the breakdown of industrial injury incidents. For every one major incident at work, there are 30 minor injuries and 300 non-injury accidents.

**held covered clause** In marine insurance, a clause that (for an additional premium) gives cover against accidental wrong description of goods.

**hidden price increase** Decline in the real value of a good or service occasioned by a decrease in its quality or quantity rather than by a rise in its price. *See **real value**.*

**hidden reserves** Reserves not declared on a company's balance sheet.

**hidden tax** Tax included in the price of goods so that it is not obvious to the consumer. Most forms of indirect taxation are hidden in this way, *e.g.* tax (duty) on tobacco and alcohol.

**hidden unemployment** Another term for *disguised unemployment*.

**higgledy-piggledy growth** Term coined in the 1960s to describe shares or companies whose earnings are relatively unpredictable.

**high-beta** Describing shares that are volatile.

**H**

**high-end** Normally describing goods that are produced for the top of the market and are consequently very expensive.

**higher rate taxpayer** Person who pays the higher rate of income tax.

**high-risk behaviour** Activity, such as hang-gliding or pot-holing, that exposes a person to more danger than normal. It attracts higher than usual insurance premiums for, *e.g.*, personal accident insurance.

**high-risk items** In household contents insurance, items that are more likely to be stolen (such as hi-fi, television and video equipment). Many policies impose a limit on the maximum cover for such items.

**high-risk occupation** Occupation, such as a test pilot or bomb disposal expert, that exposes a person to more danger than normal. It attracts higher than usual premiums for, *e.g.*, life assurance.

**high seas** Waters that are not part of the territorial waters of any particular country.

**hightech** Describing any business that makes extensive use of modern technology, particularly electronic systems.

**high-technology stock** Shares in a company involved in *hightech* activities.

**hike** Increase.

*He took a large pay hike when he changed jobs.*

**hire** To pay a sum of money (usually expressed as so much per hour, day, week, etc.) for services or the use of goods (*e.g.* equipment or transport).

**hire purchase** (HP) Form of credit, normally extended on *consumer goods*, whereby the customer takes and uses the goods and pays for them in instalments (with interest) over an agreed period of time. The seller can in theory reposses the goods at any time if the hirer defaults (unlike a credit sale).

**historical cost** Cost of an asset at the time it was acquired, rather than the current cost of its replacement.

**historical cost accounting** Method of assigning value to *e.g.* assets for accounting purposes. In historical cost accounting, the original cost of an asset is taken into account, rather than its replacement cost. *See current cost accounting.*

**historic dividend** Total *dividend* paid on a company's shares in the last financial year.

**hit bid** Bargain in which a dealer sells immediately at a price a buyer is willing to pay, instead of waiting for a possibly better price.

**hive off** Splitting off of an operating arm of a company to make it into a *subsidiary company*. It is said to hive off that part of its operation.

**holder** Someone who owns something or owns rights in something, such as bills, bonds or shares.

**holder for value** Person who holds a *bill of exchange* for which a value has at one time been given.

**holder in due course** Person who has taken up a bill for value before payment is due, and who has no good reason to suspect the title of the previous holder. *See also bearer.*

**holding** Investment in a company or in any *security*.

**holding company** Company that exists to own shares in other companies, that are (depending on the level of shareholding) its subsidiaries. An immediate holding company is one that holds a controlling interest in another company, but in turn, the immediate holding company itself may be owned by a holding company. *See also subsidiary company.*

**hold over** To defer settlement of a deal on the Stock Exchange until the next settlement day.

**holiday insurance** Insurance for holidaymakers that provides cover against death, injury, unavoidable cancellation, etc. It can be purchased at the time of booking the holiday with a travel agent or as an annual policy.

**home foreign business** In insurance, policies issued in the UK against overseas risks.

**home service agent** Employee of an insurance company that deals in *industrial life assurance* who collects weekly or monthly *premium* instalments from the homes of policyholders. He or she may alternatively be known as a home service insurance representative.

**home service insurance** *See industrial insurance.*

**homogeneous exposures** Similar risks. *See law of large numbers.*

**honorarium** Money paid to a professional such as an *accountant* or a *solicitor*, when the professional does not request a *fee*.

**honorary** Describing a position or its holder that is not rewarded with payment; *e.g.* an honorary president.

**honorary secretary** Someone who takes on the running of a society or charity in the same way as a *company secretary* but without payment.

**honour policy** Another term for *policy proof of interest.*

**horizontal diversification** Diversification into industries or businesses at the same stage of production as the diversifying company, *e.g.* a suit manufacturer might diversify into leisure wear, and a yacht builder into the construction of motor boats.
*See also* **horizontal integration; vertical diversification.**

**horizontal integration** Amalgamation of companies in the same stage of production, and which are therefore likely to possess similar skills.

**horse and pony insurance** A specialist form of insurance cover which can be an extension to a household policy or stand alone. Compensation is provided in the event of death, injury, vets' fees and loss by theft or straying. Extensions to the basic cover can be provided to cover equipment and third party liability.

**horse trading** Hard negotiations, normally ending in both parties making concessions to each other. *See also* **tradeoff.**

**hostile takeover** Attempt to purchase control of a company that is unwelcome to some of the target's shareholders and directors. Unwelcome takeovers may be resisted by a gamut of *defensive tactics. See crown jewel tactic; golden parachute; Jonestown defence; knight; poison pill; shark repellent; shark watcher; suicide pill.*

**hot issue** Issue of shares that are expected to sell extremely rapidly.

**hot money** Informal term for money obtained illegally (*e.g.,* by fraud or theft). In business, however, it is money that is moved rapidly and at short notice from one country to another to take advantage of changes in short-term interest rates or to avoid imminent devaluation of a currency. *See also* **refugee capital.**

**house** A business or *company.* It is also a popular nickname for the London Stock Exchange.

**household contents insurance** An insurance designed to cover those items that are in the home. Risks covered include fire, theft, explosion, water damage, impact, subsidence and landslip, accidental damage to specified items and liability. The range of perils can be extended to cover accidental damage to all contents in the home. *See also* **household insurance.**

**household insurance** Insurance cover for private property and/or its contents. Usually the sum insured is the cost of rebuilding the property in the event of it being damaged beyond repair. Because property values can change rapidly, most modern property insurance has index-linked premiums. *See also* **household contents insurance**.

**houseperson's permanent health insurance** (PHI) Health insurance cover for housepersons in view of the fact that their disability could lead to additional expenses for a family. The cover is limited, with a standard condition that housepersons are "confined to the house".

**HP** Abbreviation of *hire purchase*.

**hull insurance** Insurance of a vessel and its machinery. A policy is generally taken out during construction which covers the ship for the whole of its useful life. Most hull insurances provide cover against accidents caused by the negligence of crew or stevedores.

**human capital** Value of a company's employees.

**hustle** To work hard to make sales and profits. The term has connotations of forwardness and aggression.

**hyperinflation** Inflation that is running extremely high; also known as galloping inflation.
*After World War I, Germany suffered a crippling period of hyperinflation.*

**hypothecation** A firm of shippers may borrow money from a *bank* using cargo they are currently shipping as *security*. In this case, the bank takes out a *lien* on the cargo and this is conveyed in a letter of hypothecation.
In the USA, hypothecation is putting up securities as collateral on a *margin* account.

# I

**IAS** Abbreviation of *internal audit* system.

**IBA** Abbreviation of *insurance broking account.*

**IBNR** Abbreviation of *incurred but not reported.*

**IBRC** Abbreviation of *Insurance Brokers Registration Council.*

**ICC** Abbreviation of International *Chamber of Commerce.*

**ICON** Abbreviation of *indexed currency option note.*

**IDB** Abbreviation of *inter-dealer broker.*

**IFA** Abbreviation of *independent financial adviser* .

**IFSC** Abbreviation of *International Financial Services Centre.*

**ignorantia juris neminem excusat** Latin for "ignorance of the law is no defence". It is a doctrine which warns that people who break the law will be punished, regardless of whether or not they are aware that they are committing a crime.

**illiquidity** Situation in which an *asset* is not easily converted into cash, or in which a person is unable to raise cash quickly and/or easily. *See also liquidity.*

**illegal** Something that is against the law. *See also* **unlawful.**

**illustration** Quotation for life assurance or pension policies that provides an indication of future benefits based on certain growth rates. The information that must be provided is specified by the Financial Services Act.

**ILU** Abbreviation of *Institute of London Underwriters.*

**IMF** Abbreviation of *International Monetary Fund.*

**immediate annuity** *Annuity* that begins paying out an income immediately.

**impact** Special peril that can be added to most fire policies and is automatically included in most household policies. The wording in the policy may refer to impact or collision with aircraft, aerial devices, road vehicles and animals.

**impact day** Day on which a company is scheduled to publish details of a new issue.

**imperfect** Broadly, actual rather than pure theoretical structures and transactions; more precisely, any economic state that is not perfectly efficient.

**imperfect competition** Situation of competition in which the goods are not homogenous, *i.e.* they are not perfect substitutes for each other. This dissimilarity gives the producer a small amount of control over price. It is also known as monopolistic competition. *See also* ***perfect competition.***

**imperfect market** Any market that does not enjoy free competition, good communications, regular demand and uniform goods.

**imperfect oligopoly** *Oligopoly* in which the goods produced are slightly different from each other. This difference may allow the seller to alter the price in relation to other sellers without a significant effect on sales.

**impersonal account** On a *book-keeping* ledger, an account that deals with *capital* and *assets* (the *real accounts*) or income and expenditure (the *nominal accounts*) or a combination of the two. The only element of the ledger the impersonal accounts do not cover is the record of debtors and creditors (the *personal accounts*).

**implied terms** Terms of a *contract* that are not expressly stated, but that the law considers necessary to the sense of the contract and therefore implicit.

**implied warranty** In marine insurance, warranty that a vessel is seaworthy and its voyage lawful (not explicitly written into the contract).

**import** Goods and services brought into a country for sale, from abroad.

**importation** The act of importing.

**import ban** Ban of specified imports, often for political rather than economic reasons.

**importers' entry of goods** The customs regulations in force in the country to which exports are being despatched, and which the exporter must note and observe.

**import specie point** Point in the variation of exchange rates at which it becomes cheaper for a nation on the ***gold standard*** to import gold than buy foreign currency.

**imprest** Sum of money made available for petty expenses. *See* ***petty cash***.

**imputation system** UK *taxation* system, established in 1973, which partly governs the payment of *corporation tax*. Under this system, a shareholder's *dividends* are taxed at source, and he or she is issued with a *credit* for the tax imputed.

**IMRO** Abbreviation of *Investment Management Regulatory Organization*.

**inactive** Describing something not working or moving. *See also* **active**.

**inactive market** Alternative term for *dull market*.

**in-and-out trader** Stock-market trader who buys and rapidly sells a security on the same day.

**in arrears** Term with two meanings:
1. It describes a payment that is late, behind an agreed schedule.
2. For annuities, it describes the fact that income payments are made at the end of the period.

**Inc** Abbreviation of incorporated. *See* *incorporation*.

**incapacity** Situation that allows benefits to be drawn from a pension scheme before the age of 50. The member must be unable to fulfil the requirements of his normal occupation

**incentive** Positive motive (sometimes artificially generated) for performing some task.

**incestuous share dealing** Dealing in the shares of associated firms in order to win tax concessions. Incestuous share dealing is often illegal, but need not necessarily be so.

**incidental expenses** Minor expenses not directly relevant to the running of a business.

**incidentals** Non-material items, particularly those referred to in a company's *accounts*.

**income** Money, goods or services received from any activity. Income may be either a return on one of the factors of production – a *salary*, *rent*, *interest* or *profit* – or a transfer payment made for some other reason, such as unemployment benefit. The definition includes non-monetary income such as the benefit derived from the possession of *assets*.

**income and expenditure account** Similar in form to a *profit-and-loss account*, an income and expenditure account records all cash transactions over a given period.

**income bond** Type of bond that provides an income rather than capital growth. *See **National Savings**.*

**income bracket** Range of income (wages, salaries), normally rated from a specific minimum to a specific maximum. The term is also applied to people in that range.

*She is in the middle income bracket.*

**income drawdown** Method of taking money directly from a personal pension fund before retirement. Personal pension rules allow the purchase of an annuity to be deferred up to age 75, while drawing an income from the fund in the meantime.

**income option** Facility with many interest-earning accounts in banks, building societies and National Savings that allows the depositor to collect interest monthly, quarterly, six-monthly or annually.

**income statement** Alternative term for *profit-and-loss account.*

**income tax** Tax paid on income, such as fees, salaries or wages.

**inconvertible** Describing money that cannot be exchanged for gold of equal value. UK currency has been inconvertible since the country came off the *gold standard* in 1931.

**incorporation** The process of setting up a business as a legal entity.

**increasable term assurance** Term *life assurance* contract that provides the option to increase the sum assured, within limits, without further medical evidence.

**increasing life annuity** Annuity that increases annually by a fixed percentage or through index-linking to protect the investor against inflation.

**increasing term assurance** Term *life assurance* contract in which the sum assured automatically increases in line with a fixed percentage of the retail price index each year to keep pace with rising costs. *See **index-linked term assurance**.*

**increment** Amount of increase.

**incremental cost** Extra cost incurred when a company agrees to take on a new project.

**incremental increase** Increase that occurs in stages or steps, or successive increases by one unit.

**incurred but not reported** (IBNR) Insurance term applied to losses that are covered but neither claimed nor reported by the policyholder. Insurance companies maintain an IBNR reserve fund to meet such claims should they eventually be made.

**indebtedness** State of owing money or services to someone else, or the amount of money owed.

**indebtedness date** Alternative term for *indebtedness day*.

**indebtedness day** When a company issues a *prospectus*, it must make known the day on which its statement of debt (the extent of its indebtedness) was made. It is assumed that the indebtedness figure was correct at that time, called the indebtedness day.

**indemnity** Undertaking that provides an exact financial compensation for *loss* or damage. Indemnity may be in the form of replacement or repair of property lost or damaged, or provision of cash to the value of the property. The commonest indemnity is an *insurance policy*, in which the policyholder is indemnified by the insurance company in the event of a valid claim. The aim is always to place the insured in the exact financial position after a loss as he or she enjoyed immediately before that loss occurred.

**indemnity basis cover** In *household contents insurance*, a type of cover for the actual value of the item insured (taking into account age and depreciation). *See also new for old.*

**indemnity insurance** Insurance that compensates the policyholder in the event of loss with a sum of money or payments for the repair or replacement of the item lost.

**indenture** *Deed* or *instrument* to which there is more than one party. It is so called because such deeds were formerly cut or torn (indented) into portions, one for each party, to prevent forgery and provide proof of each person's involvement in the transaction. Indentures were formerly widely used to bind an apprentice to his master for the period of his apprenticeship.

**independent** Describing a person or organization that is free to act unilaterally and is not dependent on any other person or organization.

**independent company** Company that operates entirely under its own authority, and is not owned or controlled (in part or in whole) by any other company.

**independent financial adviser** (IFA) Adviser defined under the terms of the 1986 Financial Services Act who is required to recommend from a range of products and companies. He or she must recommend a suitable product from all those available in the marketplace, and is not tied to any one company. See also *polarisation*; *tied agent*.

**index** Form of measurement or comparison; a listing giving an indication of change.

**index arbitrage** Process of selling *stocks* at the same time as buying stock-index futures, or vice versa. It is a form of program trading.

**indexation** Form of *index-linking* that ties *income* to the *retail price index* and therefore prevents a fall in real wages during a period of *inflation*.

**indexed currency option note** (ICON) Document that records a debt whose value depends on the effective exchange rate between the currencies concerned. A pre-arranged rate is set between defined limits for interest payments but changes if the limits are exceeded.

**indexed portfolio** Portfolio linked to a stock index, such as the *Financial Times Stock Exchange 100 Index* (FOOTSIE).

**index fund** Investment fund that is linked directly to a share index, in that it has investments in shares on that index.

**index futures** Futures contracts that are based on the figures provided by indices.

**index-linked gilts** Gilt-edged securities that have a variable rate of interest adjusted to take account of inflation (using *index-linking* to the *retail price index*).

**index-linked term assurance** Term *life assurance* in which the sum assured automatically increases in line with the retail price index each year.

**index-linking** System of linking costs, prices or wages to the price fluctuations of an economy in order to allow for *inflation* and maintain value in real terms. Index-linking is most often used to relate *income* to the *retail price index*. In a year of 4% inflation, therefore, it would be usual for an indexed salary to rise by the same amount.

**index number** Weighted average that permits the comparison of prices or production over a number of years. The components selected for comparison are weighted according to their importance and then averaged. Figures are compared to those for a *base year*, selected for its typicality and given the index number 100 or 1000.

**index tracker fund** Investment fund that tracks an index; it is also known as a tracker fund. The make-up of the fund mirrors the make-up of a particular index such as th FTSE 100 index. *See also passive management.*

**indication-only price** Price quoted by a *market maker* that indicates what he or she thinks a security is worth although he or she is not prepared to deal in it.

**indicator** Measurable variable used to suggest overall change among a group of linked variables too complex to yield to simple analysis. Thus a variety of economic indicators – such as *price, income, imports, exports, money supply* and so on – are studied in an attempt to estimate the state of a national economy.

**indirect** Describing something that is associated with, but not immediately connected to, something else; something at one remove, *e.g.* indirect *taxation* consists of taxes levied on *expenditure* rather than *income.*

**indirect costs** Costs of items or activities, such as maintenance of buildings and machinery, that are not used in the production of goods, nor immediately necessary for their production.

**indirect expenses** Expenses incurred in production, but not directly attributable to any one factor of production; *e.g.* in life assurance, Head Office rent would be an indirect expense.

**indirect production** Production of goods for sale by employing labour and machinery and using a system of divided labour in order to make a profit.

**indirect taxation** Tax paid to one person or organization (often a retailer), who then pays it to the government. *Value-added tax* is a form of indirect taxation.

**Individual Savings Account** (ISA) Tax-free method of saving announced by the government in 1997 and planned for introduction in 1999, when *personal equity plans* (PEPs) and *tax-exempt special savings accounts* (TESSAs) are due to lose their tax-free status. There will be no lower limit to the amount that can be invested but the planned maximum is £5,000 per year. *See also* **Catmark.**

**indorsement** *See endorsement.*

**industrial life assurance** Life assurance policy with a small sum assured, with premiums paid regularly (often weekly) to the assurance company's agent calling at the policyholder's residence. It is also called home service assurance. It began in industrial areas for people without bank accounts, but is now declining.

**industrials** Shares in an industrial company, usually manufacturing. *See also* **commercials**.

**industrial sabotage** Unfair competition between competitors. The term applies to any dubious tactics, not just physical sabotage.

**industry** Agglomeration of companies involved in the production of goods or services. The term is usually applied as a generic for a group of companies dealing in very similar products, *e.g.* "the insurance industry".

**inertia** Sate of inactivity, or resistance to movement.

**inertia selling** Method of selling in which unsolicited goods are mailed to a "customer" and followed by an invoice.

**infant industry** Newly-established national industry in the early stages of growth.

**inflation** Persistent general increase in the level of prices. Strictly defined, inflation includes neither one-off increases in price (occasioned by *e.g.* a sudden scarcity of some product) nor any other increases caused by real factors. Its causes include an excess of demand over supply and increases in the money supply, perhaps brought about by increased government expenditure, which causes a decline in the real value of money.

**inflation accounting** Alternative term for *current cost accounting* or current purchasing power accounting.

**inflation-adjusted** Describing wages that have been modified to maintain real income by increasing pay in line with inflation. The term may also be applied to the economist's technique of discounting price changes to obtain a truer picture of quantitative changes in output.

**inflation tax** Extra revenue brought into the government because inflation has brought new tax payers on stream or pushed taxpayers or taxable items into higher brackets.

**infopreneur** Person who makes a living by collecting, assessing and selling information to interested parties.

**information float** Time it takes to relay information from one person or organization to another, *e.g.* the information float using the postal service is at least one day, whereas the float using computer link-up could be a matter of seconds.

**information services** Economic sector in which information is traded and sold, *e.g.* most financial services are information services, as are the City pages of newspapers.

**information technology** (IT) Area of microelectronics that combines computing and telecommunications technologies in the organization, storing, retrieval and transfer of information.

**informative advertising** Advertising that concentrates on providing the target with information about the product, thereby helping consumers to choose between products.

**infrastructure** Public utilities of a country. Also known as social overhead capital, the infrastructure includes roads, railways, airports, communications systems, (*e.g.* telephones), housing, water and sewerage systems, and other public amenities.

**inheritance** Possessions or titles passed to one or more persons on the death of another.

**inheritance tax** Tax paid on inheritances by heirs, often calculated in relation to the closeness of the relationship between the heir and the deceased person. In the UK at the present time, *capital gains tax* covers income from inheritances.

**inhouse additional voluntary contribution** Pension scheme that is offered by an employer alongside the main pension scheme. *See also free-standing additional voluntary contribution.*

**initial allowance** Amount deducted from a company's profits for the purposes of calculating tax in the first year after *acquisition*.

**initial charge** Charge made by a *fund manager* to cover such things as administration and commission when setting up a financial package.

**initial margin** *Deposit* that must be paid on selling or buying a *contract* on a *futures* market. *See also equity.*

**initial public offering** (IPO) First share offer made by a company *going public*.

**initial public offering window** (IPO window) Period of time between an announcement of an *initial public offering* and the start of dealing in the shares offered on a stock market. Grey market trading takes place in the IPO window (*see grey market*).

**initial single contribution** Lump sum paid at the beginning of a *personal pension scheme.*

**initial yield** *Current yield* of a *unit trust* or other collective investment expressed as a percentage of the *offer price.*

**injunction** Restraining order issued by a court. An injunction instructs a named person to perform a certain duty or forbids him or her to commit a specific act. Failure to comply with an injunction is considered contempt of court.

**inland bill** *Bill of exchange* that is drawn and payable within the UK. *See also foreign bill.*

**Inland Revenue** UK government department whose major responsibility is the collection of various taxes, such as *income tax, capital gains tax* and *corporation tax.*

**Inner Six** Six EU countries: Belgium, France, Germany, Italy, Luxembourg and the Netherlands.

**innoventure** *Venture capital* scheme based on an innovative product or service. Such schemes are regarded as being particularly risky.

**in play** Describing a *quoted company* for which a *takeover* bid is expected to be launched in the very near future.

**input tax** In the *value-added tax* system, the tax that is collected from the seller of goods by the *Customs and Excise. See also output tax.*

**inscribed stock** Now discontinued method of registering the name of a stockholder, by which the holder was issued with a slip indicating that the holder's name had been registered. This slip did not have the status of a certificate. It was also known as registered stock.

**insider** Person with special knowledge derived from holding a privileged position within a group or company. It is illegal for the person to use that information in dealing on the stock exchange.

**insider dealing** Also known as insider trading, illegal transactions made on the basis of privileged information. Most insider dealing concerns trading in *stocks* and *shares* whose value is likely to be affected by the release of news of which only a few people are aware.

**insider trading** Alternative term for *insider dealing.*

**insolvency** State in which total liabilities (excluding *equity capital*) exceed total *assets*; therefore, it is the inability to pay *debts* when called upon to do so. If insolvency is chronic, *bankruptcy* or *liquidation* generally follow.

**insolvency payment** Payment funded by the deposit protection scheme made to a depositor or investor in a bank or building society that fails. It is up to 90% of a deposit of up to £20,000 (*i.e.*, a maximum of £18,000 per investor).

**instalment** Part payment of a *debt*, such as one undertaken as part of a *credit sale* or *hire purchase* agreement, or of an insurance *premium*. Instalment payments fall due at fixed and specified intervals and when totalled equal the original debt, usually with the addition of *interest* payments.

**instant** Often abbreviated to inst., a little-used term meaning "of this month", *e.g.* a letter written in November mentioning the "13th inst." refers to 13 November. *See also* *ultimo*.

**Institute of Actuaries** Professional organization of actuaries, based in London. Fellowship of the Institute (FIA) is one of the qualifications of the profession.

**Institute of Certified Public Accountants** Professional organization of certified accountants in the UK.

**Institute of Chartered Accountants** Professional organization of chartered accounts in the UK, divided into the Institute of Chartered Accountants in England and Wales, the Institute of Chartered Accountants in Ireland and the Institute of Chartered Accountants in Scotland. They set educational standards and co-ordinate training, set examinations and oversee the practice of accountancy.

**Institute of Insurance Brokers** Relatively small organization that looks after the interests of insurance brokers.

**Institute of London Underwriters** (ILU) Organization that, among other things, produces the standard clauses in marine insurance contracts.

**institution** Organization, particularly one concerned with the promotion of a specific subject or some public object (*e.g.* the Royal United Services Institution). The term "*The* Institution" is used to denote the collective of *institutional investors*.

**institutional investor** Corporate rather than individual investor; a company which invests funds on behalf of clients, generally intending to reap profits only in the long term. Institutional investors include banks, insurance companies, pension funds and unit trusts. At the present time, institutional investors hold from 50% to 70% of all *negotiable securities*.

**instrument** Broadly, any legally binding document.

**insurable interest** Financial interest, recognized at law, which the insured has in the subject matter of insurance. In some cases, an unlimited insurable interest exists, *e.g.* in one's own life and the life of a spouse. However, in most cases, insurable interest is limited to the value of the property or goods, or extent of liability.

**insurable risk** Risk against which insurance cover can be obtained by somebody with an *insurable interest* in it.

**insurance** Contract under which the insurer agrees to provide *compensation* to the insured in the event of a specified occurrence, e.g. loss of or damage to property. In return, the insured pays the insurer a *premium*, usually at fixed intervals. The premium varies according to the insurer's estimate of the probability that the event insured against will actually take place (a calculation carried out by an *actuary*). *See also* *assurance*.

**Insurance Accounts Directive** Directive of the European Union (EU) concerned with the format and presentation of insurance companies' financial accounts.

**insurance agent** Person who sells *insurance* on behalf of an insurance company. *See also* *insurance broker*.

**insurance bond** Type of *bond* issued by a life assurance company. *See growth bond; guaranteed bond; income bond.*

**insurance broker** Person who arranges and sells *insurance*. He or she, who must be registered with the *Insurance Brokers Registration Council* (IBRC), is regulated by the *Personal Investment Authority* (PIA) and is paid a commission by the insurer to act as an intermediary with the client, arranging policies and processing claims issued by an insurance company

**Insurance Broker's Registration Council** (IBRC) Statutory organization established in 1977 to register *insurance brokers* and regulate their activities.

**insurance broking account** (IBA) Bank account approved for business conducted by a registered insurance broker or corporate broker.

**insurance certificate** Document issued by an insurance company certifying that a valid policy exists. *See certificate of insurance.*

**insurance claim** Claim made by a person who is insured against an insurance company for payment under the conditions of a policy.

**insurance cover** Sum of money guaranteed to the insured in the event of the circumstances insured against actually occurring.

**insurance cover note** *See cover note.*

**insurance of rent** Insurance that provides compensation to the owner of a building if damage or destruction means that it cannot be rented out.

**Insurance Ombudsman** Official in charge of a service set up by insurance companies in 1981 to arbitrate in disputes between insurance companies and their policyholders.

**insurance policy** Legally binding document issued by an insurance company defining the terms of an insurance contract. It details the cover provided (and any conditions or restrictions) and the premium to be paid. *See also* **life assurance.**

**insurance premium** Sum paid to an insurance company by a client for cover as defined in an *insurance policy*. It may be paid as a lump sum or in instalments, as one payment or annually, depending on the nature of the policy.

**insurance premium tax** Tax on insurance *premiums*, currently 3%, introduced in the UK in 1994. Not all types of insurance are taxable, but it does affect most *general insurance* such as household, motor vehicle and travel insurance.

**Insurance Regulatory Information System** (IRIS) Computerized system used by regulators in the USA to audit the operations of insurance companies.

**Insurance Technology Trade Association** Organization that promotes the application and development of technology as it is used by the insurance industry.

**insurance tied agent** *Insurance agent* who acts for only one insurance company for pensions or life assurance, or up to six companies for *general insurance.*

**insured** Person or company that holds an *insurance policy* (a contract with an insurance company); a policyholder.

**insured pension scheme** Pension scheme with its assets/fund placed with an insurance company.

**insured peril** Peril that is specifically stated in an insurance policy as being covered or included.

**insurer** Insurance company or other person or company that agrees to indemnify someone against particular risks, usually as defined in an *insurance policy* and for an *insurance premium*. *See also* **underwriter**.

**integration**  Amalgamation of two or more companies to improve efficiency. Also, an industry is said to be integrated if products from different partaking companies are compatible.

**intellectual property**  Expression of the theory that ideas as well as tangible inventions and innovations are unique to one person or group and should be patentable. Intellectual property currently has no clear standing in UK law, other than in *copyright*.

**inter-dealer broker**  (IDB)  Person who matches deals between anonymous buyers and sellers on behalf of two *market makers*.

**interest**  Term with three possible meanings:

1. It is a charge made by a lender to a borrower in exchange for the service of lending funds. It is usually expressed as a percentage of the sum borrowed, but may be paid in kind.

*The bank made me a loan at 10% interest.*

*In 1997 Niger borrowed £11 million from neighbouring Libya, paying interest that included 1,500 camels per year.*

2. It is a payment made by a bank or building society to customers on some forms of savings account.

*My building society pays 7% interest.*

3. It is money that is invested in a company, usually in return for *equity* or *shares*, thus making the investor "interested" in the performance of the company. In this sense, an interest may be in anything that yields a return.

*He has an interest in several small companies.*

*See also* **insurable interest**.

**interest cover**  Ratio of earnings to the fixed-*interest* payments necessary to service loan *capital*.

**interest-only mortgage**  Mortgage in which the mortgagee pays back only interest during the mortgage period because he or she has an endowment, a personal equity plan (PEP) or other asset to repay the capital at the end.

**interest rate**  *Interest* charged to a borrower or paid to an investor, usually expressed as a percentage per annum.

**interest rate futures**  Financial *futures* purchased as a hedge against an adverse change in *interest rates*. If interest rate changes on the hedger's financial instruments produce a loss, the futures contract offsets it. *See also* **hedging**.

**interest yield** On a fixed-interest security, the rate of interest expressed as a percentage of the price paid. It is also termed the running yield.

**interim** In the meantime. The term usually refers to the halfway point in a financial year.

**interim accounts** Short financial statement produced by a company (often unaudited) in the middle of the year, halfway between publication of the *annual accounts.*

**interim dividend** Any dividend other than the final dividend declared at the conclusion of each trading year. Interim dividends may be made as a reward for a particularly good economic performance or simply as an effective advance on the final dividend, which will be correspondingly reduced in value. Most UK companies quoted on the stock market make interim dividend payment per annum; it is unusual for a firm to exceed this frequency of interim payments.

**interim receiver** Person appointed by a court to act as receiver, until a receiver proper is appointed. *See receivership.*

**interim report** Short statement published at the end of the first half of a public company's financial year, detailing results for the previous six months and declaring any *interim dividend.*

**intermediary** Person who acts between and deals with two parties who themselves make no direct contact with each other, such as an *insurance broker.*

**internal audit** Audit of a company's books that takes place virtually continuously and is undertaken by internal staff, rather than by an external auditor. Internal auditing is carried out in order to monitor company profitability and guard against fraud.

**internal check** System of *accounting* that ensures that each person's work and financial dealings are checked by an independent third party within the company. Together with an *internal audit*, internal checks act to promote efficiency and prevent fraud.

**internal control** Combination of self-regulatory measures by which a company ensures that each employee is accountable, safeguards its *assets* and institutes an accurate system of *accounting*, therefore enhancing its own efficiency.

**internal rate of return** (IRR) Term with two meanings:

1. It is a hypothetical *interest rate*, equivalent to the marginal efficiency of *capital*, which is used to assess the investor's *yield* and therefore determine the viability of an investment. If the internal rate of return is higher than the current rate of interest at which the investor could borrow, the investment is worthwhile.

2. It is the discount rate at which, applied to the expected pattern of cash expenditure and income of a capital project, would give a net present value of zero. It may be compared with the return on alternative investments, or on some target rate of return.

**Internal Revenue Service** (IRS)  US equivalent to the UK's *Inland Revenue*.

**International Financial Services Centre** (IFSC)  Organization based in Dublin with the function of attracting foreign financial institutions to the Republic of Ireland.

**international funds**  Another name for *global funds*.

**International Monetary Fund** (IMF)  International organization set up in 1944 after the Bretton Woods conference, to organize and administer the international monetary system. It was designed to help countries in financial difficulties, especially with their *balance of payments*. It makes loans and provides financial advisers.

**intervention order**  Order issued by a *self-regulatory organization* (SRO) to limit or halt the business of a financial service provider. It can also freeze assets until the situation is resolved.

**intervention price**  Price slightly below the *threshold price* at which the *European Commission* intervenes to purchase agricultural surpluses, thus supporting home markets and helping to achieve the average or *target price*.

**inter vivos policy**  Life assurance policy that can be used to cover the potential inheritance tax liability of a *potentially exempt transfer* (PET). It is written as a special type or decreasing term assurance for the amount of the initial potential inheritance tax liability.

**intestacy**  Situation in which a person dies without making a will, leaving the estate without a designated heir. If a person dies intestate, the Crown divides the estate between surviving relatives, making provision first for the spouse, and then for any children. If neither spouse nor children are living, other relatives are entitled to share in the estate. If no relatives can be traced, the estate goes to the crown.

**in-the-money option**  Term with two meanings:

1. It is an option to buy shares (*call option*) for which the price on the open market has risen above the price fixed (called the option's *exercise price*).

2. It is an option to sell (*put option*) for which the market price has fallen in relation to the *exercise price*. An in-the-money option is said to carry *intrinsic value*.

**in the window** Describing anything obviously for sale, *e.g.*, a company may put an unquoted subsidiary in the window by discreetly inviting potential purchasers to make themselves known. The term is also a virtual synonym for *in play*.

**intracapital** *Capital* placed at the disposal of an *intrapreneur*.

**intrapreneur** Member of the staff of a company who is given relative autonomy in order that he or she may make use of entrepreneurial skills to the advantage of the company. *See also* **entrepreneur**.

**intrinsic value** Value of the materials from which an object is made rather than its market or face value, *e.g.* a coin may be said to be worth so much and is exchanged on the basis of that stated value, but the metal used in minting it may be worth much less. Intrinsic value is also the value (if any) of a traded *option* that is in-the-money, brought about by a favourable difference between *market price* and *exercise price*.

**introduction** Means of offering a new share issue to the public, through the medium of a stock exchange but without the publication of a *prospectus* and the provision of an application form. Introductions are possible only if there is a large number of potential shareholders and no large *bargains* have been struck to market the *stock*.

**introductory commission** *Commission* payable to somebody who introduces business to an insurance company or other financial service provider. It is usually a very high percentage of the first year's *premiums* and must be disclosed to the client.

**inventory** Term with two meanings:

1. It is the list of the stocks of raw materials, goods in production or finished goods owned and stored by a company, giving details of their *cost*, *value* and *price*.

2. It is an itemized account of the contents of a rented property, against which the contents are checked when the tenant leaves.

**inventory control** Stock control. Most efficient businesses are managed, using inventories, in such a way that minimum levels of *stock-in-trade* sufficient to meet any likely demand are always maintained.

**investment** Term defined in two different ways by two schools of thought:

1. It is expenditure on real or financial assets rather than the funding of consumption. In this sense, investment consists of the purchase of any asset which is expected to increase in value.

   *We have invested our money in short-term treasury bonds.*

2. To an economist, it covers spending that results in economic growth, *e.g.* money spent on the purchase of machinery or the building of plant that will produce goods and services for sale. Investment extends to funds applied to the improvement of the *infrastructure*, and the term may also be applied to the expenditure on human resources.

   *In an effort to improve the nation's economy, the government is investing in a huge road-building programme as well as making an enormous investment in the re-education of its workforce.*

**investment adviser** Person who advises individuals or institutions on financial matters related to investment in its widest sense. The function is performed by everyone from turf accountants to chartered accountants.

**investment allowance** Alternative term for *capital allowance.*

**investment bank** US bank that is similar to a UK merchant bank.

**investment bond** *See insurance bond.*

**investment instrument** Any medium of investment, including *stocks, shares* and *securities* of all kinds, *unit trusts* and funds, grouped investment media, and so on.

**investment manager** *See fund manager.*

**Investment Management Regulatory Organization** (IMRO) *Self-regulatory organization* (SRO) that regulates any company that offers to manage investments, from friendly societies to unit trust companies. It is to be incorporated into the *Financial Services Authority.*

**investment services directive** (ISD) *Directive* of the European Union (EU), issued in 1966, that deals with cross-border transactions by investment banks and dealers in securities.

**investment trust** Pooled investment scheme in which a small investor is able to invest in a range of shares through the agency of the scheme's managers. It is not a "trust" but is a limited liability company and is close ended. However, it does offer similar advantages to unit trusts.

**investment trust warrant** Security that guarantees an investor the right to buy shares at the *exercise price* on a certain date.

**Investor's Compensation Scheme** Scheme set up under the 1986 Financial Services Act. It provides compensation for individuals who lose financially due to an authorized person becoming insolvent. The maximum payout is £48,000.

**invisible assets** Also called intangible assets, assets that cannot be seen (such as goodwill or staff expertise). *See also tangible assets.*

**invisible earnings** *Income* earned from payment for services rather than goods, on a national scale. Invisible earnings include profits from tourism, shipping, and the provision of insurance, banking and other financial services. They are also called simply invisibles.

**investment grant** Grant of money made available by the government to companies for certain purposes.

**inward investment** Alternative term for *foreign investment.*

**invisibles** *See invisible earnings.*

**invisible exports** Services (rather than goods) provided to foreign people, organizations and countries. Invisible exports include banking, shipping and insurance services.

**invisible trade** Trade in services rather than goods. *See invisible exports.*

**invitation to treat** Suggestion, made by one person to another, that he or she enter into negotiations which may result in a formal offer to trade. The difference between an invitation to treat and an *offer* proper is that an invitation does not bind the parties concerned to the conditions of the invitation, whereas the terms of an offer are legally binding.

**invoice** Document that summarizes a business transaction and often doubles as a request for payment. An invoice lists and describes the goods (or services) ordered and details their price, and usually records the dates and times of dispatch and delivery.

**invoice discounting** *Discount* offered on unpaid *invoices* sold to a *factoring* company, which will then try to claim the money owed on its own account. The size of the discount will reflect the likely difficulty of securing payment. *See also discounting bank.*

**involuntary betterment** In insurance, a situation in which a policyholder is in a better position after his or her insurer meets a claim that before the event that led to it (because the original situation cannot be reproduced).

**IOU** Abbreviation of "I owe you," a non-negotiable written note recording a *debt*.

**IPO** Abbreviation of *initial public offering.*

**IRIS** Abbreviation of *Insurance Regulatory Information System.*

**IRR** Abbreviation of *internal rate of return.*

**irrevocable** Describing something (*e.g.* an order or letter of credit) that is unalterable and cannot be revoked.

**IRS** Abbreviation of *Internal Revenue Service.*

**ISA** Abbreviation of *Individual Savings Account.*

**ISD** Abbreviation of *investment services directive.*

**issuance** Procedure of issuing *securities*, carried out by a *company* or *issuing house.*

**issue** Term with two meanings:

1. It is the quantity of a particular *stock* or *share* offered to the public.

2. It is the total number of banknotes in print at a given time.

**issue by tender** *Stocks* and *shares* may be issued by the process of inviting tenders above a stated minimum price and then selling to the highest bidder. *See also* **application and allotment.**

**issued capital** That part of a company's capital that comes from a share issue. It is also known as subscribed capital.

**issue price** Price at which a new issue of shares is sold to the public.

**IT** Abbreviation of *information technology.*

# J

**jajo** Abbreviation of January, April, July, October, the months in which some stock *options* expire.

**jobber** Also known as a stockjobber, a member of the London Stock Exchange who deals in securities with stockbrokers and other jobbers, but not with the public. Before the **Big Bang**, the London Stock Exchange was the only exchange in the world on which the activities of the stockbrokers and jobbers were kept separate. This practice has now been discontinued and jobbers have been replaced by *market makers*. In the USA, a jobber is any middleman between a wholesaler and a retailer, or a person on a stock exchange who deals in securities that are worthless (*e.g.* junk bonds). The US synonym for jobber in the UK sense is *dealer*.

**jobber's book** Before the **Big Bang**, a book showing the *position* a *jobber* held in the market: whether he holds stock for which he has yet to find a buyer, or whether he is short on stock that he has already sold.

**jobber's pitch** On the London Stock Exchange, trading position on the floor of the exchange from which *jobbers* operated.

**jobber's turn** Profit made by a *jobber* on a deal.

**jobbing backwards** Looking back at past decisions, transactions or events, often – with hindsight – regretting them and perhaps considering how different actions could have been taken.

**job lot** Collection of *stocks* or *goods* sold together, perhaps to somebody who wants only some of them.

**joint** Describing something that is a combination of two or more things, *e.g.* a joint company or a joint treasurer.

**joint and several** Concept by which joint debtors (*e.g.* two or more partners in a company) are responsible for the debt, both jointly and as individuals. Joint and several liability gives the lender recourse to each of the partners in the debt in the event of default.

**joint-life annuity** See *joint-life and last-survivor annuities*.

**joint-life and last-survivor annuities** *Annuities* involving a husband and wife (or any two people). The joint-life annuity starts paying on a defined date and continues until both people are dead. The last survivor annuity starts paying on the death of one of the people and continues until the other person is dead.

**joint lives policy** Life assurance policy involving two people that pays when one of them dies.

**joint-stock company** Alternative term for limited company.
*See* **limited liability company.**

**joint tenancy** Situation in which two or more people have equal rights to the tenancy of a property. The difference between a joint tenancy and a *tenancy in common* is that if a joint tenant dies, the property reverts to the other tenants, and so on until one tenant remains, with sole tenancy rights.

**Jonestown defence** Any form of defensive tactics against a hostile takeover bid that is so extreme as to appear suicidal. *See also* **poison pill.**

**journal** In accounting, a book in which daily transactions are recorded before being transferred to the books of account.

**judgement** Ruling made by a court in a particular case (also spelled judgment).

**judgement debt** Debt that has come before the courts and which has been ordered to be repaid.

**jumpy** Description of a market in which dealers are nervous and so likely to jump at the slightest movement.

**junior capital** Company shares that represent the company's *equity.*

**junior stock** Shares offered to a company's executives at below the market price. Initially, junior stock has a low dividend rate, but may be converted to ordinary shares to provide a capital gain.

**junk bond** Bond, especially common in the USA, issued by a company with a low credit rating. It is often used to raise funds for *leveraged buyouts*, secured against the assets of the target company.

# K

**K** Thousand (1,000), often in finance expressed in units of currency. *She was earning 50K as a consultant.*

**kaffir** Racist stock exchange nickname for shares in South African mining companies.

**kangaroo** Stock exchange nickname for shares in Australian companies, especially those dealing in tobacco, property and mining.

**kerb** On the London Metal Exchange, a period of time during which all metals are traded simultaneously.

**kerb market** Trading in securities that takes place outside an official exchange.

**kerb trading** Closing a deal on a financial futures market after hours. It is so called because originally traders would emerge from the exchange after official trading closed for the day and remain outside (on the kerb) to close any unfinished business.

**key features document** Document required to be given to all prospective purchasers of "investments" under rules of the *Financial Services Act*. It is client-specific and gives basic details about the policy, its benefits and any limitations.

**key money** Premium paid by a new tenant of a property to the previous leaseholder in return for the granting of the lease or licence.

**Keynesianism** School of economic thought, named after John Maynard Keynes (1883-1946), an economist greatly influential in the late 1930s. Keynesians believe that the best way to bring about economic change is by government intervention in the form of market controls and public investment. *See also* **monetarism**.

**key person insurance** Insurance to cover the health of an essential employee (a key person) in a company. This form of insurance covers the cost of replacing such personnel at short notice by equally qualified temporary staff and any loss of profits incurred in the meantime.

**kick-up** Chance offered to holders of bonds to convert them into shares at a profit.

*By offering an equity kick-up, the company was able to offer lower coupons on the issue.*

**killer bees**  People who help a company to resist a *takeover bid* by making the target less attractive financially.

**kite**  Another name for *accommodation bill*. It is also slang for a cheque.

**kite flying**  Raising money by way of an *accommodation bill*.

**knee-jerk**  Reflexive movement in a market that is sudden and largely artificial.

**knight**  Third party who appears at the scene of a *takeover* battle. *See also white knight; grey knight.*

**knock-for-knock agreement**  In motor insurance, agreement between a group of insurers that no question of responsibility will be discussed and that each company will pay for damage to its own policyholders' vehicles, so long as the policyholder is covered for such damage.

**knowledge engineer**  Person who collects and files information on a sophisticated computer system, in order to produce knowledge rather than mere data.

# L

**labour** People used in the production of goods or services.

**labour costs** Expenses incurred in providing labour in the production process. Labour costs can include not only wages and salaries, but also National Insurance contributions and contributions to pension schemes.

**labour-intensive** Describing an industry in which labour is the most important and costly factor of production. Thus, an industry in which the major cost is the payment of salaries, incentives and bonuses is labour-intensive.

**laches** Legal term for negligence in performing a duty, asserting a right or claiming a privilege.

**lacklustre** Describing uninspiring corporate performance, normally indicated by a poor stock market rating. *See also price/earnings ratio*

**Lady Macbeth strategy** During a hostile *takeover*, a strategy undertaken by a party that seems at first to be acting as a *white knight*, but subsequently joins the aggressor.

**laesio enormis** Latin for "extraordinary injury". It is a doctrine (derived from Roman law) which states that a contract price must be fair and reasonable. An unfair or unreasonable price is grounds for terminating the contract.

**laggard** Share that does not keep up with the average price of comparable shares.

**lame duck** Weak individual or company; one ripe for *takeover* or unable to provide effective competition.

**land tax** Tax on the ownership of land, normally paid in the form of rates.

**lapse** Status of an insurance policy following failure to pay premiums.

**lapsed policy** Insurance policy that is worthless because premiums have not been paid.

**last in first out** (LIFO) Term with two meanings:

   1. It is an accounting term for a system of stock-keeping, whereby the

latest items manufactured or bought are used or sold before old stock is cleared. In a period of deflation this has the effect of maximizing profit, because new goods or materials have cost less to manufacture or buy. *See also* **base stock method**; **first in first out**.

2. It describes the method by which some companies make employees redundant, on the basis of length of service. Thus, the last people to be employed are the first to be laid off.

**last-survivor annuity** *See* **joint-life and last-survivor annuity**.

**last-survivor policy** *Life assurance* policy involving two or more people. It pays when the last person dies. It is also known as a second-death policy.

**last trading day** In trading in *financial futures*, the last day on which trading may take place before delivery.

**late-kerb** Trading in metals that goes on after hours, usually over the telephone. *See* **kerb trading**.

**laundering** Method of disguising the origin of funds by moving them rapidly from one account or country to another. It thus becomes a complicated business to trace their origins, movements and eventual destination. Counterfeit or stolen money may be laundered.

**LAUTRO** Abbreviation of *Life Assurance and Unit Trust Regulatory Organization*.

**lawful visitor** In insurance, person non-domiciled at a property but covered (up to a stipulated amount) by a domestic policy. Such people include family members, guests, workmen and persons allowed to enter by law (such as excise officers and police officers).

**law of large numbers** Principle whereby the insurer benefits due to large numbers of homogeneous exposure being insured. The principle states that the actual number of events occuring will tend towards the expected number, where there is a large number of similar situations.

**lawyer** Somebody licensed to practise law. The term may be applied to a solicitor, but is most usually (and loosely) used as a synonym for "attorney" or "barrister".

**lay day** Day on which a vessel may unload cargo without incurring port charges.

**layer** Term used in reinsurance where successive treaties are "layered" on an excess of loss basis. Once the first excess of loss layer has been used up, the second layer treaty is called upon, and so on.

**LBO** Abbreviation of *leveraged buyout.*

**LCA** Abbreviation of *Lloyd's Central Accounting.*

**LCE** Abbreviation of *London Commodities Exchange.* Now also known as London FOX (*Futures and Options Exchange*).

**LCO** Abbreviation of *Lloyd's Claims Office.*

**leading indicator** Measurable variable (such as factory construction) that moves in advance of the indicated item (such as the level of employment).

**leading insurer** Insurer (or underwriter) who accepts the first share of a *coinsurance* arrangement, and often the largest share.

**lead manager** In a *syndicate*, the company that does the administration. For this service, the lead manager usually receives a higher *commission* than the other members of the syndicate.

**lease** Contract giving temporary possession of a property, often in areas where prices are appreciating so rapidly that it is not in the owner's best interests to sell. Buildings are the most common subjects of a lease, although it is possible to lease land and other possessions, such as vehicles and machinery. Long-term leases are often mortgaged, bought and sold. *See also* **tenancy**.

**lease-back** Arrangement by which a property is sold on condition that it is immediately leased back to the original owner. *Capital* tied up in property is therefore freed for other uses.

**lease financing** Form of off-balance-sheet financing whereby goods (*e.g.* machinery) are leased rather than being purchased outright. Lease financing is therefore generally thought of as a type of disguised *borrowing*. It is generally frowned upon by accounting authorities.

**leasehold** Describing property held by *lease*. On leasehold land, the lessee pays *ground rent* to the owner of the *freehold*.

**ledger** Book in which trade transaction, credits and debits are recorded. The term is most accurately applied to the principal volume in a series of account books, which collates the details made in the *books of original entry*.

**leg** One of the divisions of a corporation or company.

**legal charge** Another name for a *mortgage*.

**legal expenses insurance** Insurance that provides cover to individuals and businesses for legal costs incurred. It can be taken out as a stand-alone policy, but is usually included within household and motor policies.

**legal reserve** Minimum sum that building societies and insurance companies have by law to hold as security for their customers.

**lending** Temporary grant of money, goods, equipment, people and so on, made on the understanding that the thing lent, or its equivalent, will be returned, often with additional (*interest*) payment.

**lessee deposit** Deposit that is paid by the lessee on rented property, intended to cover the lessor against damage or loss and returnable on termination of the lease.

**letter** Written document of agreement, often listing the terms and conditions of a business relationship.

**letter of acceptance** Document issued by a *life assurance* company when a proposal has been accepted. The policy does not come into effect until the *premium* has been paid.

**letter of allotment** Means by which shares are allotted. A letter of allotment may be used as proof of ownership and entitles the holder to a *certificate* for the number of shares stated in the letter. It should not be confused with *allotment note*.

**letter of indemnity** Document sent with a shipment for export which states that the manufacturer is prepared to rectify any damage that occurs during transit, due to inadequate packing, handling, and so on.

**letter of intent** Letter outlining some intended action sent to establish intent in the eyes of the law.

**letter of regret** Letter informing an applicant that he or she has been unsuccessful in applying for a new share issue.

**letters of administration** Court order that appoints someone to act as *administrator* in the winding-up of a deceased person's estate in the absence of an executor or if someone dies intestate, or to administer the winding-up of a company.

**letters patent** Document issued by the Patent Office attesting the holder's right to possession of a *patent*.

**level premium** In *life assurance*, a *premium* that remains unchanged for the duration of a policy.

**leverage**  Alternative term for *gearing*; the ratio of a company's debts to total *capital* or shareholders' funds. In a buoyant market, a high proportion of debt has a beneficial effect on share earnings, because it is usually possible for the company to earn more on its loan capital than it is paying in *interest*. In such circumstances, high gearing is beneficial to shareholders. Conversely, a fall in demand or a rise in interest rates affects a highly-geared company adversely. A company's leverage or gearing often has a significant effect on its share price in an open market. *See also* **leveraged buyout**.

**leveraged buyout**  (LBO)  Buyout of a large company by a smaller one, the capital for which has been borrowed from a friendly source, secured on the assets of the company being bought. *See also* **leverage**.

**leveraged company**  Company that is seriously in debt.

**LGS**  Abbreviation of *Loan Guarantee Scheme*.

**liability**  A company's or person's debt. Long-term (or deferred) liabilities are usually distinguished from current liabilities, as are secured debts from unsecured debts.

**liability insurance**  Insurance policy that covers the cost of paying compensation and court costs if the policyholder's negligence results in injury to somebody or damage to property. *See* **employer's liability insurance**.

**LIBA**  Abbreviation of *Lloyd's Insurance Brokers Association*.

**LIBOR**  Abbreviation of *London Inter Bank Offered Rate*.

**licence insurance**  Type of insurance that provides cover for a hotelier or publican against the non-renewal or revocation of a liquor licence.

**lien**  The right to possession of property until such time that an outstanding *liability* has been repaid. A lien gives a *creditor* the right to retain or sell the property of a *debtor* in lieu of payment.

**lien on shares**  The right to take possession of *shares* if a borrower defaults on payment.

**life annuity**  Annuity for which payment ceases when a specified person dies (who need not be the annuitant).

**life assurance**  Insurance policy for which the policyholder pays a premium and when the person whose life is assured dies, payment is made to the *beneficiary*. Policies can be for a specific term or for the whole of life. *See also* **endowment**; **term assurance**.

**Life Assurance and Unit Trust Regulatory Organization** (LAUTRO) Former *self-regulatory organization* (SRO) that regulated companies that dealt in *life assurance* and *unit trusts*. In 1994 it was taken over by the *Personal Investment Authority* (PIA) and LAUTRO ceased to exist in 1995.

**life assurance premium relief** Income tax relief in respect of personal *life assurance* premiums (or those of one's spouse), on policies taken out before 14 March 1984. It is no longer available on policies taken out after that date, but continues to be available at a rate of 12.5% for those policies effected before the date, as long as they are not varied.

**life assured** The person whose death results in payment of the agreed sum under a *life assurance* policy. He or she need not be the policyholder.

**life insurance** *See life assurance.*

**life of another policy** Way of writing *life assurance* in which the policy-holder (the person to whom the proceeds are paid) or grantee is not the person whose life is assured. *Insurable interest* needs to exist when such policies are taken out.

**life office** Company that provides *life assurance.*

**life policy** *Life assurance* policy that contains personal details of the insured, the premium payable, and the amount to be paid by the assurance company when the assured person reaches a certain age or dies.

**life table** Statistical table of life expectancies at different ages, used by assurance companies in calculating premiums. *See mortality table.*

**LIFFE** Abbreviation of *London International Financial Futures and Options Exchange.*

**LIFO** Abbreviation of *last in first out.*

**LIMEAN** Abbreviation of *London Inter Bank Mean Rate.*

**limit (order)** On a stock or commodity exchange, an instruction given by a client to his or her *stockbroker*, which specifies the maximum price the broker is authorized to pay to buy a shareholding, or the minimum he is to demand before selling.

**limit (up/down)** The maximum and minimum limits within which the price of some commodity futures and *financial futures* are permitted to fluctuate in one day's trading. *See fluctuation.*

**limitation of benefit clause** Clause included in *personal health insurance* (PHI) policies that limits the benefit payable to 2/3 (66%) of pre-disability earnings, including state benefits, employer payments and other PHI policies. This provides an incentive for the claimant to return to work.

**limited** In a business context, something of restricted *liability*, as in a *limited company*.

**limited company** Also called a limited liability company, a company formed from a group of people, whose *liability* is limited to the extent of the investment they have made (usually to purchase shares in the company).

**limited liability** Restriction of the owners' loss in a liquidated company to the amount of *capital* each has invested. The loss of the individual shareholder in such an eventuality is limited to the value of his or her holding. In the event of *liquidation* the company itself remains liable for its outstanding debts; creditors are generally paid by selling off or dividing up the bankrupt company's *assets*. *See also* **limited company**.

**limited order** Instruction to a *broker* containing conditions about price and timing.

**limited partner** Partner whose liability for the debts of the partnership is limited in law to the sum he or she invested in it. A limited partner does not generally share in the management of the firm. He or she may, however, offer advice and examine the books of account. *See* **limited partnership**.

**limited partnership** Partnership in which one or more partners have only *limited liability* for the firm's debts. In each limited partnership there must be one general partner with unlimited liability. A limited partnership is therefore unpopular and a *public limited company* is preferred, because all shareholders in such a company have only limited liability. *See* **general partnership**.

**limited payments policy** Type of *life assurance* for which *premium* payments cease when the assured attains a certain age (often 65 years).

**limit of indemnity** Maximum amount an insurance company is liable to pay out on a given insurance policy.

**limit of liability** Maximum amount an insurance company will pay under a liability policy.

**limit order** US term for a *stop loss order*.

**LIMNET** Computerized management system for the London insurance market.

**line** Acceptance of risk by an underwriter. Also, in reinsurance, it is the retention limit under a surplus reinsurance treaty.

**line management** Management system in which a chain of command is formed from top executives, down the line to junior staff. Line management is concerned only in the major activities of a company.

**line of credit** *See credit line.*

**line slip** Arrangement by which an insurance *broker* who has placed many similar risks with a group of *underwriters* need deal with only the lead or second underwriter instead of all of them.

**liquid** Something that is readily accessible, such as *assets* that can be immediately realized in *cash* form. *Money* is by definition fully liquid. Treasury bills and Post Office Savings are similarly liquid. Cash kept in a bank is the most obvious liquid asset.

**liquid assets** Assets that may be readily converted into money. *See tangible assets.*

**liquid assets ratio** Ratio of the value of total assets held to the value of assets that may be converted into cash without loss.

**liquidated damages** Damages of an amount already specified in a *contract*. The terms of the contract provide for liquidated damages to be paid. *See also unliquidated damages.*

**liquidation** The *winding-up* of a company, so-called because the company's *assets* are liquidated – converted into cash money – in order that outstanding *creditors* may be paid (in whole or in part).

**liquidity** The ease with which an *asset* can be converted into money. Cash deposits in current bank accounts may be quickly withdrawn and are said to be highly liquid; money in most deposit accounts is slightly less so because notice must usually be given before withdrawal. *See also illiquidity.*

**liquidity ratio** For any business, current assets divided by current liabilities. It is also termed the current assets ratio.

**(LIRMA)** Abbreviation of *London Insurance and Reinsurance Market Association.*

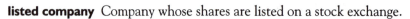

**listed company** Company whose shares are listed on a stock exchange.

**listing** *Flotation* of a company on a stock exchange; the sum of the actions that permits *securities* to be traded on a stock market. The issued shares are then listed in the exchange records and their price fluctuations recorded and published.

**listing agreement** Agreement to abide by the rules of the London Stock Exchange when applying for *listing*.

**Little Bang** First stage of deregulation of the UK stock market, which applied only to overseas trading. *See* **Big Bang**.

**living debt** Part of the *National Debt* used to pay for the infrastructure, hospital building, schools and other national assets.

**Lloyd's adviser** Person who provides corporate members of *Lloyd's of London* with data and analyses, and negotiates their participation in a *syndicate*.

**Lloyd's** *See Lloyd's of London.*

**Lloyd's broker** Insurance *broker* who is registered to deal at *Lloyd's of London*.

**Lloyd's Central Accounting** (LCA) Centralized accounting system used by *syndicates* and traders of *Lloyd's of London*.

**Lloyd's Claims Office** (LCO) Centralized system for assessing and agreeing insurance claims used by *Lloyd's of London syndicates*.

**Lloyd's Insurance Brokers Association** (LIBA) Former trade association of insurance brokers, which ceased to exist in 1977 with the founding of the British Insurance Brokers Association, now the *British Insurance and Investment Brokers Association* (BIIBA).

**Lloyd's List** Daily newspaper that covers matters relating to shipownership and shipping, listing arrivals and departures of merchant vessels throughout the world. *See also* **Lloyd's Register**.

**Lloyd's of London** Incorporated association of insurers that specializes in *marine insurance*. Formally established by Act of Parliament in 1871, the Corporation developed from a group of 17th-century *underwriters* who met at Edward Lloyd's coffee house in London.

Lloyd's supervises about 20,000 individual insurers ("names") grouped into *syndicates*, each of which has unlimited *liability* and accepts a fraction of the *risk* of business brought to them by one of more than 200 registered *brokers*. Lloyd's involvement in marine insurance currently comprises less than half the total business transacted by Lloyd's underwriters. From 1988 to 1994, Lloyd's lost over £8 billion and many names went bankrupt. As a result limited liability companies are now allowed to become "corporate names".

**Lloyd's Outward Reinsurance Scheme** (LORS) Computerized system for processing reinsurance transactions between *brokers* and *syndicates* of *Lloyd's of London*.

**Lloyd's policy** *Marine insurance* policy written by underwriters at *Lloyd's of London* and sealed by the Corporation.

**Lloyd's Policy Signing Office** Office at *Lloyd's of London* that checks insurance policies and slips drawn up by *brokers* and has them signed on behalf of *syndicates*, for whom it also prepares monthly reports and accounts.

**Lloyd's Register** List that gives details of all the registered merchant ships in the world. *See also Lloyd's List.*

**LME** Abbreviation of *London Metal Exchange*.

**loading** Term with two meanings in insurance:
1. It is an extra sum added to a *premium* for a risk that is regarded as greater than normal for the type of policy.
2. It is the part of a *premium* that funds costs and profits. *See front-end loading*.

**loading broker** Someone who acts for a ship's owner, obtaining cargoes for the vessel to transport.

**loan** Sum of money borrowed by one person or organization from another on condition that it is repaid, generally for a specified time and often at an agreed rate of *interest*. *See also back-to-back loan; personal loan.*

**loan account** *Account* (produced by a lender, such as bank) that records the amounts repaid on a bank loan and interest charged to the borrower.

**loanback** Loan made by a *pension fund* to a contributor to that fund. Loanback pensions are secured not against the total value of the contributions to date, but against some other asset. However, the maximum available loan is usually equal to the total value of the accumulated units. The loan becomes an asset of the borrower's *pension plan* and interest payments are, therefore, part of the income of the plan.

**loan creditor** Person or organization from which a business has borrowed money.

**loan capital** That part of a company's capital that is lent over a fixed period of time.

**loan drawdown** *See drawdown.*

**Loan Guarantee Scheme** (LGS) UK government scheme introduced in 1981 to promote the establishment and development of small businesses. The government agrees to underwrite 70% of approved loans made to such firms in exchange for a 2.5% annual *premium* on this portion, and on condition that the lending institution underwrites the balance of 30%.

**loan-loss provisions** Reserves held by a bank or other lending institution against loans that are not repaid by the borrower.

**loan on policy** Sum advanced against the security of a *life assurance* policy that is charged against the *surrender value* of the policy until the loan is repaid (together with accrued interest).

**loan protection insurance** Type of insurance that provides cover against default on loan repayments because of personal accident, sickness or (except for self-employed people) unemployment or redundancy. It is also termed accident, sickness and unemployment insurance (ASU).

**loan rate** *Rate of interest* charged for a *loan*, often expressed as a certain percentage above *base rate*.

**loan selling** Selling of a loan by one bank or financial institution to another. The borrower is not necessarily informed.

**loan shark** *Moneylender* who (quite legally) charges excessive rates of interest, usually for only short-term loans.

**loan stock** Security issued by a company in respect of loan funds made available by investors. It is similar to a *debenture*, although loan stock is often unsecured.

**local authority bond** Bond issued by a local government authority. It is also known as a municipal bond.

**local currency** Currency of a foreign country with which an exporter or trader is dealing.

**lockbox** Security chest or safe for personal use. The term also includes safe-deposit boxes provided by some banks.

**lock-up** On financial markets, an investment expected to yield profit only in the long term, and in which capital will therefore be "locked-up" for some time.

**lock-up option** In a situation in which a company is being threatened with an unwanted *takeover*, a defensive tactic whereby the target company promises to sell its most attractive *assets* to a *white knight*. *See also crown jewel tactic.*

**locus poenitentiae** Latin for "opportunity to repent". It is an option open to the parties of an illegal *contract*, who may save it by deciding not to carry out that part which is against the law.

**Lombard Street** Street in London whose name, because it is the location of the head offices of many UK banks and discount houses, stands for the London *money market*. The US equivalent is *Wall Street*.

**London Commodities Exchange** (LCE) Market that deals in cocoa, coffee, rubber, spices, tea and other commodities. In 1996 it merged with the *London International Financial Futures and Options Exchange*.

**London Foreign Exchange Market** Market that deals in sterling and various foreign currencies, using contracts that are made verbally (using telephone lines or other electronic means) and later confirmed in writing.

**London Futures and Options Exchange** (London FOX) *Commodity market* that deals in *futures* and *options*.

**London Insurance and Reinsurance Market Association** (LIRMA) Organization that provides central accounting services and policy signing facilities for member general insurance companies.

**London Inter Bank Mean Rate** (LIMEAN) Average of the London Inter Bank Bid Rate (LIBID) and the London Inter Bank Offered Rate (LIBOR).

**London Inter Bank Offered Rate** (LIBOR) Rate of interest that commercial banks offer to lend money for on the London Inter Bank market. Along with the *minimum lending rate*, LIBOR has a significant effect on bank *interest rates*.

**London International Financial Futures and Options Exchange** (LIFFE) Financial futures market established in 1982 for dealing in options and futures contracts within the European time zone. Originally the London International Financial Futures Exchange, its name changed in 1992 when it merged with the London Traded Options Market. (LTOM). A further merger in 1996 with the London Commodity Exchange (LCE) gave it unique status in the financial world.

**London Money Market** *See money market.*

**London Metal Exchange** (LME) Market established in 1877 to deal in non-ferrous metals, including aluminium, copper, lead, tin and zinc.

**London Stock Exchange** Market that deals in securities in London. Established in the 17th century, it became the International Stock Exchange of the UK and Republic of Ireland in 1986. It provides the main market and the *Alternative Investment Market* for companies.

**London Traded Options Market** *See London International Financial Futures and Options Market.*

**London Underwriting Centre** (LUC) Business centre founded in 1993 for non-marine company insurance in London. It houses underwriters and the offices of the *London Insurance and Reinsurance Market Association* (LIRMA).

**long** Term with two meanings:

1. In the UK, it is the position taken by a *bull* speculator, who acquires quantities of a stock or commodity in excess of the amount contracted for, in expectation that the price will rise and permit the surplus to be sold at a profit.

2. In the USA, it is a *security* that someone has bought and owns.

**long bill** *Bill of exchange* with more than ten years to maturity.

**long bond** Bond with more than fifteen years to maturity. *See also medium bond; short bond.*

**long credit** Loan that may be repaid over a long period of time. *See also short credit.*

**long-dated gilt** *Gilt-edged security* with a redemption term of more than fifteen years.

**long hedge** Hedge against a fall in the interest rate on the futures market. *See also short hedge.*

**long liquidation** Long-term *self-liquidating* company.

**longs** Fixed-interest securities with redemption dates more than fifteen years in the future. *See fixed-interest security.*

**long-tail business** Insurance term for the issuing of policies on which claims are not expected for a considerable time.

**long tap** Long-term government securities issued in unlimited numbers.

*See tap.*

**long-term** In describing securities, a period exceeding fifteen years, but more loosely applied to *stocks* issued for an indefinite period of time or in perpetuity. In the City, the phrase "long-term" is loosely applied to any period over one year.

**long-term business** Insurance business that includes ordinary and industrial life assurance annuities and pensions.

**long-term insurance** *See long-term business.*

**long-term liability** Debt that need not be repaid in the next three years. In *accounting*, the term is sometimes applied to loans that are not due to be repaid in the current accounting period.

**loop** Circular chain of *shareholdings*, *e.g.* A owns 20% of the stock of B; B owns 20% of the stock of C; C owns 20% of the stock of D; and D owns 20% of the stock of A.

**loophole** Any circumstance that permits the evasion of a custom or rule, but especially a legal inexactitude that offers an escape from a *contract*.

**LORS** Abbreviation of *Lloyd's Outward Reinsurance Scheme*.

**loss** Disadvantage, forfeiture of money or goods, or negative profit. It is possible to insure against most kinds of loss.

**loss adjuster** Person who assesses a loss and arranges payment of a claim to the policyholder on behalf of an insurer.

**loss assessor** Person who negotiates an insurance claim with an insurer on behalf of the claimant (the policyholder).

**loss leader** Product or service offered for sale at a substantial loss in order to attract customers. The hope is that shoppers who come to buy the loss leader will also purchase other goods.

**loss-of-profits insurance** Type of insurance that provides cover against loss of trade and profits resulting from some disaster such as a fire. In the latter case the policy would typically pay a business the equivalent of the expected net profits lost while repair work and restocking were carried out, plus salaries, rates and rent due in that period. Fire damage itself will probably be covered by a separate *fire insurance*. A loss-of-profits policy is sometimes also called a business-interruption policy. *See also business interruption insurance.*

**loss ratio** In insurance, the value of all claims expressed as a percentage of total *premiums* for a period. The figure is used as a guide to the profitability of the business when considering rates.

**losses occurring insurance** Type of insurance in which the insurer must pay claims for losses that occur during the term of the policy, no matter when the claim is discovered or made.

**lot** Method of deciding by chance which *stocks* will be redeemed in a given year.

**low-beta** Describing shares that are relatively stable.

*Some analysts expect the current trend to continue and so believe that low-betas are good buys.*

**low-cost endowment mortgage** Insurance policy that repays capital on a mortgage while also providing death benefit and long-term savings in the form of a tax-free lump sum on maturity (although not usually guaranteed).

**low-load fund** Mutual fund that charges a low initial fee.

**lump sum** Sum of money paid to someone all at once, as opposed to being paid as a series of separate sums. The term is used in life assurance and pensions business to describe the sum paid at the end of term or retirement.

**lump system** System of payment under which workers receive a *lump sum* for each day's work or for the fulfilment of a daily quota. The lump system is common in the building industry, but frowned upon because it can enable employees to avoid *taxation*.

**Lutine Bell** Bell that hangs in the underwriting room at *Lloyd's of London*. It was formerly rung before the announcement of important news, such as that concerning the fate of a missing ship. It was recovered from the *Lutine*, a ship which sank in 1799 and which was insured at Lloyd's for £1.4 million.

# M

**M0** *See money supply.*

**M1** *See money supply.*

**M2** *See money supply.*

**M3** *See money supply.*

**£M3** *See money supply.*

**M4** *See money supply.*

**M5** *See money supply.*

**Maastricht Treaty** An Agreement signed by EU states in 1992 which paves the way for *European Monetary Union* and eventual political union. The UK government opted out of certain parts of the Treaty.

**macroeconomics** Study of broad or *aggregate* economics. Macroeconomics concerns itself with the relationship between such major aggregates as prices, incomes, total consumption and total production, together with interest and exchange rates, savings and investment. *See also microeconomics.*

**made bills** *Bills of exchange* traded in the UK but drawn and payable overseas.

**mail order** System for buying and selling by post; the customer purchases goods direct from the manufacturer or distributor without the intervention of a *middleman* or retailer.

**mainstream corporation tax** Company's overall corporation tax liability payable on gross profits. Tax actually paid is the mainstream corporation tax minus any *advance corporation tax* (ACT) payments.

**maintenance** Broadly, the financial provision made by a husband for his ex-wife and any children after a divorce.

In law, also used to describe a contribution towards the cost of a legal action made by a person who has no legal or moral interest in the case.

**major** US equivalent of a *blue chip* company; a very large company within its market sector.

**majority interest**  Shareholding that gives the holder control of a company, *i.e.* one of over 50%. *See also **minority interest**.*

**making a price**  Action of a stockbroker or market-maker when he or she quotes a ***bid price*** or ***offer price*** for a stock or share.

**mala fide**  Latin for "in bad faith"; fraudulent. *See also **bona fide**.*

**malpractice insurance**  Type of ***liability insurance*** that provides cover for a US ***accountant*** against claims connected with his or her professional performance.

**managed account**  Investment account managed for a depositor by a bank's investment department.

**managed float**  *See **dirty float**.*

**managed fund**  Fund that is set up by a life office, unit trust or investment company which is made up of a range of securities and managed by a fund manager. The spread of investments and size of a fund manager's expertise means that this type of fund usually offers lower risk for a small investor.

**managed PEP**  *See **personal equity plan** (PEP).*

**managed unit trust**  Type of ***unit trust*** that is actively managed by a fund manager and invested in a range of securities.

**management**  Control and supervision of a company, asset or operation; the group of people who control and administer a company, as distinct from the workforce. The effectiveness of a firm's management is often of vital importance to its ***performance***, and management is therefore sometimes taken as a ***factor of production***.

**management accountant**  Accountant who is involved in the day-to-day running of a business, providing information upon which managers are able to make decisions. The distinction between cost and management accountancy is now becoming increasingly blurred.

**management buyout**  Purchase of a company by its managers, one of the most common forms of buyout.

**management company**  Company that practises management consultancy.

**manager**  *See **fund manager**; **management**.*

**managing director**  Senior executive director of a company, junior only to the *chairman*, and charged with implementing the decisions made by the *board*.

**M & A** Abbreviation of *mergers and acquisitions*.

**mandate** Written authority empowering one person to act on behalf of another. Mandates are issued when the mandator dies, is declared bankrupt, or certified insane. They are generally used to give access to the mandator's accounts.

**mandatory grant** Grant that must be paid to all people or organizations that fall into the qualifying categories. *See also* **discretionary grant**.

**manufacturing costs** All expenses incurred by the manufacturer in the production of goods and services. They are also known as production costs.

**manufacturing industry** The aggregate of companies that produce goods rather than providing services.

**manuscript signature** Hand-written signature, as opposed to a *facsimile signature*.

**Mareva injunction** Injunction that prevents the transfer of funds overseas until a case concerning them has been heard in the UK courts.

**margin** Term with four meanings:
1. It is the proportion of the total cost of a product or service that represents the producer's profits.
2. When trading commodities or financial futures, it is the proportion of the contract that is put up.
3. It is the proportion of the total price of a *share* paid by the purchaser to his or her *stockbroker* when the broker buys *securities* on *credit*. The practice in more common in the USA than in the UK, where most dealing is done on account.
4. It is the price added by lenders to the market rate of interest to provide a profit.

**marginal** In economics, the difference between two figures, *e.g.* a marginal unit is the last unit produced, or the first unit supplied, and is defined as the smallest additional amount that is economically viable to produce or buy.

**marginal analysis** Method used in *microeconomics* to study the effect of successive small changes in demand, output, prices and costs.

**marginal cost** Cost incurred in raising the level of output beyond the original target. Marginal cost calculations are used to justify going beyond that target (or, indeed, not doing so).

**marginal relief** Tax relief granted to a taxpayer whose *income* only marginally exceeds a specified level or tax *bracket*. He or she receives a portion of the relief available to those in the lower bracket.

**margin call** In futures trading, if an adverse price movement more than eradicates a party's *margin*, the balance of the deficit is called upon, often cancelling the *bargain*. *See also* *call option*.

**margin dealing** Term with three meanings:

1. It is the method of dealing commodities or financial futures in which only a proportion of the value of the contract is put up. *See* *margin cover*.
2. It refers to high-gear dealing on the edge of a security's price; *i.e.* betting for low stakes on a high-risk change of price.
3. It describes transactions conducted on the margin of a loan from a broker or a speculator. The speculator deposits stock as collateral, but may still trade with any surplus accumulated as the result of a rise in market price.

**margin loan** Loan commonly made on limited *security*, *e.g.* a group of several lenders may advance money secured on property to 75% of its value. A margin loan would then be secured on the remaining 25%. This would carry a higher risk and therefore attract a slightly higher rate of interest. It is also known as a top-up loan.

**margin of solvency** Amount by which a company's total assets are greater than its total liabilities (excluding share capital). *See* *solvency margin*.

**marine insurance** Insurance of ships and their cargoes which provides indemnity for property loss, damage and injury to third parties. Marine losses arise in four areas:

*hull* – damage to or loss of vessel.

*cargo* – goods that have been sold and are being shipped to the buyer.

*freight* – the cost of transporting cargo.

*liability* – damage or injury to third parties.

**marine insurance broker** *Agent* who acts for a Lloyd's *underwriter* in dealing with a shipper wanting to insure a vessel or its cargo.

**marine surveyor** Surveyor who specializes in ships.

**market** Term with three meanings:

1. It is a place where goods and services are bought and sold.
2. It is the actual or potential demand for those goods and services.
3. It is an abstract expression denoting any area or condition in which buyers and sellers are in contact and able to do business together.

**market agreement** Agreement between all the companies in a particular part of the market, *e.g.* life offices have made a market agreement to limit payouts on all permanent health insurance policies to 2/3 of pre-disability income. This maintains an incentive for claimants to return to work.

**market capitalization** Value of all the securities of a company at current market prices.

**Market Financial Services** (MFS) At *Lloyd's of London,* a department of the Corporation that provides accounting services for *brokers* and *syndicates* and administers trust funds for North America.

**market forces** Forces of *supply and demand,* which together determine the price of goods and services on the open market.

**market if touched** (MIT) Instruction to a broker to sell shares as soon as the price reaches a designated level.

**marketing** Distribution, promotion and presentation of a product.

**marketing research** Alternative term for *market research.*

**market leader** Company that has the largest share of a particular market. Individual products that have the largest share of a market are known as *brand leaders.*

**market maker** Market principal who encourages dealing by varying the price of his stock to promote its sale or purchase. The term is used especially with reference to the stock market.

**market order** Order to buy or sell securities on the stock market or a financial futures exchange at the best obtainable market price.

**market research** Survey that is conducted to assess consumer demand. Companies carry out market research in order to maximize the efficiency of their output and to determine potential markets which may be exploited in the future. In addition, market research often suggests ways in which goods and services may be more attractively presented to the public.

**market risk** Part of the total risk inherent in buying a stock, which depends on market movements as a whole rather than on the particular characteristics of the stock itself, *e.g.* during a market *crash*, the share prices of many sound companies whose earning prospects remain unchanged may fall in line with less sound stock. This illustrates the market risk, rather than the specific risk inherent in stock market dealings.

**market saturation** Situation in which a *market* has as much of a product as it can sell.

**market tending** Control of a market's stock index, by intervention buying and selling.

**market value** Price at which something is traded on the open market.

**marking up** Adjustment of price (say, by a retailer) to allow for a profit *margin*. The retailer's mark up is equal to *gross profit*.

**mark to market** On a financial futures exchange, the adjustment of a customer's account to allow for profits or losses on his or her *open contracts* during the previous day's trading.

**mark-up** *See marking up.*

**married couple's personal allowance** Amount allocated to a married couple in the UK to offset against income for *income tax* purposes. However, relief is restricted to 15%. A married couple will have the allowance initially allocated to the husband; however they can elect to transfer the allowance wholly to the wife, or for it to be divided equally between them.

**master policy** Group *life assurance* scheme for a company's employees, usually paying death benefit and widow's or widower's benefit, and often linked to a pension scheme.

**matched bargain** Deals made by finding clients who wish to sell particular *stocks* and ones who wish to buy those same stocks.

**matching** Action of a bank in striking a balance between its assets and liabilities.

**material damage warranty** Clause in *business interruption insurance* that specifies that a material damage claim under another property insurance must be admitted before the interrupted cover is effective.

**material facts** In insurance, any fact which would influence the judgement of an underwriter in determining a premium or in deciding whether to accept a proposed risk. *See also utmost good faith.*

**maturity date**  Date, specified in advance, on which a financial instrument, such as a bill of exchange or insurance policy, may be exchanged for its cash value. It may also be called the redemption date.

**maximum fluctuation**  Also known as maximum slippage, the upper limit to which a price may change on any exchange in one day's trading. It is fixed in advance as a percentage of the current price, and trading in a contract is halted for the rest of the day if the maximum fluctuation price is reached.

**maximum investment plan** (MIP)  Unit-linked *endowment policy* aimed at producing maximum investment rather than *life assurance*. Regular premiums over a period of ten years accumulate to provide a tax-free lump sum at maturity.

**maximum possible loss** (MPL)  In insurance, the worst possible case with regard to claims (often calculated for fire insurance).

**maximum slippage**  *See maximum fluctuation.*

**medical insurance**  In the UK, insurance that covers the cost of medical treatment in private rather than National Health hospitals and clinics. Such policies normally offer to pay the cost of specialist treatment and home nursing, but no cover is provided for emergency treatment, which is still provided by public hospitals. Also known as private medical insurance.

**medium bond**  Bond with between five and fifteen years to maturity. *See also **long bond**; **short bond**.*

**medium-dated gilt**  *Gilt-edged security* with a redemption term of between five and fifteen years.

**medium-dated stock**  Stock with a redemption term of between five and fifteen years.

**medium-term capital**  Loan capital lent in the medium-term, *i.e.* for between five and fifteen years.

**meltdown**  Sizeable financial crisis; a severe crash. The term is taken from the nuclear power industry, where a "meltdown" in a reactor would trigger a major disaster.

**members' syndicate premium limit**  Limit to the amount of business that can be underwritten to a Lloyd's of London *name* by a given *syndicate*.

**memorandum**  Broadly, a reminder, very often a document that records the terms of an agreement or sets out an argument. It is often abbreviated to memo.

**memorandum of association** Document that has to be registered and filed at Companies House in the UK, giving details of a company's particulars and aims. It is accompanied by the *articles of association*, which sets up the internal regulations of the company's operations, and states, among other things, the powers of the directors.

**memorandum of satisfaction** Document issued to certify that a *mortgage* has been paid in full.

**mercantile agent** Person or company that takes part in *factoring*.

**merchant bank** Bank that originally specialized in financing trade, but today offers long-term loans to companies, venture capital, management of investments and underwriting of new issues. Merchant banks also function as *accepting houses*.

**merger** Fusion of two or more companies, as distinct from the *takeover* of one company by another. Mergers may be undertaken for various reasons, notably to improve the efficiency of two complementary companies by rationalizing output and taking advantage of *economies of scale*, and to fight off unwelcome takeover bids from other large companies. The companies involved form one new company and their respective shareholders exchange their holding for shares in the new concern at an agreed rate.

**mergers and acquisitions** (M&A) Field of arranging *mergers* between companies or *takeovers* of companies, or the department within a large company that is formed to carry out this function.

**megamerger** Merger of two major companies to form one gigantic corporation, *e.g.* the 1986 merger between British Petroleum and Standard Oil of Ohio.

**mergermania** Fever that is believed to grip sectors of the business world from time to time. Mergermania occurs after a well-publicized merger or series of mergers; other companies become concerned that they will become adversely affected by the creation of larger and more powerful rivals and seek to merge themselves with other concerns as a protective measure.

**mezzanine finance** Money lent to a small and growing, but financially viable, company. It is so called because the risk of making the loan falls between that of advancing *venture capital* and the safer course of putting the finance into established debt markets.

**MFS** Abbreviation of *Market Financial Services.*

**microeconomics** Study of the individual components of an economy in isolation. Microeconomics examines the choices open to specific people, companies and industries and has been developed to enable the study of subjects such as utility, price mechanisms, *competition* and *margins.* *See also macroeconomics.*

**middleman** Intermediary, usually a wholesaler, retailer or broker who acts as an *agent* between a buyer and a seller. Middlemen tend to push up prices by adding their own profit margin to the difference between buying and selling prices, and it may therefore be in the interests of the buyer and seller to "cut out the middleman" (as in *direct insurance).*

**middle-market price** Price mid-way between the *bid price* and *offer price* on the open market. It is the price the Inland Revenue takes into account when calculating *capital gains tax* on share dealings.

**middle price** Alternative term for *middle-market price.*

**minimerger** *Merger* between two small companies.

**minimum contributions** Amounts required as a minimum to contract out on a money purchase basis. *See contracted-out money purchase scheme.*

**minimum fluctuation** Also known as the basis point, the lower limit to which a price may fall in one day's trading on an exchange. As with the *maximum fluctuation,* it is fixed in advance and trading is halted for the day if the minimum fluctuation is reached.

**minimum guarantee fund** Minimum amount of capital that an insurance company has to set aside, specified by solvency regulations. *See guarantee fund.*

**minimum lending rate** (MLR) Minimum rate at which the Bank of England, acting in its capacity of *lender of the last resort,* is willing to discount *bills of exchange* and at which it offers short-term loans. The government suspended MLR in 1981.

**minimum offering period** Minimum period of time for which an offer to the public to purchase shares may be left open. In the UK this period is usually 14 days.

**minimum wage** Lowest amount a company may pay a worker, often fixed by legislation or trade union agreements.

**minor** In English law, a person under the age of 18; one who cannot legally conduct certain transactions or purchase certain goods.

**minority** Term with two meanings:

1. It is the status of a person under the age of 18; the state of being a minor.
2. It is the smaller portion of something, *i.e.* less than half the whole.

**minority interest** Shareholding that does not give the holder control of a company, *i.e.* a holding of less than 50%.

**minority shareholder** Person who holds a *minority interest* in a company.

**MIP** Abbreviation of *maximum investment plan.*

**MIRAS** Acronym for *mortgage interest relief at source.*

**mirror syndicate** Lloyd's of London *syndicate* with the same *agent* and composition as another syndicate.

**misfeance** Act by an officer of a company that is a breach of duty or trust relating to company assets.

**misfeance summons** Application requesting that a court investigate the actions and conduct of a director of a company in *liquidation*. The summons may be issued by any interested party, such as the official receiver, a creditor or a shareholder, and it requests the court to force the director concerned to compensate them for money misapplied or misappropriated.

**misery index** Index that estimates the relative ill-health of the economy by incorporating variables such as the level of *inflation*, unemployment and economic growth.

**misrepresentation** Any false statement that encourages a person or company to enter into a *contract*. Misrepresentation may be either fraudulent, *i.e.* a deliberate intent to deceive, or innocent, *i.e.* the result of a genuine mistake. The latter type is also termed negligent. Under English law the injured party may have the contract dissolved and claim restitution and/or damages.

**mistake** In law, a fundamental mistake is one that undermines a whole contract, rendering it void. It includes mistakes as to the subject matter of the contract, or identity of the contracting party.

**MIT** Abbreviation of *market if touched.*

**mitigation** Reduction in the severity of something.

**mitigation of damage** Minimization of a *loss*. Mitigation of damage is the responsibility of the sufferer, and must be attempted if he or she is to win full *compensation* in court. Mitigation of damage, therefore, acts as a check against such acts as insurance fraud.

**mixed economy** Economy in which elements of free-market economies and planned economies co-exist.

**MLR** Abbreviation of *minimum lending rate.*

**MMC** Abbreviation of *Monopolies and Mergers Commission.*

**mock auction** Auction that is in some way illegal. This may occur in several ways: when goods are sold for a price lower than the highest bid; when some goods are given away in order to attract bidders; when those who have not already bought lots are excluded from bidding; when part or all of the agreed price is privately returned to the bidder.

**model code** Stock Exchange code of conduct that sets out guidelines for share dealings by company directors. It specifies, broadly, that directors should not engage in questionable dealings with company stock, and in particular forbids share dealings in the two months preceding a company announcement of profit, loss, dividend, a proposed merger, takeover, sale of assets, and so on.

**modem** Short for modulator-demodulator, an electronic device that allows computer data to be transmitted (to another computer, possibly over a network) using telephone lines.

**modern portfolio theory** Theory of stock valuation developed in the early 1980s. It values *stocks* by estimating their future earnings discounted back to the present.

**momentum** In finance, the rate at which a *price* increases or decreases.

**monetarism** Group of economic theories which state in general that the level of prices and wages in an economy is ultimately determined by the amount of money in circulation (the *money supply*); that variations in the amount of money (monetary growth) have no long-term effect on the level of real activity (*e.g.* output and hence unemployment); and that monetary growth can be controlled by government in order to control price inflation.

**monetary control** Method used by a government to control the *money supply* through its *central bank* (in the UK the Bank of England).

**monetary inflation** Inflation that is caused by an increase in the *money supply.*

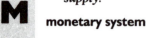

**monetary system** System that controls the exchange rates of a group of countries, or a system that a single country uses to control its own currency exchange while ensuring there is enough money in circulation for internal use.

**monetary union**  Agreement between countries in an economic union to have a common currency, fixed exchange rates and free movement of capital between countries. It is a short-term aim of the European Union (EU).

**money at call**  Loans that may be called in at short notice, and which therefore attract only low rates of *interest*.

**money broker**  *Money market* dealer in short-term loans and securities. On the London Stock Exchange, six firms act as money brokers, channelling borrowed *stocks* from institutions onto the market, thereby enhancing the *liquidity* of the *gilt-edged security* and *equity* markets in particular.

**money had and received**  In law, money in the possession of one person that belongs to another. The term is applied whether or not the possessor obtained the money in good faith.

**money insurance**  Insurance that provides compensation for money stolen from business premises, the home, or while being carried to and from the bank.

**money laundering**  *See laundering.*

**moneylender**  Person licensed by the government to lend funds to others. The term is, however, used informally to describe any person lending money independently of banks and other financial institutions, often at high rates of interest; and as such carries certain negative connotations.

**money market**  Market operated by banks and other financial institutions to facilitate the short-term borrowing and lending of money. In the UK, the Bank of England is the *lender of last resort*. A wider money market includes also the markets in bullion and foreign exchange.

**money-market fund**  *Unit trust*, the income from which is invested in high-yield, short term instruments of credit. Money-market funds are particularly popular when interest rates are high.

**money-market instruments**  Financial products traded on the *money market*, including certificates of deposit and other short-term instruments.

**money-market unit trust**  Risk-free unit trust that invests in short-term *money-market instruments*.

**money-purchase pension scheme** Pension plan based on contributions to the pension fund rather than on salary immediately before retirement. At retirement, the pension fund is used to purchase an annutiy. There is no guarantee as to the level of pension income; the annuity depends on the level of contributions to the fund, investment returns achieved and annuity rates at retirement. *See also* **contracted-out money-purchase scheme**; *occupational pension scheme*; *personal pension plan.*

**money runner** Informal US term for a person who invests in markets throughout the world, probably creating *hot money* in the process.

**money supply** Total amount of money available at short notice in a given country. There are several categories of money supply: M0, M1, M2, M3, M4 and M5.

M0 is defined as notes and coins in circulation and in bank tills, plus the operational balances that banks place with the *Bank of England*. M0 is the narrowest category and is sometimes called narrow money.

M2 is defined as notes and coins in circulation plus non-interest bearing bank deposits, building society deposits and National Savings accounts.

M3 is defined as M1 plus all other private sector bank deposits and certificates of deposit. M3 is the broadest definition of the money supply and may also be known as broad money. £M3 excludes non-sterling deposit accounts.

M4 is defined as M1 plus most private sector bank deposits plus holdings of money market instruments.

M5 is defined as M4 plus building society deposits.

**Monopolies and Mergers Commission** (MMC) Government organization that monitors *takeover bids* and *mergers* (in the public and national interest) and acts as watchdog over *monopolies* and restrictive trade practices.

**monopolistic competition** Alternative term for *imperfect competition.*

**monopoly** Strictly, an industry with only one supplier. The term is also applied more widely to an industry controlled ("monopolized") by one company, which produces a sufficient proportion of the total output of that industry to effectively control *supply* and therefore *price*. In the UK, monopolies, and mergers or takeovers that might lead to the creation of a monopoly, are subject to the scrutiny of the Monopolies and Mergers Commission.

**monopsony** Industry in which there are many manufacturers but only one customer for the goods produced. By controlling demand the consumer can, in theory, set the price. Monopsonies generally evolve to serve nation states; the market for warships, for example, is a virtual monopsony in that the vessels produced are purchased only by the government of the nation concerned, or by other governments that have its approval.

**moonlighting** Informal term for the practice of having two jobs, one of them generally involving work in the evening or at night.

**moral hazard** In insurance, it is behaviour by the insured that could increase the chance or size of a loss. It includes the inclination to be careless if there is no penalty for so doing (such as car owner with motor insurance who does not take precautions against the theft of the vehicle).

**moral obligation** Obligation, usually to perform some service or complete some transaction, that cannot be enforced in law but which is nevertheless met out of honour.

**moratorium** Grant of an extended period in which to repay a loan, or a period during which the repayment schedule is suspended.

**morbidity** Probability or risk of disability.

**mortality rate** Number of deaths per 1,000 of the population per year; the probability of someone dying at a given age.

**mortality table** Another name for *life table*. It is a table of mortality rates produced by actuaries and providing life assurance offices with the necessary basis for calculation of life and annuity rates.

**mortgage** Transfer of the deeds to a property as *security* for the repayment of a *debt*, e.g. building societies that provide a loan for the purchase of a house take legal possession of the property until the loan and interest have been repaid. It is a temporary assignment, since once the loan plus interest is repaid, the morrgager has the right to have the property reassigned. Types of mortgage include *endowment mortgage*; *pension mortgage*; *PEP mortgage* and *repayment mortgage*.

**mortgage bond** Certificate stating that a mortgage has been taken out and that a property is security against default.

**mortgage debenture** Debenture secured by the mortgage of a property or other asset owned by the institution concerned.

**mortgagee** Person who lends money using a *mortgage* as security.

**mortgage guarantee insurance** *See mortgage indemnity guarantee.*

**mortgage indemnity guarantee** Single-premium insurance to cover a *mortgagee* (lender) for the amount of a mortgage in excess of a certain sum (usually 75% of the value of the property) should the mortgagor (borrower) default on the loan. It is paid for by the *mortgagor* (borrower).

**mortgagee in possession** *Mortgagee* who has taken possession of a mortgaged property, usually because the *mortgagor* has defaulted on repayments.

**mortgage interest relief at source** (MIRAS) Method by means of which income tax relief is granted immediately on *mortgage* interest. It is being phased out.

**mortgage protection policy** Type of life assurance (taken out by a *mortgagor*) that covers the outstanding debt on a repayment mortgage. The sum assured decreases during the term of the mortgage but premiums remain level throughout the payment term.

**mortgagor** Person who takes out a *mortgage* in order to borrow money (usually to buy a property).

**most-favoured-nation clause** In bilateral international trade agreements, clause stating that each country agrees to look upon the other as its "most-favoured" trading partner, thus offering each other the best tariffs, first refusal, etc.

**motor insurance** Insurance taken out by drivers of motor vehicles. Under the Road Traffic Acts, third party insurance covering injury, death or property damage to third parties is compulsory. This cover is often extended to third party fire and theft or comprehensive cover.

**MPL** Abbreviation of *maximum possible loss.*

**multilateralism** Broadly, international trade. Multilateralism is the use of the proceeds of a sale in one country to fund purchases in another. Thus, a nation selling arms to Iran and using the proceeds to purchase weapons in Nicaragua is practising multilateralism.

**multinational** Concerning more than one nation.

**multinational corporation** *Corporation* that has operations and offices in more than one country.

**multiple** Term with three meanings:

1. It is a chain store; a group of shops in numerous locations but selling the similar goods and under one *management* group.

2. It is the factor by which one multiplies the cost of producing a unit of goods, to arrive at a satisfactory selling price.

3. It means manyfold.

*It would contravene the terms of the issue of British Gas shares if one person made multiple applications for the shares.*

**multiple exchange rate** Variable *exchange rate* that some countries quote, often giving a more favourable rate to importers of wanted goods and to tourists.

**municipal bond** Equivalent to a *local authority bond.*

**muster roll** Register of the holders of a *security.*

**mutual** Describing a company owned by its depositors or members but which does not issue *stocks* or *shares.* Many building societies and insurance companies in the UK have this status. They exist for the benefit of their members. Mutuals can change their status to a *public limited company* by *demutualization,* but only with the agreement of their members.

**mutual fund** Alternative US term for *unit trust.*

**mutual indemnity association** Mutual organization that accepts business from members of a particular trade or profession.

**mutual insurance company** Insurance company that is owned by its policyholders. *See mutual life assurance company.*

**mutual life assurance company** Kind of life assurance company owned by its policyholders. It has no shareholders and so all the profits available as surplus are distributed to with-profits policyholders in the form of bonuses.

# N

**Naamloze Venootschap** (NV)  Dutch equivalent of the British *public limited company* (plc).

**naked debenture**  Alternative term for *unsecured debenture.*

**naked option**  Option to buy shares in which the seller of the option (the option writer) does not already own the shares. In this instance, the option writer hopes to buy back the option before it is exercised and so avoid having to supply the shares. If the option is exercised and the market price of the shares has risen, then the option writer makes a loss. An option writer who sells naked options is known as a naked writer.

**naked writer**  *See naked option.*

**name**  Member of a Lloyd's of London *syndicate*, who underwrites insurance business. *Liability* of a name is unlimited.

**NAPF**  Abbreviation of *National Association of Pension Funds.*

**narrow money**  Alternative term for M0. *See money supply.*

**NASD**  Abbreviation of *National Association of Security Dealers.*

**NASDAQ**  Abbreviation of *National Association of Securities Dealers Automated Quotations.*

**NASDIM**  Abbreviation of *National Association of Securities Dealers and Investment Managers.*

**National Association of Insurance Commissioners** (NAIC) US organization made up of *Commissioners of Insurance.*

**National Association of Pension Funds** (NAPF)  Trade association of UK providers of *occupational pensions.*

**National Association of Security Dealers** (NASD)  US organization that issues licenses to people dealing in personal finance and life assurance in the USA.

**National Association of Securities Dealers and Investment Managers** (NASDIM)  Former organization that represented licensed security dealers, superseded by *the Security and Futures Authority* (SFA) and other self-regulatory organizations (SROs) after the 1986 Finance Act.

**National Association of Securities Dealers Automated Quotation**  US equivalent of *over-the-counter market* (OTC), now trading in the UK.

**National Debt**  Debts owed by the government, *i.e.* the sum of government borrowing, covering such things as National Savings, Treasury bills, and government bonds. The US equivalent is called the Federal Debt.

**National Insurance contributions** (NIC)  Payments made by those with earned income into the National Insurance Fund, from which various benefits are paid. There are five classes of contributions:

*Class 1* – primary contributions are paid by employees; secondary contributions by employers.

*Class 1A* – introduced in 1991, it is payable by employers on the taxable value of company cars and fuel provided to employees.

*Class 2* – flat rate contribution paid by the self-employed.

*Class 3* – voluntary flat-rate contributions paid by those who want to make up their contribution record.

*Class 4* – profit-related contributions paid by the self-employed once profit exceeds a certain amount.

**National Insurance Fund**  UK government fund into which the self-employed, employees and their employers pay contributions. The fund is administered by the Department of Social Security (DSS) and provides state pensions and various social security benefits, including invalidity benefit, unemployment benefit, maternity benefit, sickness benefit and widow's benefit.

**nationalization**  Government policy whereby industries previously in private ownership are bought by the state and subsequently controlled by the government. *See also* **privatization.**

**nationalized industry**  Industry that is owned by the state and controlled by the government, which was previously in private ownership. *See also* **privatization.**

**National Savings**  Established in 1969 from the former Post Office Savings Department, this organization offers a wide range of savings schemes and accounts to individual savers. These include *National Savings Certificates* (NSCs), income and capital bonds, *premium savings bonds*, pensioners' bonds and ordinary and investment accounts. Some schemes are tax free, *e.g.* NSCs Schemes are offered through the Post Office.

**natural economy**  Economy in which barter is the most common form of *exchange*.

**natural increase**  Increase in population over a specified time, calculated by subtracting the number of deaths in that period from the number of births. A falling population is therefore subject to natural decrease.

**natural justice**  Rules to be observed by an arbitrator when adjudicating a dispute. Broadly, he or she must act in good faith and demonstrate a lack of bias or personal involvement. All the documents pertaining to the case must be made available to both parties, and no evidence may be presented without each being present. Each party must have an equal opportunity to state its case.

**natural rate of growth**  Used in theoretical economics to describe a rate of growth in an economy that is in equilibrium, *i.e.* an economy with no *inflation* and with unemployment at its natural level.

**natural rate of interest**  Rate of interest at which the demand for and supply of loans is equal.

**NAV**  Abbreviation of *net asset value*.

**nearby futures**  Futures contracts that are closest to maturity. *See also deferred futures.*

**near money**  Liquid asset that can be transferred immediately (such as a *bill of exchange* or *cheque*), although not as liquid as cash. It is also known as quasi-money.

**near-term**  Short term; in the near future. US securities markets have been criticized for near-termism, the practice of examining price performance over a period of days rather than years.

**negative cash flow**  *Cash flow* in which outgoings are greater than income.

**negative easement**  Right of a landowner to prevent a neighbour from exploiting or affecting his or her land.

**negative equity**  Asset that is currently worth less than the money borrowed to pay for it. An all-too-common example is a house whose current market price is less than the remaining value of the mortgage taken out to buy it.

**negative income tax**  (NIT)  System of taxation by which those earning less than a specified income receive tax credits to bring their income in line with a guaranteed minimum income.

**negligence** Tort, defined as a breach of a duty to take reasonable care. Negligence may be displayed by a manufacturer supplying a defective product, a doctor failing to make an accurate diagnosis, by a lawyer who fails to advise his or her client of the law, by a company chairman who fails to consider the interests of his shareholders, etc. A person who has suffered as a result of negligence can claim damages. Individuals and organizations can protect themselves against the consequences of negligent actions by taking out *liability insurance*.

**negotiable** Transferable, or subject to adjustment by negotiation.

*The company made a preliminary bid for the contract, but indicated that their terms were negotiable.*

**negotiable instrument** Document that may be freely exchanged, usually by *endorsement*, and which entitles the *bearer* to a sum of money. Negotiable instruments include *cheques, bills of exchange, certificates of deposit* and *promissory notes.*

**negotiable security** Security that is easily passed from one owner to another by delivery. In the UK, very few instruments are negotiable in this way.

**negotiation fee** Charge made by a bank for arranging a loan.

**net** That which remains after all deductions and charges have been made. *See also gross.*

**net assets** Difference between an organization's assets and its current liabilities.

**net asset value** (NAV) Value of a share in a company. It is calculated by dividing the net assets of the company by the number of issued shares.

**net claims** Claims made after any recovery from reinsurance arrangements.

**net current assets** Difference between current assets and current liabilities, equal to the *working capital.*

**net dividend** Dividend paid to a shareholder which excludes the tax credit.

**net domestic product** Value of *gross domestic product* after a figure for capital consumption has been deducted.

**net interest** Any *interest* paid on a deposit or investment after deduction of income tax at source (such as interest paid into a tax-payer's account at a building society).

**net margin** Difference between the selling price of an article and all the costs incurred in making and selling it.

**net premium** Remainder of the yearly *premium* paid to an insurance company after it has deducted its charges (for such things as brokerage, commission, and so on).

**net profit ratio** Ratio of net *profit* to sales.

**net relevant earnings** Relevant earnings less capital allowances and allowable losses. It is the basis for calculating maximum personal pension contributions.

**net worth** Another term for *net asset value*.

**NEWCO** Company set up to reinsure debts of Lloyd's up to 1985 (the so-called Old Years).

**new for old** Feature of a household insurance policy that meets a claim with a payment equivalent to the cost of total replacement at current (new) prices; there is no deduction for wear and tear, and depreciation. It is not available for articles of linen and clothing.

**new issue** *Stocks* and *shares* that are about to be placed, or have recently been placed on the *open market*. New issues may consist of stock in a recently-established *limited company* or supplementary issues made by established companies.

**new issues market** Alternative term for *primary market*.

**new time** On the London Stock exchange, the last two days of an *account*. Transactions conducted in new time are settled at the end of the next account; therefore, new time is effectively part of the next account period.

**New York Metals Exchange** (NYMEX) Organization that, with the Chicago Metals Exchange, conducts a significant part of the world's hard commodity trading. The two institutions are usually in fierce competition.

**New York Stock Exchange** Main US stock exchange which was founded in 1792 and is based in Wall Street.

**NIC** Abbreviation with two meanings:

1. It is short for *National Insurance contribution*.
2. It stands for newly industrializing country, a country which,

although part of the Third World, has rapidly developed a substantial industrial base. In the 1980s this status was accorded to South Korea and Taiwan.

**niche**  Market or section of a market controlled by an operator who is catering for a well-defined and usually small group of customers.

**Nikkei Average**  Index of share prices on the Japanese Stock Exchange.

**nil paid**  *New issue* of shares for which the issuing company has yet to be paid. The term is most commonly applied to rights issues.

**NIT**  Abbreviation of *negative income tax.*

**NL**  Abbreviation of *no liability.*

**no-brainer**  Fund that tracks the performance of a stock *index.* Its manager buys all the *stocks* listed on a major index, and hence no discretionary management is required. *See also passive management.*

**no-claims bonus**  In household insurance and motor insurance, a payment made if the insured has made no claims against the policy in a year. It usually takes the form of a discount on the next year's *premium.* It is also termed a no-claims discount, and can rise to 60% of a premium if a person has four claims-free years in motor insurance. It is not dependent on blame for an accident so a discount is lost if a claim occurs even if it is not the insured's fault.

**no liability**  (NL)  Australian equivalent of a *public limited company* (plc).

**no-load share**  Share sold at net asset value with no *commission* charge.

**no-loan fund**  Form of US *unit trust* that employs no salesman and therefore incurs no commission or distribution costs. An investor thus avoids paying a commission on shares purchased, the only expense remaining being a relatively modest management fee. *See mutual fund.*

**nominal**  Existing in name only.

**nominal accounts**  One of the three parts into which a book-keeping *ledger* is divided. The nominal accounts are the records of *income* and *expenditure. See also impersonal accounts; personal accounts; real accounts.*

**nominal damages**  Damages awarded by a court which is satisfied that the plaintiff is in the right, but has suffered no actual loss.

**nominal interest rate**  Rate of interest without an allowance for inflation. *See also real interest rate.*

**nominal partner**  *Partner* who lends his or her name to a firm, but who has invested no capital and does not take an active part in the company. He or she remains liable for the partnership's debts.

**nominal value**  Also known as face value, the nominal value of something is the value or price written on it, *e.g.*, the denomination of a banknote or the par value of a share.

**nominee**  Agent, frequently one who purchases shares on behalf of an undisclosed client. *See **nominee shareholder**.*

**nominee shareholder**  Usually an institution that acquires shares in a company on behalf of somebody else (the beneficial owner). This enables the true shareholder's identity to be concealed and is often used when a person wishes to build up his or her shareholding prior to a *takeover* bid.

**non-amortizing mortgage**  *See **balloon mortgage**.*

**non-business days**  Sundays and bank holidays, when banks are closed for business. They are not included in *days of grace*, and *bills of exchange* that fall due on a non-business day are postponed until the next day.

**non-contract market**  Alternative term for *spot market*.

**non-contribution clause**  Clause that removes the requirement for an insurer to pay a claim if the insured is entitled to indemnity under another insurance policy. However, if both policies covering an event each contain such a clause, they cancel each other out and both pay a rateable proportion.

**non-contributory pension**  *Occupational pension scheme* in which the employee makes no contribution. The employer is responsible for paying all of the necessary contributions and offers the pension scheme as a benefit to its employees.

**non-cumulative preference share**  Type of *preference share* for which any unpaid interest (dividend) is not carried over to the next year.

**non-discretionary personal equity plan**  *Personal equity plan* (PEP) in which the *fund manager* acts on the instructions of the investor as to the investment medium.

**non-equity investment**  Any investment in securities except shares in a company (*equity*).

**non-executive director**  Member of the *board* of directors who plays no active part in the day-to-day running of the company. He or she may attend board meetings and offer advice. Non-executive (or outside) directors are often well-known public figures whose appointment lends cachet to a company, or whose presence on the board is valued for their expertise, impartiality or wide-ranging contacts.

**non-forfeiture clause** Clause in a *life assurance* policy that allows it to continue even though premiums have not been paid. Usually the surrender value is used to pay the premiums for a set period, or until the value is exhausted.

**non-marine insurance** All general insurance except for aviation, marine and transport.

**non-marketable securities** That part of a *national debt* not traded on the stock market. Non-marketable securities include *National Savings* Certificates, Premium Savings Bonds, certificates of deposit, official funds in perpetual or terminable annuities, and the whole of the external national debt. About one-third of the total national debt is currently in the form of non-marketable securities.

**non-participating policy** Type of *life assurance* policy in which there is no additional bonus from an investment element. *See also* ***non-profit insurance***.

**non-participating preference share** Type of *preference share* in which holders are paid a fixed dividend before ordinary shareholders but do not receive extra dividends in a very profitable year. It is the usual type of preference share.

**non-performing asset** That part of a company's *capital* that is currently yielding no *return*, and on which none is expected. *Fixed assets* are generally classified as non-performing.

**non-profit insurance** Type of *life assurance* with no investment element included in the policy. On death, only the basic sum assured is paid. It is also known as a ***without-profits policy***.

**non-profit making organization** (NPO) Company or institution that has a legal obligation to make no profit. The term is most usually applied to registered charities.

**non-proportional reinsurance** Reinsurance arrangements in which the reinsurer does not participate pro rata. It includes excess of loss and excess of loss ratio (stop loss) methods.

**non-qualified** Employee share option plan in which the gain made by the employee (*i.e.* the difference between the grant price and the market price) is taxed as *income* and not as a capital gain. *See* **capital gains tax**.

**non-qualifying policy**  Type of *life assurance* policy that does not satisfy the qualifaction rules. Before 1984, a non-qualifying policy would not have qualified for premium relief. The effect of holding a non-qualifying policy now is that policyholders who are higher rate taxpayers when payment is made may be subject to 17% tax on any gain made on the policy. However, basic rate taxpayers have no liability.

**non-resident**  Person who does not live in an area or state, or who lives there but does not meet the legal requirements for residence.

**non-taxable income**  Income which for one reason or another is not subject to normal *income tax*. Non-taxable income includes, for example, save as you earn schemes, statutory redundancy pay, certain profit-related pay, Premium Bond and National Lottery prizes, and the capital element of an annuity payment.

**non-voting shares**  Shares that carry no voting rights. Non-voting shares are issued to raise additional capital for the company, while permitting existing shareholders to retain control of the company. Such shares are often known as A-shares and generally rank *pari passu* with voting shares in respect of other rights.

**no par value** (NPV)  Describing shares that have no stated value, but are valued at the current stock exchange price.

**normal market size** (NMS)  Method of classifying shares, introduced in 1991, equal to 2.5 times the average daily customer turnover last year divided by the price of the share. It has replaced the classification into alpha, beta, gamma and delta shares.

**notary public**  Official licensed to attest the validity of documents and of the signatures on them by signing and/or sealing them. Dishonoured or protested bills also require the seal of a notary public.

**note**  Token or proof of a transaction.

**note of hand**  Alternative term for *promissory note*.

**notes to the accounts**  Information that by law must accompany a company's accounts, such as details of assets, debentures, investments, reserves and paid-up share capital.

**notice**  In insurance, advice to a life office of an assignment of a *life assurance* policy. Under the 1867 Policies of Assurance Act, a life office must have a system of recording notices of assignment and must acknowledge the notice given if requested to do so.

**notice in lieu of distringas** Notice issued by a shareholder and supported by a statutory declaration, that formally advises the issuing company of his or her holding. Such notices prevent any attempt by the company to transfer the shares in question to a third party. it is also known as a stop notice.

**notice of assessment** Document issued by the *Inland Revenue* detailing a person's taxable income and the amount of *income tax* payable.

**notice of coding** Document issued by the *Inland Revenue* detailing a person's tax code for *income tax* purposes. A copy is also sent to the person's employer if he or she pays income tax *pay as you earn* (PAYE).

**notice of second charge** *See second mortgage.*

**noting and protest** First two stages in the dishonouring of a *bill of exchange*. The bill is first "noted", or witnessed, by a *notary public*, who thereby testifies to its existence but not necessarily to its validity. It is then presented again, and if refused for a second time it is protested by being returned to the notary, who then testifies to its refusal. Noting must be completed within one working day of the bill's first being dishonoured.

**notional income** Non-financial benefit that an owner receives from an *asset*. The term is most usually applied to the benefit received by the owner-occupier of a property. In such a case, the notional income is equal to the amount that would otherwise have had to be spent on *rent*.

**not negotiable** Description applied to a document that may not be freely exchanged, and to which the holder has no better claim than any previous bearer. Cheques, postal orders and bills of exchange may be crossed "not negotiable" as a safeguard against theft.

**novation** Discharge of one contract in favour of the creation of another, *e.g.* a builder may contract to start work on a certain day, and later notify the client that he or she will be unable to do so. In this case the client may discharge the contract and sign another on the same terms with a second builder.

**novus actus interveniens** Latin for "new act intervening". *See proximate cause.*

**NPO** Abbreviation of *non-profit-making organization.*

**NPV** Abbreviation of *no par value.*

**nuisance** Tort that covers unlawful interference with someone's enjoyment of land, for example, excessive noise or obstruction of light.

**null and void** Phrase used when a contract is invalidated.

*The court ruled that the contract be made null and void.*

**number fudging** Informal term for creative accountancy; the creation of a favourable account sheet without resort to actual fraud. It is also known as window dressing.

**NV** Abbreviation of *Naamloze Venootschap.*

**NYMEX** Abbreviation of *New York Metals Exchange.*

**NYSE** Abbreviation of *New York Stock Exchange*, the largest security market in the United States. *See* **stock exchange**.

**N**

# O

**obligation**  The duty to repay a loan.

**obsolescence**  Loss of the value of something when it becomes out of date. In accounting, obsolescence refers to an asset that has to be written off, not through deterioration, but when its continued use becomes uneconomic, *e.g.* a piece of machinery may be superseded by a new, faster version; it is therefore uneconomic for the company to continue to use it, and the asset becomes obsolete. *See also **wear and tear**; **write off**.*

**obvious damage**  Damage to goods in transit that can be seen from the outside of the packaging. *See also **hidden damage**.*

**occupational pension scheme**  Pension scheme set up by an employer for the benefit of its employees, or certain categories of employees. It can be contributory, where the employee pays a set percentage contribution as well as the employer, or non-contributory, where the employer pays the full amount.

It can be insured with an insurance company responsible for collecting premiums and paying benefits, or self-administered, where the trustees are responsible for all administration.

Occupational schemes can also be either final salary or money purchase, and either contracted-in or contracted-out.

Legally, the occupational scheme must be set up under irrevocable trust, approved by the Pension Schemes office for tax concessions, and approved by the Occupational Pensions Regulatory Authority for contracting out. An employer must contribute to an occupational scheme. *See also **contracted-in**; **contracted-out**; **contributory pension**; **final salary pension scheme**; **insured pension scheme**; **money-purchase pension scheme**; **non-contributory pension scheme**; **self-administered pension scheme**.*

**odd lot**  Collection of **stocks** and **shares** that is so small and varied that they inconvenience the **broker** who agrees to deal them, and which he or she will therefore buy only at a low price. In the USA, an odd lot of fewer than 100 shares are dealt at a higher commission rate than larger quantities. *See also **round lot**.*

**offer**  Statement that one party is willing to sell something, at a certain price and under certain conditions. If a particular buyer is unwilling to buy at the offer price or under the conditions of the offer, he or she may make a *bid* against the seller's offer, called a counter-offer.

**offer by prospectus** In contrast to an *offer for sale*, an offer by a company to sell shares or *debentures* directly to the public by issuing a *prospectus*, instead of selling the shares to an *issuing house*.

**offer document** Document sent to a company's shareholders by the maker of a *takeover bid*, setting out the bidder's point of view and intentions for the company should the bid be successful.

**offer for sale** Offer by a company to sell shares to an *issuing house*, which then publishes a *prospectus* and sells the shares to the public. *See also offer by prospectus; offer for sale by tender.*

**offer for sale by tender** Similar to an ordinary *offer for sale* except that the prospective buyers state the price they are willing to pay for a certain number of shares (above a minimum price specified in the *prospectus*).

**offer period** During a *takeover*, the length of time an offer of shares must remain open (at least 21 days).

**offer price** Price at which a *market maker* is prepared to sell a security. *See also bid-offer spread; bid price.*

**offer to purchase** Alternative term for *takeover bid.*

**offering circular** Document that in the USA contains information regarding offers of shares exempt from *Securities and Exchange Commission* regulations and registration.

**office premium** Premium (or price) charged by an insurer for insurance cover.

**Official List** Formally the Stock Exchange Daily Official List (SEDOL), the official publication of the London Stock Exchange which appears daily at 5.30pm detailing price movements and dividend information for almost all securities quoted on the Exchange.

**official quotations** Figure quoted daily for almost all securities on the Stock Exchange *Official List.*

**official receiver** (OR) *See receivership*

**official reserves** Gold and currency reserves kept by the government. *See gold and foreign exchange reserves.*

**offset** Cancellation of the requirement to deliver commodities sold on a *futures* contract by buying an equal amount of the same commodity for the same delivery period.

**offshore** Describing a business that operates from a *tax haven* (such as the Isle of Man).

**offshore financing** Raising of capital in countries other than one's own.

**offshore fund** Investment scheme operated from a *tax haven,* by which investors may benefit from the haven's taxation privileges without leaving their home country. *See tax shelter.*

**old-age pension** Popular name for the UK state retirement pension paid to women over 60 years and men over 65. Strictly, the term describes a state pension that is paid to people over the age of 80 years.

**Old Lady** Popular name for the *Bank of England. See Old Lady of Threadneedle Street.*

**Old Lady of Threadneedle Street** The Bank of England, situated in Threadneedle Street in the City of London. It is a popular term of endearment dating from the early 19th century.

**Old Years** Business years at *Lloyd's of London* up to (and including) 1985, when heavey losses were made. *See also* **NEWCO.**

**oligopoly** Industry in which there are many buyers but few sellers. Such conditions give the producer or seller a certain amount of control over price, but leave him or her especially vulnerable to the actions of competitors. *See also monopoly.*

**Ombudsman** Official in charge of a complaints and dispute service offered to individuals who are unable to resolve problems directly with their financial institution. Various Ombudsmen exist for different types of financial service, including the Banking Ombudsman, Building Societies Ombudsman, Insurance Ombudsman, Investment Ombudsman, Pensions Ombudsman and Personal Investment Authority Ombudsman. Services offered are independent from the financial institutions they represent and the Ombudsman's decision is generally binding on the institution but not on the individual. Services are offered free of charge to the individual and are ultimately paid for by levies on the relevant financial institutions.

**on call** Describing a repayment that must be made whenever the lender requires it (without notice).

**oncost** Another name for *overheads.*

**on demand**  Describing a *bill of exchange* that is payable to the bearer immediately on presentation, such as an uncrossed cheque.

**one-man**  Describing a business, company or operation involving only on person,

**one-month money**  Money placed on the *money market* that cannot be withdrawn without penalty for one month.

**one-year money**  Money placed on the *money market* that cannot be withdrawn without penalty for one year.

**on-floor**  Describing transactions that are conducted and concluded on the floor of an exchange in the usual manner.

**on-line**  Describing an electronic facility that is connected directly to a computer.

**on stream**  When an asset or investment begins to function, it is said to come on stream.

**open**  Unrestricted or unlimited. Also, to open is to take out a futures option.

**open contract**  Contract that has been bought or sold on a financial futures market, but has not been closed by making an offsetting transaction or taking delivery of the financial instrument involved. *See also open position.*

**open cover**  Form of declaration policy used in marine insurance. Shipments are declared as and when they are made.

**open-end fund**  Alternative term in the US for *unit trust.*

**opening bid**  First bid at an auction.

**opening price**  Price of a share at the beginning of a day's business on a stock exchange. This may differ from the previous evening's closing price, generally because the price has been adjusted to take into account events that occurred overnight and the performance of other exchanges.

**opening range**  On a financial *futures* market, the highest and lowest prices recorded at the opening.

**opening sale**  Sale of an *option* contract where the seller becomes in effect the writer of the option by assuming responsibility for its performance.

**open insurance policy**  Type of *marine insurance* that provides cover for all shipments made during a particular period (as opposed to a single shipment). The nature and value of each cargo must be declared to the insurers.

**open market** Market in which goods are available to be bought and sold by anyone who cares to. Prices on an open market are determined by the laws of *supply and demand*.

**open market option** Right to buy an annuity from the retirement fund of a *personal pension scheme* from any insurance company or friendly society in the market.

**open policy** Another name for an *open insurance policy*.

**open position** Exposed position of a speculator who has bought or sold without making any hedging transactions, and who therefore gambles that the market will rise or fall as he or she predicted.

**operating budget** Alternative term for *cash budget*.

**operating costs** Expenses incurred in the day-to-day running of a company.

**operating margin** *Operating profit* expressed as a proportion of price or operating costs.

**operating profit** Earnings from normal business transactions. It does not include interest on loans or return on other investments.

**operation** Another term for a business (such as a company, partnership or firm) or the activities it undertakes.

*She was called in to mastermind the company's new printing operation.*

**operation of law** If one party obtains a legal judgement on a contract under which the party's liabilities are discharged, the contract is said to be discharged by operation of law, in that the legal requirements of the contract become merged with the requirements of the judgement

**operational (or operations) research** Mathematical technique that can be applied, *e.g.* to discover how the various activities within an industry may be regulated to coexist with maximum efficiency.

**operative clause** Clause in an insurance policy that sets out exactly when the insurer will pay a claim.

**opinion poll** Survey of opinion carried out by interviewing a sample number of people, in person or by telephone, and detailing their preferences and opinions, usually in statistical form. Opinion polls are most commonly associated with politics, but are also widely used by manufacturers and advertisers to assess public taste and preferences.

**OPL** Abbreviation of *overall premium limit*.

**opportunity cost** Cost involved in using an asset (*e.g.* machinery) for one purpose rather than another, *e.g.* a company owning a building which it uses as storage space could rent it to someone else for, say, £500 per week. That sum is the opportunity cost of the building.

**option** An investor may pay a *premium* in return for the option to buy (a *call option*) or sell (a *put option*) a certain number of securities at an agreed price (known as the *exercise price*), on or before a particular date. The dealer may exercise his or her option at any time within the specified period and normally does so at an advantageous time depending on market prices. Otherwise the dealer may allow the option to lapse.

**option dealing** Buying and selling in *options*, which usually involves buying or selling goods or shares at some future date and at a prearranged price.

**option money** Premium paid in return for an *option*.

**options date** Date on which a children's assurance is terminated or converted to a *whole life assurance* or *endowment assurance* in the child's name (often set at the date of the child's 18th birthday).

**option writer** Someone who sells *call options*, thereby agreeing to supply shares, or someone who sells *put options*, agreeing to buy shares.

**OR** Abbreviation of official receiver. See *receivership*.

**order and disposition** In *bankruptcy*, a means whereby a bankrupt's creditors may seize property to which the bankrupt has no title. Order and disposition comes into effect only if title is not obviously someone else's and if the bankrupt has led a third party into believing the goods are his or hers in order to receive credit. See also *bankrupt*; *reputed owner*.

**order-driven** Describing an economy, industry or trading on a stock market that reacts in relation to the flow of incoming orders. See also *quote-driven*.

**ordinary business** *Life assurance* that is not industrial life business.

 **ordinary life assurance** Another term for *ordinary business*.

**ordinary shares** Shares whose holders are the owners of a company. They are entitled to a dividend after other preferential payments have been made (although payment of the dividend is at the discretion of the directors). Ordinary shares are sometimes classed as voting or non-voting shares, and are sometimes also known as equities.

**original documentation** *See* *advance documentation.*

**original terms** Method of reinsuring life assurance business whereby the reinsurance is based on the same rate of premium as the original *cession*. The reinsurer pays a proportion of the commission to the ceding company, and a proportion of any claim.

**OTC** Abbreviation of over the counter. *See* *over-the-counter market.*

**outcry market** On commodity markets, trading is recorded from the outcries of traders on the floor, although deals are sealed by private contract. Markets on which trading is carried on in this noisy manner are known as outcry markets and the style of trading is known as open outcry.

**outgoer** Farmer who accepts financial inducements to turn his or her agricultural land to another function, *e.g.* for leisure pursuits or a caravan site.

**outgoings** Money paid for something; expenditure.

**outlay** Money paid for something; expenditure.

**out-of-the-money option** Option to buy shares (*call option*) for which the market price has fallen since the price was fixed. Equally, it is an option to sell (*put option*) for which the price on the market has risen above the agreed exercise price. In either case, the dealer makes a loss if he or she decides to exercise the option. *See* *exercise price.*

**output tax** In a *value-added tax* system, the tax that is charged by a supplier to a customer. *See also* *input tax.*

**outright buy stock** Stock that is recommended unreservedly by market analysts.

**outside broker** Dealer in *stocks* and *shares* who is not a member of any exchange.

**outside director** Alternative term for *non-executive director.*

**outstanding claims reserves** Funds set aside by an insurer to meet the cost of claims that have been incurred but not yet settled or paid.

**overall premium limit** (OPL) Maximum value of insurance that can be underwritten by a member of *Lloyd's of London.*

**overbought** If there are many buyers on a market, prices (*e.g.* of shares) are pushed to artificially high levels and the market is said to be overbought. *See* **oversold.**

**over-capitalization** Situation in which a company has more capital than it can employ to its profit. *See also* **gearing.**

**overexposure** Overabundance of risk. *E.g.* if a *stockbroker* is paid a salary largely dependent on the performance of a company and maintains a substantial shareholding in the firm, he or she is over-exposed to the possibility of a downturn in the broking business.

**overhead expenses** Term sometimes used for *indirect expenses,* sometimes for *fixed costs,* and sometimes for both. Its precise meaning varies from company to company. *See also* **overheads.**

**overheads** (US **overhead**) Costs incurred in the everyday running of a business and not variable according to output. Also known as indirect costs, fixed costs or supplementary costs, overheads include heating, lighting and energy costs, administration, insurance, rent and rates.

**overheating** Describing an unhealthy economic situation in which bank borrowing, balance of payment deficit, prices and wages are all rising.

**overinsurance** Practice of insuring property or another item for more than it is worth. Overinsurance is futile, because an insurer does not normally pay more than the true value of the thing insured. *See also* *contribution;* **double insurance;** and **underinsurance.**

**overnight loan** Bank loan to a *discount house,* secured by **bills of exchange** and repayable the next day.

**overriding commission** Term with two meanings:

1. Commission paid to a broker in return for finding **underwriters** to an issue of shares. *See* **share issue.**

2. In reinsurance, commission paid to the ceding company which is more than the acquisition cost to allow for additional expenses.

**overshoot** Describing price trends on a currency market that continue to rise above levels anticipated by analysts.

**oversold** Describing a market in which there are too many sellers, so the price falls to an artificially low point, too rapidly. *See also* **overbought.**

**oversubscribed** A sale of shares by *application and allotment* is said to be oversubscribed if the number of shares applied for exceeds the number of shares available. The situation is often remedied by a *ballot*. *See also allotment*.

**over the counter** Something that is legal, above board. *See also over-the-counter market*.

**over-the-counter market** (OTC market) Market on which securities not listed on any stock exchange may be bought and sold. In practice, the OTC market is operated by a limited number of market makers, often on the basis of matched bargains. *See also* **unlisted securities market**.

**over-trading** Describing a potentially dangerous situation in which a company tries to take on more business than its working capital will allow.

**ownership** Basic right to possess something. It should not be confused with possession, for whereas a person may own something, he or she may still lose possession of it, *e.g.* to a bailee or to a thief. *See* **bailment**.

**own life policy** Type of *life assurance* in which the policyholder is both the person who receives the benefits (the grantee or the assuree) and the person whose life is assured. On death, the lump sum payable becomes part of the deceased's estate (and is therefore liable to inheritance tax).

# P

**pa** Abbreviation of *per annum*.

**PA** Abbreviation of *personal account* or personal assistant.

**package deal** Deal that is all-inclusive, *i.e.* one that provides for the settlement of most or all the outstanding issues between the parties concerned.

**package policy** In insurance, a policy in which several different types of cover are packaged together and combined into one policy (*e.g.* household comprehensive insurance).

**packing** Adding, to the payments on a loan, charges for services such as insurance, etc. without the borrower requesting them, or indeed fully understanding what he or she is buying. This practice is illegal.

**pacman defence** Method of defending against a hostile *takeover*, whereby the target company makes a tender *offer* for the shares of the aggressor.

**paid up** Term with two meanings:
1. It is used either as a verb or an adjective to mean that a person has paid the money he or she owes or, more specifically, that he or she has paid a subscription. It is also used to distinguish fully-paid from *partly-paid* shares.

   *After we chased them for two weeks, they finally paid up.*

   *He is a paid-up member of the union.*
2. It is used in life assurance to describe the status of a policy for which no further premiums will be paid and a reduced sum assured is payable. See *paid-up policy*; *paid-up value*.

**paid-up capital** Capital obtained by a share issue in which the shares are fully paid. *See also* **called-up capital; uncalled capital.**

**paid-up policy** *Life assurance* policy where, before the end of the term of the policy, the assured has stopped paying premiums. The policy continues with a reduced sum assured but no further premiums are paid.

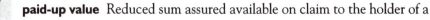

**paid-up value** Reduced sum assured available on claim to the holder of a *life assurance* policy if he or she ceases paying premiums without surrendering the policy.

**painting the tape** Method of creating an impression of activity around a share, by reporting fictitious transactions. Painting the tape is illegal.

**P&I Clubs** Protection and Indemnity Associations. These are associations of shipowners organized to provide mutual aid for members for liabilities not covered by marine hull policies. Each shipowner contributes to the fund on a tonnage basis but could be called upon to make further contributions if claims in a year are heavy.

**paper** Describing any form of *loan*, but particularly a short-term loan such as a *Treasury bill*. It refers to the paper on which a pledge to repay money at a specified time is recorded. Most paper is negotiable and can be bought or sold like any other commodity.

**paper company** Company established, usually with little capital, merely for financial purposes. *See also* **shell company**.

**par** Equal to the face value or current rate. *See parity*

**parcel** Block of shares that changes hands during a *bargain*.

**parent company** Company that owns or part-owns, but more importantly controls, several *subsidiary companies*.

*pari passu* Latin for "with equal step", indicating simultaneous effect, often applied to new share issues. In this context, it means that the designated share will rank equally for *dividends* with comparable existing shares.

**Paris Club** *See Group of Ten*

**parity** Equality (in value).
*It is unlikely that the US dollar will reach parity with sterling.*

**par of exchange** Rate of exchange between two currencies for which there an equal supply and demand.

**parole contract** Simple, unwritten (*i.e.* verbal) contract.

**par priced** Describing a security that is trading at its par value.

**partial loss** In insurance, a term describing only partial damage to property, *i.e.* it is not totally destroyed.

**participating loan** Syndicated loan, for which there are two or more lenders. The lead bank or manager arranges the loan and its terms using agreed contributions from other banks or lenders.

**participating policy**  Type of *life assurance* policy that pays, in addition to a lump sum, a bonus based on investments made by the assurance company. *See* **with-profits policy.**

**participating preference shares**  *Preference shares* that entitle the shareholder to additional dividends or bonuses from the remaining profits of a company if the dividend on ordinary shares exceeds a specified amount.

**particular lien**  The right to take possession of specified *assets* in the event of default. A particular lien cannot be transferred to other goods or assets.

**particular risk**  In insurance, an event such as a fire, injury at work or motor vehicle accident that is personal (in cause and effect), as opposed to a widespread risk. *See also* **fundamental risk.**

**part load**  Portion of the part of the share capital of open-ended investment companies not covered by underlying *assets. See* **share capital.**

**partly-paid**  Describing securities and shares for which the full *nominal value* has not been paid and on which the holder is liable to pay the balance either on demand or on specified dates. Formerly, it was common for a company to *call up* only a part of the nominal value of each share, retaining the right to demand the balance when it became necessary to increase its *capital.* This gave the company access to capital without the need for new share issues. The term also applies to new issues in which the issue price is to be paid in instalments.

**partly-paid shares**  Shares that have not yet been fully-paid for by the shareholder. Many large new issues are paid for in two stages, to avoid liquidity problems for investors. *See also* **fully-paid shares.**

**partner**  Person engaged in a business enterprise jointly with, and generally with the same status and responsibility as, another or others. *See* **partnership.**

**partnership**  Business association, in the UK normally formed by between two to twenty partners. The partners are jointly and severally liable to the debts of the partnership, so that if one partner dies or deacamps, the remainder are responsible for any debts. *See* **deceased partner.**

**partnership agreement**  Written formal agreement between partners which sets out requirements on death, retirement or dissolution of the partnership.

**partnership at will** Partners are normally bound by a formal agreement; if not, the partnership is called a partnership at will, and may be broken at any time by any partner. *See also partnership agreement.*

**par value** Normal price of a share or security. It is also known as face value or nominal value.

**passing a name** Provision to a seller of the name of a potential buyer. A broker often "passes a name" in this way, but rarely guarantees the buyer's solvency when so doing.

**passive management** Form of mutual fund management, increasingly popular in the USA, in which a fund's investments are selected automatically to match the exact performance of the stock index. *See also index tracker fund.*

**patent** Authorization that grants the addressee the sole right to make, use or sell an invention for a specified period of time. Applicants for a patent must establish the novelty of their invention.

**pay-as-you-earn** (PAYE) System of income tax collection whereby tax is deducted from current earnings at source. The employer is responsible for collecting the tax, and the employee receives only *net* wages.

**PAYE** Abbreviation of *pay-as-you-earn.*

**paying agent** Organization that pays capital or interest to holders of bonds, for which the agent may charge a fee.

**payment** Remuneration of someone in money or kind.

**part payment** Interim payment or instalment.

**payment in kind** Payment, generally of wages, made in goods or services rather than in money. Payment of total wages in kind was made illegal in the UK in the 19th century, but part payment in kind is still common, *e.g.*, workers who receive luncheon vouchers or the use of a company car are receiving payment in kind. *See also fringe benefit.*

**payment on account** Part payment of an outstanding debt, usually coupled with an agreement to repay the balance on a specified date. The method is used by the Inland Revenue under self-assessment to collect income tax in two instalments.

**payout** Issue of the money paid to the insured in the event of a successful claim for an article lost, damaged or destroyed.

*He was disappointed that the payout on his insurance claim was so little.*

**payroll tax** Tax on business undertakings, levied in relation to the number of people employed, or as a percentage of the total wage bill. Payroll tax is often used to control the relative elasticities of the supply and demand for labour. Its imposition deters companies from employing more workers than they currently require.

**peculation** Embezzlement, particularly the appropriation of public money or goods by an official.

**pecuniary insurance** Insurance that relates to the loss of money as opposed to property damage. It includes fidelity guarantee and loss of profits insurance.

**pegged exchange rate** Form of floating *exchange rate* in which the value of the currency is pegged between a pre-determined maximum and minimum value.

**pegging the exchanges** Maintenance of a fixed currency *exchange rate*, by government intervention in the markets. Pegging the exchanges is generally resorted to in order to prevent an unfavourable rise or fall in the value of a currency.

**penalty clause** Clause in a *contract* stating that if one party breaks the contract (*e.g.* by late delivery of goods) it will be liable to pay a penalty, usually in money.

**penny shares** Shares in a company that are traded in low denominations (usually under 50p). Penny shares are often highly volatile.

**pension** Regular payment, made weekly, monthly or annually after a person retires from full-time employment, generally for the rest of the pensioner's life. *See basic state pension; occupational pension scheme; personal pension scheme; State Earnings-Related Pension.*

**pensionable earnings** For the purposes of an *occupational pension scheme*, the part of a person's earnings that is used to calculate pension contributions and benefits. Pensionable earnings are often defined as basic salary only.

**pensionable service** Time spent in a particular employment that qualifies an employee for benefits from an *occupational pension scheme*. It may not be the whole length of service, usually because an employee cannot join the pension scheme until he or she reaches a certain age.

**pensioneer trustee** Person authorized by the Pension Scheme Office to oversee the management of a *small self-administered pension scheme* (SSAS). He or she must be independent of the employer.

**pension fund** Pool of money from which *pensions* are paid.

**pension fund withdrawals** Drawing of income from a pension fund rather than purchasing an annuity.

**pension mortgage** Type of mortgage in which the borrower pays back only interest while funding a pension plan that will provide a lump sum to pay off the capital as well as providing a pension at retirement.

**pension scheme** System set up to pay its members a *pension*. *See occupational pension scheme; personal pension scheme.*

**Pensions Ombudsman** Official established in 1990 to arbitrate in grievances between pensioners and their *pension schemes* (excluding state pensions). *See Ombudsman.*

**PEP** Abbreviation of *personal equity plan.*

**PEP mortgage** Type of *interest-only mortgage* funded by a *personal equity plan* (PEP).

**P/E ratio** Abbreviation of *price/earnings ratio.*

**per capita** Latin for "by the head". It usually indicates that a sum will be divided equally among a group. Thus per capita income is calculated by dividing the total income received by a group by the number of people in that group.

**per capita gross national product** Value of gross national product divided by the number of people in the nation's population. It gives an indication of the wealth of the nation and its people.

**per contra** Latin for "by the opposite side". In accounting, an entry on the opposite side of an account or balance sheet. It is therefore a self-balancing item.

**per diem** Latin for "by the day". It usually applies to an allowance, rental or charge made on a daily basis.

**perfect competition** Situation of competition in which the products are perfectly similar, so that the consumer has no preference. There are a large number of producers and consumers, so that any producer who tries to raise the price of a product above market price is undercut by competitors, and consumers only buy at the lowest price. This model is frequently used by economists.

**perfecting the sight** Supplying the full details demanded on a *bill of sight.*

**perfect oligopoly** *Oligopoly* in which the goods being produced by each seller are of the same type.

**performance** Earnings or losses made on a security or by a company.

*This year, the company's performance was poor – it made substantial losses in most areas.*

**performance bond** Bond delivered by a contractor to a public authority for a sum in excess of the value of a contract, and which is to be paid in the event of breach of contract. It is therefore a form of *guarantee*. It is also known as a contract bond.

**peril** In insurance, any event that causes a loss and which may be included or excluded on an insurance policy, *e.g.* an insured peril in a fire policy is fire; an excluded peril is war.

**peril of nature** In insurance, a class of *peril* that includes earthquake, flood, hailstones, storm, thunderbolt and subsidence; such perils are usually covered by property insurance.

**period bill** Fixed-term *bill of exchange* payable on a specified date, and not on demand.

**perk** Abbreviation of perquisite, a casual *benefit*. In general terms it is a *benefit in kind*, but is more specifically applicable to informal rather than formally agreed benefits.

**permanent health insurance** (PHI) Insurance that provides an income should the insured be unable to carry out his or her own occupation (as defined in the policy) due to sickness or disability. The income commences after a *deferred period* and continues until the insured recovers, dies or until retirement. Benefits can be level or increasing but the maximum available is 66% of pre-disability earnings.

**permission to deal** Authorization issued by a stock exchange that permits dealings in the shares of a company. Permission to deal must be sought three days after the issue of a *prospectus*.

**perpetual** Eternal; valid for an indefinite time.

**perpetual annuity** Payment of a constant annual amount in perpetuity.

**perpetual debenture** Debenture that may not be repaid on *demand*.

**perpetual inventory** Running record of all materials, parts or items of stock. Most frequently it is used in retailing, where stock turnover is relatively fast.

**perpetual succession** Continuation of a company after the departure or death of its directors. A company is an individual legal entity which exists irrespective of its personnel, and which ceases to exist in law only after its *liquidation*.

**persistency rate** Proportion of investment contracts that remain in force after a specific period.

**personal** Pertaining to an individual, or private as opposed to public.

**personal accident and sickness insurance** Type of general insurance that provides two benefits: firstly a lump sum on death or injury as a result of an accident; secondly, a weekly sickness benefit for a maximum of one or two years. It is an annually renewable contract.

**personal account** Term with two meanings:

1. On the stock market, it is an account maintained by a dealer on his or her own behalf and at personal risk, independent of the company for which he or she works.

2. In *book-keeping* it is an account that lists *creditors* and *debtors*.

**personal allowance** Amount a person may earn before he or she is obliged to pay *income tax*. This amount may vary from year to year.

**personal annuity scheme** Type of *contributory pension* for self-employed people or those not in an *occupational pension* scheme. *See personal pension plan; retirement annuity policy.*

**personal disposable income** (PDI) Gross income less income tax, National Insurance contributions (NICs) and any other statutory deduction. *See also personal savings ratio.*

**personal equity plan** (PEP) Government scheme, dating from 1986, that encourages people to invest in *equities*. PEP investments can include unit and investment trusts. Corporate-bond PEPs, introduced in 1995, allow investment in fixed-interest securities. The growth and proceeds from a PEP are completely free of income and capital gains tax. In 1997 the government announced that PEPs would lose their tax-free status in 1999, at which time the new *Individual Savings Accounts* (ISAs) will be introduced.

General PEPs invest in the shares of more than one company. The maximum limit per investment is £6,000 per tax year. Single-company PEPs contain shares of one company only and have a limit of £3,000 per tax year. PEPs can be *managed* (by a fund manager), **self-select** (the investor makes the decisions) or advisery (a stockbroker advises the investor).

**personal equity plan mortgage** Type of *pension mortgage* in which the pension element is a *personal equity plan* (PEP).

**personal equity plan share exchange scheme** Type of *personal equity*

*plan* (PEP) in which the *fund manager* will accept shares or unit trusts as contributions to the PEP.

**personal insurances** Types of insurance pertaining to an individual, *e.g.* motor, household, health insurance.

**Personal Insurance Arbitration Service** Organization for resolving disputes between policyholders and insurance companies, introduced by the *Insurance Ombudsman.*

**Personal Investment Authority** (PIA) *Self-regulatory organization* (SRO) established in 1993 that oversees businesses dealing with private investors. It took over responsibilities of the *Financial Intermediaries, Managers and Brokers Regulatory Association* (FIMBRA) and the *Life Assurance and Unit Trust Regulatory Organization* (LAUTRO) in 1994. It is to be incorporated into the *Financial Services Authority.*

**Personal Investment Authority Ombudsman** Official established to resolve complaints against PIA members. *See Ombudsman.*

**personal lines insurance** Any general insurance bought by individual people and households, such as household buildings and contents, accident and sickness, motor, travel, etc.

**personal loan** Loan made (usually by a bank, but now increasingly by registered brokers) to a private individual. This form of loan is generally fairly modest and intended for some specific purpose, such as the purchase of a car.

**personal pension scheme** Arrangement that allows someone to contribute part of his or her earnings to an insurance company or other pension provider, which invests the money in a *pension fund.* The lump sum that becomes available on retirement purchases an *annuity*, which provides the pensioner with regular payments. It is therefore a *money purchase scheme.* Part of the fund at retirement can be taken as a tax-free cash lump sum, but this is restricted to 25% of the fund. The pension annuity income is taxed in full as earned income. *Appropriate personal pensions* (APPs) can be used to contract out of the *State Earnings-Related Pension Scheme* (SERPS). The benefits from a personal pension are not limited (except for the tax-free cash sum), but contributions to the plan are restricted to a percentage of *net relevant earnings*, the percentage ranging from 17½% to 40%, depending on age.

**personal reserve** Profits from underwriting insurance made by a member of *Lloyd's of London*, held in trust with his or her funds at Lloyd's.

**personal savings ratio** For an individual, one hundred times total earnings divided by total *personal disposable income.*

**PET** Abbreviation of *potentially exempt transfer.*

**petties** Abbreviation of *petty cash,* used most commonly on an invoice to denote charges made for various small items not separately enumerated.

**petty cash** Money in notes and coins kept for payment of small bills and day-to-day expenses. *See also float.*

**petty cash book** Book in which *petty cash* transactions are recorded.

**PHI** Abbreviation of *permanent health insurance.*

**physical hazard** Physical features of a risk that increases the chance or size of a loss, *e.g.* a thatched roof or proximity to a river.

**physical risk control** Techniques and physical operations used by a *risk manager* to reduce the size and/or frequency of potential losses.

**PIA** Abbreviation of *Personal Investment Authority.*

**pipeline premiums** For an insurance company, *premiums* relating to risks that are written but not closed.

**pit** On a commodity exchange, the equivalent of a stock exchange *trading floor.* It derives from the local nickname for the floor of the Chicago Commodities Exchange. Now, a pit is the floor of any open outcry exchange.

**pitch** Area in which a trader operates.

**placement** Process of issuing shares through an intermediary, usually a stockbroker or *syndicate.* The intermediary "places" the shares with clients, frequently institutional investors, or with members of the public. A certain proportion of any share issue quoted on the London Stock Exchange must be made available to the public through the Exchange.

**placing** Security issued to raise new capital in a placement. Stockbrokers acting on behalf of the company concerned "place" shares by selling them to financial institutions and to the public. The term is also used as a synonym for *placement.*

**plain English policies** Insurance policies that are written in everyday language to aid understanding by the policyholder.

**planned economy** Economy in which some or all economic activity is planned and undertaken by the state, directly or indirectly, irrespective of the market forces of *supply and demand*, and without *private enterprise*. *See also controlled economy.*

**PLC** Abbreviation of *public limited company*, also expressed as plc.

**pledge** Transfer of personal property from a debtor to a creditor as security for a debt. Legal ownership of the property concerned remains with the pledger. *See also pawnbroker.*

**pluvius insurance** Alternative name for *weather insurance*.

**point** Unit of price in which *stocks* are traded. One point generally equals £1 or $1.

**poison pill** Technique used by companies facing a hostile *takeover* bid to make their stock as unattractive or inaccessible as possible. Stock may be diluted by new issues and company articles changed to require the approval of a greater proportion of the shareholders for the takeover. Expensive subsidiary companies may be purchased to reduce the attractiveness of the company's balance sheet, and provision is often made for *greenmail* payments and for *golden parachutes*.

**Polaris** Computerized system that interchanges data which enables non-direct insurers and brokers to do *personal lines* insurance business.

**polarisation** Requirement under the 1986 Financial Services Act that all persons advising on investments (as defined in the Act) must be either tied to one particular company (and sell only its products) or be totally independent (give recommendations from all companies in the market).

**policy** Term with two meanings:

1. It is an agreement that a group of people (e.g. a company) will, in certain circumstances, act in a certain way.
   *It was the store's policy not to give refunds on any goods.*
2. In insurance, it is a document setting out exactly the terms of the insurance contract. *See insurance policy.*

**policy fee** Flat fee charged on an insurance policy. It can be added to the basic premium or deducted from the premium before allocating units.

**policyholder** Person who has an *insurance policy*; it is usually the insured person or the grantee.

**policy loan** Loan from a life office against the security of an endowment policy. The loan is limited to 90% or 95% of the surrender value accrued.

**policy proof of interest** (PPI)  Type of *insurance policy* most common in marine insurance. In the event that the contingency insured against actually occurs, the holder of a PPI need not suffer material loss in order to claim against the policy; possession of the policy itself is regarded as sufficient proof of interest.

**policyholder's funds**  Part of the insurance fund set aside to cover any outstanding liabilities. *See also* **technical reserves**.

**Policyholder's Protection Board**  Organization set up by the 1975 Policyholder's Protection Act to compensate private policyholders in the event of an insurance company's winding up. In the case of compulsory private insurance, the Board pays 100% of the liability; for other general and long-term insurances, a sum equal to 90% of the liability (or benefits in the case of life assurance) is provided. The Board can also arrange for a cash injection to prevent insolvency or a transfer of business to another insurer.

**policy schedule**  *See* **schedule**.

**policy underwriter**  In marine insurance, the person who signs his or her name on a policy, thereby validating it. The term is also used for a member of a *syndicate* of *underwriters* at Lloyd's of London.

**ponzi scheme**  Scheme in which investors are paid off by using capital from the investments of later investors. A ponzi scheme is fraudulent.

**pool**  Organization of insurers and reinsurers through which particular risks are written. Premiums, losses and expenses are shared in agreed proportions, usually fairly small percentages. Pools exist for extremely hazardous risks such as nuclear risk.

**pooled investment**  Investment in which many small amounts paid by individuals are pooled together to spread the risk and gain the advantages of economies of scale. Examples include *unit trusts* and *investment trusts*.

**popular capitalism**  Capitalism that has reached a large number of the country's population, through increased personal investment, growth in small businesses, proliferation of profit-sharing schemes, etc.

**porcupine provision**  Provision written into a company's *articles of association*, or into a corporate charter or bylaw, designed to act as a deterrent to hostile *takeovers*. An example of a porcupine provision is the *poison pill* defence.

**portable pension**  Description applied to a pension that can be taken from job to job, employment to self-employment and vice versa. The term is used to describe an advantage of a personal pension or *free-standing additional voluntary contributions*.

**portfolio** Selection of securities held by a person or institution such as a bank or insurance company. Portfolios generally include a wide variety of *stocks* and *bonds* to spread the *risk* of investment, and the contents of a portfolio are managed – that is, continually changed in order to maximize income or growth. *See* **managed fund**.

**portfolio analysis** Technique of strategic analysis used to distinguish the characteristics of different business units in a multi-business corporation.

**portfolio insurance** Protection for a *portfolio* of investments provided by financial *futures* and *options*. Decisions about buying and selling these are made by the *fund manager*.

**position** In general terms, the place of an investor in a fluctuating market.

**postdate** To affix some future date to a document, thereby preventing the occurrence of actions or transactions concerning that document before the specified date.

**post-entry** Events or developments that occur after a company's entry into a stock market.

**Post Office** Organization responsible for the UK postal services and, through its 20,000 post offices, the payments of pensions, social security benefits, etc. This aspect is run by Post Office Counters Ltd. Its branches are used as outlets for *National Savings* products.

**potentially exempt transfer** (PET) Transfer of a gift from one individual to another, or certain types of trust (disabled, accumulation and maintenance or interest in possession) which does not attract inheritance tax immediately. Tax is only paid if the donor dies within 7 years of making the gift and then on a sliding scale. Once the donor lives for 7 years, the gift becomes fully exempt. *See* **inter vivos policy**.

**pot is clean** Term that indicates that all shares allocated during an issue for offer to institutional investors have been taken up.

**power of attorney** Legal agreement giving one person the authority to act in legal matters on behalf of another.

**power lunch** Substantial lunch, over which large deals are often finalized.

**PPI** Abbreviation of *policy proof of interest*.

**preamble** Clause in an insurance policy that gives the basic essentials of a contract. It is also known as the recital clause.

**precautionary savings**  Savings invested in very "safe" media (such as bank deposit accounts, building societies and National Savings) for meeting unforeseen needs.

**pre-emption**  Right to purchase shares before they become generally available, usually offered in the case of new issues to existing shareholders. Rights of pre-emption are often proportional to the value of an existing holding.

**preference**  Prior right; the superiority of one person or thing over another.

**preference shares**  Also known as preferred stock, preference shares offer the shareholder preferential claims to dividends, usually at a fixed rate, and a prior claim to ordinary shareholders on the company's assets in the event of *liquidation*. The market price for preference shares tends to be more stable than that of ordinary shares. Preference shareholders may not vote at meetings of ordinary shareholders. Preference shares fall into five categories: cumulative, non-cumulative, redeemable, participating and convertible. *See also* ***participating preference share.***

**preferential creditor**  Creditor entitled to repayment before the debts of other creditors are met. Secured creditors have preference over unsecured creditors, and in the case of the liquidation of a company, payment of outstanding taxes and salaries have preference over the settlement of debts.

**preferred ordinary shares**  Ordinary shares that carry additional rights, usually in respect of payment of dividend.

**preferred stock**  Alternative term for *preference shares.*

**preliminary expenses**  Costs incurred during the formation of a company, including registration and promotion.

**preliminary statement**  Announcement of a company's full year results made a month or two before publication of its annual report.

**premium**  Very broadly, a price, payment or bonus valued higher than the norm. The term has a number of specific meanings:

1. It is used to describe the payments, usually annual, made to an insurance company to maintain an *insurance policy.*
2. It is the difference between the offer price of a new share issue and the price at which it begins trading, if the latter exceeds the former. The term is also used to describe the positive difference between the face value and redemption value of any stock or bond.

**premium holiday** Short period during which a *life assurance* policyholder is allowed to miss paying premiums (rather than allow the policy to lapse), although there may be a consequent reduction in benefits.

**premium income** Income that an insurance company receives from *premiums* on *insurance policies.*

**premium pool** In insurance, an arrangement whereby a single *broker* generates business for a group of insurance companies.

**premium rating** Calculation of the insurance premium on a risk.

**premium receipt book** Record of industrial life policyholder's premium payments kept by the insured.

**premium relief** *See life assurance premium relief.*

**Premium Savings Bonds** *National Savings* product that gives purchasers a stake in a lottery. Bonds are bought in multiples of £10 and offer regular draws for holders for tax-free prizes. Bonds are repaid at their face value at any time.

**Premium Trust Fund** (PTF) Fund into which *underwriters* at *Lloyd's of London* must put premiums and from which liabilities are met.

**prepaid expense** Money already paid out (such as an insurance premium) that will not be treated as an expense until a later accounting period.

**prepayment** Payment made in advance. When applied to a *bill of exchange*, prepayment is the payment before the bill matures, and in the context of mortgages it is the repayment of the debt before its maturity.

**pre-placement** Activity that takes place before a share issue has been placed.

**pre-refunding** Practice of issuing shares to re-fund (*i.e.* pay for debts that are about to mature), not immediately before maturity of the old issue, but in advance of it, in order to take advantage of good *interest rates.* *See also refinancing.*

**present value** Assessment of the current net *cost* or value of future expenditure or benefit. Most frequently it is used to measure return on *capital* investment.

**preserved benefits** Pension benefits accrued in an *occupational pension scheme* that the employee has left. Preserved benefits are not paid until retirement, although they can be transferred to other types of pension scheme.

**preserved pension**  Another name for a *deferred pension*.

**president**  Chief executive of a US company, equivalent to a *managing director* in the UK.

**pre-tax profit**  Profit calculated before allowance has been made for tax.

**price**  Cost of purchasing a unit of goods or services. Very broadly, prices are generally set by the manufacturer and retailer, taking into account all *fixed costs* and *variable costs* and allowing for a *profit* margin.

**price earnings ratio**  Known also as the P/E ratio, a way of measuring the demand for a particular share equal to the market price of an *ordinary share* divided by the *earnings per share*.

**prices and incomes policy**  Government policy for controlling wages and prices as a means of checking *inflation*. Five prices and income policies have been operated in the UK since World War II, all but one of them Labour governments acting with the sometimes reluctant co-operation of the trade unions.

**price/earnings ratio**  (P/E ratio) Market price of the shares of a company compared to the dividends those shares produce.

**pricing**  Method used to set a *price*, specifically by equating supply with demand.

**primary capital**  Capital that is used in the start-up of a business. *See also venture capital*.

**primary commodity**  Commodity that is essential to a nation, *e.g.* food, fuel and raw materials for industry.

**primary dealer**  Regulated dealer in US *government securities*.

**primary market**  Market in a new securities issues, also known as the new-issues market. *See also secondary market; tertiary market*.

**prime**  Of high quality. In finance, the term is most often used to describe the debts incurred by a person or firm with a good credit rating.

**prime entry**  In international trade, describing imported goods on which customs *duty* is levied as soon as they enter the country, and which are impounded until the duty is paid. *See also books of prime entry*.

**prime rate**  Preferential interest rate charged in the USA for short-term loans made to people or organizations with a high credit rating. It is approximately equivalent to the *minimum lending rate* in the UK.

**principal** Term with two meanings:

1. It is a person who gives instructions to an *agent*.
2. In finance, it is the original sum invested or lent, as distinct from any profits or interest it may earn.

**private** Describing a person or institution that is independent of the public or government sector.

**private enterprise** Undertaking by an individual or a private group working without significant support from the state.

**private company** Company whose shares are not available to the general public through the medium of a stock exchange, and whose members do not exceed 50 in number.

**private medical insurance** (PMI) Type of insurance that covers the policyholder for the expense of having private medical treatment. It is sometimes offered as a *perk* to a company's senior employees. *See also medical insurance.*

**privately held** Describing a company, capital, company or other possessions in the hands of a person or group of people.

**private pension** Pension scheme outside any state scheme by which people provide a pension for themselves or pay into a *pension plan* provided by others.

**private placing** Sale of the whole of a new issue of shares to a financial institution.

**private sector** That part of the business activity of a country that is financed and controlled by individuals or private companies (e.g. shareholders or investment institutions). *See also privatization.*

**privatization** Practice of offering shares in previously national industries, for sale to the general public. During the 1980s and 1990s Britain's Conservative government privatized several national industries including: British Aerospace, British Gas, and British Telecom.

**probability** Likelihood that an event will occur.

**probate** Acceptance of the validity of a will by a proper authority. A will that has not been probated has no legal force. A grant of probate is the document issued by the probate registry to confirm that the will is valid.

**probate price** In finance, a share price calculated for tax purposes by taking the lower of the bid and offer prices and adding to it one-quarter of the difference between the two. This process is known as quartering up.

**produce exchange**  Alternative term for a *commodity exchange*.

**product**  That which is produced, either in terms of goods or services, or in terms of income.

**product diversification**  Decision to begin the manufacture of new products, usually by horizontal or vertical diversification. The main purpose is to lessen the risk of commercial failure caused by a sudden fall in demand for a particular product. Diversification is also attractive to companies dependent upon seasonal or cyclical business.

**production**  Broadly, practice of manufacturing goods for sale.

**production costs**  Alternative term for *manufacturing costs*.

**products-guarantee insurance**  Type of insurance that covers a manufacturer or supplier for failure of a product to fulfil its intended function and to replace or repair a defective product. *See also* **products-liability insurance**.

**products-liability insurance**  Type of insurance that covers a manufacturer or supplier against claims for compensation made by purchasers of a faulty product (such as an electric appliance that electrocutes someone). The policy covers compensation that the insured is legally liable to pay to customers who are killed, injured or have property damaged as a result of the defect. Legal costs are also covered.

**products recall insurance**  Type of insurance that covers the cost of recalling a defective product from the market. It is often combined with *products-liability* and *product-guarantee* insurance.

**professional**  Originally, a member of one of the professions (*e.g.* medicine, law, accountancy). Increasingly the term is used to describe someone paid to do a job or perform a duty, particularly one requiring special skills or long training, or merely someone who takes his or her job seriously.

**professional indemnity insurance**  Type of *liability insurance* that covers a *professional* against claims for damages resulting from professional negligence, *e.g.* a doctor would use professional indemnity insurance as a protection against legal action brought as a result of alleged incorrect diagnosis or treatment.

**professional reinsurer**  Reinsurance company that does not offer insurance direct to the public. It specializes in reinsurance only.

**profit** Surplus money, after all expenses have been met, generated by a firm or enterprise in the course of one accounting period.

**profit-and-loss account** Annual summary of a company's financial operations, required by law to be submitted by every trading company. The profit-and-loss account has three sections: the trading account, the profit-and-loss account and the appropriation account. The profit-and-loss section of the account takes the profit or loss figure from the trading account, and after accounting for income not concerned with trading and expenses such as those incurred in administration, deducts *tax* from the final profit or loss figure. *See also account.*

**profit commission** Additional *commission* payable by a reinsurer depending on the results of business ceded under a treaty.

**profit margin** Gross *profit*, usually expressed as a percentage of net *sales*, or as simple *net* profit. Company policy generally specifies some profit margin below which it is hardly worthwhile producing goods.

**profit-sharing** Distribution of some or all of a firm's profits to its employees as a *bonus*. The distribution may be in the form of cash or shares.

**profit-taking** Selling stock and taking the profit on the transaction, instead of waiting for a better price. Profit-taking occurs when dealers believe that the market will not improve much more, at least in the short term.

**pro forma invoice** Form of invoice submitted before goods are despatched and used to confirm an order and to advise of despatch.

**projection** Estimate of future developments made on the basis of, or projected from, a knowledge of past and present events.

**promissory note** Document that states that a person promises to pay a certain sum of money on a certain date. It is also known as a note of hand.

**promoter** Entrepreneur, especially a person involved in the organization or launch of a business.

**proof of loss** Requirement in insurance that, once a loss has occurred, the insured is under an obligation to produce evidence of loss to the insurer.

**property** Legally, property is divided into real and personal property. Real property may be defined as land and buildings held freehold. Personal property consists of other personal possessions. More specifically, property is sometimes defined as something appreciating in value or yielding income.

**property company** Company that develops, invests in or trades properties (buildings).

**property enterprise trust** Form of *mutual fund* that invests solely in *enterprise zone* properties in order to gain tax advantages for its investors.

**property insurance** Type of insurance that provides cover against the loss of or damage to any kind of *property* (often up to a stated maximum limit). The property may be personal possessions, buildings or industrial plant.

**proportional reinsurance** Method of reinsurance in which reinsurers take a proportion of the insurer's premium and pay that same proportion of any loss. It includes *surplus* and quota share reinsurance.

**proposal** Form filled in a by a person wanting to take out insurance. Innaccuracies or omissions (accidental or deliberate) in a proposal may invalidate any insurance policy issued. *See also* **utmost good faith.**

**proprietary insurance company** Insurance company that is a *limited company* and owned by its shareholders, as opposed to a *mutual company*, which is owned by its policyholders.

**pro rata** Latin for "in proportion", *e.g.*, the total amount of dividend received by a shareholder is pro rata to his or her holding. *See also* **pari passu.**

**prospectus** Document that describes a proposal, *e.g.* issued to prospective shareholders by a company intending to make a public issue of shares, giving details of past and present performance and of prospects. In insurance, it is a document that details the extent of policy cover and which incorporates a proposal form.

**protected bear** Alternative term for *covered bear.*

**protected rights** Benefits provided under an *appropriate personal pension* or a *contracted-out money-purchase scheme* in place of the *State Earnings-Related Pension Scheme.* They represent the money purchase value of the rebates paid and are subject to special rules.

**protected transaction** Transaction, generally made in faith, that occurs after a company goes into liquidation or a person is declared bankrupt. A protected transaction cannot be nullified by the liquidator.

**protectionism** Policy based on self-interest, *e.g.* one that shields an industry from overseas competition, usually by the imposition of selective or general *quotas* and tariffs. *See also* **tariff barrier; dumping.**

**provision** Allowance for some eventuality. In insurance, an insurer may put aside reserves as a provision for future claims.

**proximate cause** In insurance, the immediate effective cause of an insured loss. It was defined in the case of *Pawsey v. Scottish Union & National* as "the active efficient cause which sets in motion a train of events, which brings about a result, without the intervention of any force, started and working actively from a new and independent source".

**proxy** Authorization given by a voter to another person to allow that person to vote on his or her behalf, *e.g.* a shareholder may give someone proxy to vote at a company meeting which he or she is for some reason unable to attend.

**prudence concept** In accounting, the prudence concept calls for the exclusion on the *balance sheet* of all monies or goods owed but not yet received, and the inclusion of all liabilities, whether or not they must be met immediately. It is, therefore, a *worst-moment concept*. *See also accounting principles.*

**prudent insurer** Hypothetical insurer who is in possession of all relevant information (material facts) before issuing an insurance policy. *See also proposal.*

**PSBR** Abbreviation of *public sector borrowing requirement.*

**public** Describing something that is the hands of the people and, as such, managed or controlled by the government; or that which is open to anyone.

**public liability insurance** Type of insurance that covers the insured's legal liability to pay compensation to a third party or member of the public in the event of injury, death or damage to a third party's property. It also covers legal costs.

**public limited company** (PLC or plc) Company whose shares are available to the general public through a stock exchange.

**public sector** That part of the business activity of a country that is financed and controlled by the government. Public sector industries are often known as *nationalized industries.*

**Public Sector Borrowing Requirement** (PSBR) Difference between the government's expenditures and receipts, generally financed mainly by issuing *gilt-edged securities* and other long-term loans.

**public sector liquidity** Obsolete measure of the *money supply.*

**public trustee** Person appointed by the state who undertakes to act as a trustee, executor, or investment adviser to any member of the general public.

**puisne mortgage** Mortgage issued despite the failure of the lender to take possession of the title deeds to the property offered as security for the loan. The lender may instead register the property with the Land Register or the Land Charges Register; this ensures that any transaction concerning the property must have the approval of the lender.

**pull** Colloquial for to withdraw, *e.g.* to cancel a deal just as it reaches the final stages of negotiation.

**pullback** After a period when market prices have been fluctuating erratically, the movement or return to more recognizable and predictable trends.

**purchase** To buy something, or the thing that has been bought.

**purchased life annuity** Type of *annuity* that pays an income for life (after a specified date) in return for the payment of a single *premium*.

**pure competition** Alternative term for *perfect competition*.

**pure demand** Demand that may not be expressed by purchase for a variety of reasons.

**pure endowment** Type of *life assurance* policy that pays a specified sum if the policyholder is alive on a specified date. No payment is made if he or she dies before then.

**pure risk** In insurance, a risk that can result in either a break-even situation, or a loss.

**put** *See put option.*

**put band** Period for which a *put option* is valid.

**put option** Option to sell shares, commodities or financial futures at an agreed price on or before an agreed future date.

**put-through** Stock exchange dealing procedure used in cases of very large orders, whereby a stockbroker finds both a buyer and a seller and is therefore able to "put the shares through the market" in a single quick transaction.

# Q

**qualifying life assurance policy** Type of *life assurance* policy, which has to meet various conditions, whose proceeds are free from tax liability. Policies effected before 14 March 1984 are eligible for *life assurance premium relief* if qualifying.

**qualifying period** Time during which a valid insurance policy does not provide cover (or gives only part cover), such as a six-month period on a redundancy insurance before which claims in respect of redundancy are not allowed.

**qualifying shares** Fixed number (or percentage) of shares a person must hold before he or she is entitled to a position on the board of directors or a bonus issue.

**quantum meruit** If a supplier only half-completes the work he or she has been contracted to do, the suppler may in some cases claim payment in proportion to the work completed, known as payment quantum meruit (as much as he has earned).

**quarter day** Four days that are generally taken to mark the quarters of the year. Traditionally these are the days on which payment such as rent are made. In England and Wales, the quarter days are Lady Day (25 March), Midsummer Day (24 June), Michaelmas (29 September) and Christmas Day (25 December).

**quartering up** *See probate price.*

**quasi-contract** Contract that is either verbal or partly voidable, which a court decides is enforceable in part.

**quasi-equity** Loan stock or debt *instrument* that offers its holder rights and benefits similar to those offered to the holders of shares. *See loan stock.*

**queue (or queuing) theory** Mathematical theory that can be used to analyse the problems involved in the physical provision of services, taking into account the arrival of customers, the time they have to wait to be served, how they queue, how long the service takes to be rendered and the length of time a service unit remains idle. It is especially useful in the design of such establishments as airports, banks, etc.

**quick assets** Another term for *liquid assets.*

**quid pro quo** Literally, this for that. The principle of quid pro quo under-lies all contracts in that a contract is an agreement to exchange some-thing such as services in return for something else, such as cash.

**quiet time** Time between the registration of a new share issue and its being offered for sale.

**quorum** Minimum number of people who have to be present at a meeting for it to go ahead and the decisions made by it to be valid. In the UK, the quorum for a members' meeting is noted in a company's articles of association.

**quota** Amount of something (*e.g.* goods) allowed to one person, or company, normally fixed by a body in authority.

**quota share** Form of *proportional reinsurance* in which the reinsured amount is expressed as a percentage and premiums and claims are shared according to the same percentage.

**quota share treaty** Agreement between an insurer and reinsurer that all risks will be reinsured on a percentage basis. *See treaty.*

**quotation (quote)** Term with two meanings:
1. It is an *estimate* of how much something will cost. In *life assurance*, a quotation is called an *illustration*.

*I have asked our suppliers to quote on the job in hand.*
2. It refers to the *Official List* of the stock exchange. Appearance of a company's shares on this list is known as a quotation.

**quotation spread** The difference between the *offer price* and the *bid price* on a security. It is also known as the *bid-offer spread.*

**quoted company** Company that has received listing on a stock exchange. The shares of such a company may thus be traded on the open market. *See Official List.*

**quoted investment** In accounting, an investment in shares or debentures that are quoted on an official exchange.

**quoted price** Price of a security as it is quoted on an exchange. The quoted price may fluctuate from day to day, or even minute to minute.

**quote-driven** Describing a stock market that reacts (in terms of prices) to the quotations of market makers rather than to the number and flow of incoming orders. *See also order-driven.*

**quote machine** Computer that allows a broker access to up-to-the-minute information on quoted prices.

# R

**R & D** Abbreviation of *research and development.*

**raid** To buy significant numbers of a company's shares, sometimes as a prelude to a takeover bid.

**raider** Person or group initiating a hostile *takeover* by buying quantities of the *target* company's shares.

**rally** Rise in market prices after a period when prices have stagnated or consistently fallen, usually followed by a further fall. *See also reaction.*

**random walk theory** Theory of stock movements developed in the 1950s and 1960s, which states that share prices move in a random way, and so their movements up or down cannot be predicted. Later this theory was developed into the Efficient Market Hypothesis. *See also higgledy-piggledy growth.*

**rate** Amount of money charged or paid, calculated according to a certain rule or ratio. In insurance, it is the sum a policyholder pays an insurance company, usually stated per £100 or £1000 of *cover.*

**rate of exchange (exchange rate)** Rate at which the various currencies are exchanged for each other.

**rate of interest (interest rate)** Amount charged for loan services, normally expressed as a percentage of the loan, or the amount paid to an investor or lender (*see rate of return*).

**rate of return** Amount of money made on an investment (in the form of interest or a dividend), normally expressed as a percentage of the amount invested.

**ratification** Official approval, giving something (*e.g.* a document) validity.

**rating** Grade assigned to *e.g. bonds* or preferred *stocks* by an official agency such as Standard & Poor's or Moody's, in order to guide investors. *See also beta; triple-A rating.*

**ratio** Way of comparing quantities using proportions.
*The ratio of men of marriageable age to women of marriageable age will shortly become two to one.*

**reaction** Fall in market prices after a period of continuous price rises. *See also rally.*

**real accounts** On a book-keeping *ledger*, the record of *assets* and *capital*. *See also* **nominal accounts**.

**real interest rate** Actual interest rate minus current inflation rate, a more accurate indicator of the likely yield of an investment. *See also* **nominal interest rate**.

**realization account** When a company is being wound up and its assets are being realized in order to pay creditors, or a partnership is being dissolved, a bank account may be opened in which to deposit receipts and upon which to draw payments to creditors. This is known as a realization account.

**realize** To put a plan into action, or sell assets for cash; the act of doing so is realization.
*He had to realize his assets in order to pay his creditors.*

**realty** In insurance, land (as opposed to personality, which comprises personal assets).

**real value** Value of something when compared to fluctuations in price indexes, *i.e.* during times of *inflation* or *deflation*, *e.g.* the real value of a 10% wage increase at a time of 5% inflation is only 5%, because the cash represented by the 10% increase will only buy 5% more goods. *See* **retail price index**

**rebate** Sum of money returned to a payer because he or she has paid too much, or a discount on the price of something.
*At the end of the year you will receive a tax rebate.*

**rebuilding costs** Usual method of calculating a sum insured under a buildings policy. The Royal Institute of Chartered Surveyors publishes costs of rebuilding in different areas of the UK.

**receipt** Note stating that money has been paid or that goods have been received, such as a wharfinger receipt.
*If you leave your watch with the jeweller to be repaired, make sure you get a receipt.*
*See also* **warrant**.

**receipts** Payments received (as opposed to expenditure).

**receiver** *See* **receivership**.

**receivership** A receiver is an official into whose hands a company with financial difficulties is placed, to ensure that, as far as possible, the creditors are paid. Thus, receivership is the company's state when a receiver is called in.

*After several attempts at solving their financial problems, the company went into receivership.*

**receiving order**  Court order placing a company into the hands of a receiver.

**recession**  Stage in a trade cycle during which the decline in economic activity accelerates, causing investment values to fall, companies to have to deal with adverse trading conditions, and unemployment to rise and so income and expenditure to fall. A recession may end in a *depression* unless there is a *recovery*.

**reciprocity**  Practice of requiring incoming reinsurance business in exchange for reinsurance.

**recognizance**  Contract between a court and a person by which the person is bound to perform a certain act, such as to appear in court on a certain date, to be of good behaviour so as not to cause a breach of the peace, or to stand bail for someone else.

**recognized investment exchange** (RIE)  Market for securities recognized by the UK *Securities and Exchange Commission* (SEC).

**recommendation**  Normally refers to financial advice, *e.g.* the recommendation of a market analyst to a broker or of a stockbroker to a client.

**recommended retail price** (RRP)  Price at which a manufacturer suggests goods should retail. The RRP is often specified on the *packaging* to indicate to the customer that the retailer is not overcharging him or her and to allow a comparison to be made between the prices of competing brands. *See also* **retail**.

**reconciliation**  Act of making two accounts, statements or people agree.

**reconciliation statement**  Report that explains why two accounts do not agree.

**recourse agreement**  In *hire purchase* transactions, agreement that enables the seller to repossess the goods in the event of the purchaser being unable to make the payments required.

**recovery**  Upturn in the economy, the financial position of a company or in share prices. *See also* **boom**; **depression**; **recession**.

**recovery shares**  When a company's performance is improving after a period of difficulty, its share price is likely to go up. Shares in such a company are known as recovery shares.

**recovery trust**  Type of trust invested in low-priced *equities* (on the supposition that the company's fortunes will improve).

**rectification of register** If a court believes that an official list (*e.g.* a company's list of its shareholders) is incorrect it may make an order, known as a rectification of register, to have the list amended.

**red** To be in the red is to be in *debt*; to have an *overdrawn* account.

*At the end of last quarter, the company went into the red.*

**redemption** Repayment of an outstanding loan or debenture stock by the borrower.

**redemption date** Date on which a *loan* or *debenture* is to be repaid. Redemption dates (plural) are those on which a *stock* is redeemable at par. In the case of Treasury stocks, the precise date of repayment is decided by the government. *See also parity.*

**redemption fee** *Premium* paid to shareholders who surrender redeemable shares when asked to do so by a company.

**redeemable preference shares** *Preference shares* that the issuing company has the right to redeem, *i.e.* buy back under special circumstances.

**redemption price** Price at which forms of indebtedness (*e.g.* bills of exchange or bonds) are redeemed by the institution or government that issued them.

**redemption yield** Refers to *bonds* with a fixed *redemption date*. Redemption yield takes into account capital gain upon redemption plus the dividend, and relates them to the market price of the bond.

**red herring** On Wall Street, an initial prospectus for a share issue, circulated before the price has been fixed and the issue has been ratified by the appropriate regulating authority.

**red ink** Appearing on a balance sheet, red ink shows that a company is making a loss, has debts or has greater liabilities than assets.

**reducing balance depreciation** Method of accounting for depreciation by calculating it in a period as a fixed proportion of the residual book value of an *asset* at the start of the period.

**re-export** To import goods from one country and to then export them to another.

**refinancing** Taking out a loan to pay back other borrowing. It is also known as refunding in the USA.

**reflation** Government action that attempts to boost a country's economy.

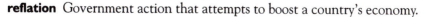

This is done by increasing the money supply, usually by reducing interest rates and taxation. *See also* **deflation**; **inflation**.

**refugee capital**  Foreign funds invested in a country that is politically more stable. *See also* **flight capital**.

**refunding**  Another term for *refinancing*

**register**  Official list, normally of names.

**registered bond**  Bond that is registered in the name of the holder. It may be transferred to another holder only with the consent of the registered holder. *See also* **bearer bond**.

**registered stock**  Alternative term for *inscribed stock*.

**registered office**  Address of a company as listed on the register of companies at Companies House. This need not be the actual working address of the company.

**register of charges**  List of charges payable by a company on its property, such as mortgages. A copy of this list must be filed by all UK companies at Companies House in London.

**Register of Companies**  List of UK companies kept at Companies House in London, detailing registered addresses and names of directors.

**register of debentures**  List drawn up by a company of those people who hold *debentures*

**regulated loan**  Loan of £15,000 or less, regulated by the 1974 Consumer Credit Act, that is not exempt under the 1974 Finance Act (which exempted loans for the alteration, improvement, purchase or repair of a private dwelling). *See also* **cooling-off period**.

**reinstatement of the sum assured**  After a claim has reduced the amount of cover provided by an insurance policy, the payment of an extra premium to bring it up to its previous amount. If the claim was for total loss, the whole original premium must be paid again.

**reinstatement value**  In insurance, the cost of restoring an asset in the event of a loss (which may exceed the current market value of the asset).

**reinsurance**  Transfer of an insurance (or part of the risk covered) from one insurance company to another for a premium, not necessarily with the knowledge of the policyholder.

**Reinsurance and Insurance Network** (RINET)  Computer network that allows the interchange of data between insurance companies in EU countries.

**reinsurance brokerage** Deduction made from a reinsurance premium by the reinsurance broker as commission for business placed.

**reinsurance to close** (RITC) Method used by a *syndicate* at *Lloyd's of London* to carry over future liabilities to the next year. Legally, each syndicate must be reformed annually, and so it pays a premium to reinsure its existing policies for the "new" syndicate.

**relevant benefits** To gain the approval of the Pension Schemes Office, an *occupational pension scheme* must provide only relevant benefits, which include benefit payable on retirement or death.

**relevant earnings** Basis of eligibility for *personal pension scheme*. It means income from self-employment or employment not covered by an occupational scheme.

**relative efficiency** A company is relatively efficient if it combines, distributes, allocates or uses limited resources more effectively than a rival. Thus if two firms have the same input but different outputs, the firm producing the larger output is said to be the more efficient of the two.

**relative strength** Usually expressed as a ratio, the relative strength of a share, commodity or anything else traded on the markets or elsewhere, is the performance of the particular investment compared to the performance of its market *index*. *See also* **beta**.

**relief** Help; normally referring to allowances made to certain taxpayers for various reasons. *See* **tax relief**.

**rendu** Form of contract by which an exporter pays to have goods delivered to a buyer's warehouse. It is also known as a franco or a free contract.

**renewable increasable convertible term assurance** (RICTA) Term *life assurance* contract which incorporates renewable, increasable and convertible options.

**renewable term assurance** Term *life assurance* contract for 5 years, with the option to renew at the end of the term for a further 5 years without medical evidence.

**renewal notice** Document sent by an insurance company to the insured reminding him or her that the next *premium* payment on an existing policy is due.

**rent** Money paid for the occupation or use of something for a period of time (*e.g.* a building, office, factory, car or television set). *See also* **lease**.

**rent back** To sell one's property (offices, factory space, etc.) on the understanding that the new owner will lease back the property to its original owner. It is a good way to raise capital by realizing property assets without having to vacate the premises.

**renunciation** Act of giving up ownership of shares.

**repatriation** Act of transferring capital from overseas to the home market.

**repayment mortgage** Mortgage in which repayments consist of interest payments and a contribution towards the repayment of the capital.

**replacement cost** *See replacement value.*

**replacement value** Amount paid by an insurance company to replace an insured item exactly as it was when lost or damaged. It is the item's replacement cost. *See also* **new-for-old**.

**replevin** In a case of *distraint*, the return of goods to their owner while the court is deciding whether the distraint was lawful.

**repo** Abbreviation of repossession, or of *repurchase agreement*.

**report** Verbal account or document that describes and explains a state of affairs or an incident that has taken place.

**repressed inflation** Alternative tern for *suppressed inflation*.

**repudiation** Act of informing the other party in a *contract* that one does not intend to honour the contract. Repudiation may also refer to the repayment of a debt, or to the termination of any form of agreement.

**reputed owner** Person who acts as the owner of a property, even if he or she is not. If the reputed owner becomes bankrupt, the property is divided among the creditors. *See also* **bailment**; **estoppel**; *order and disposition*.

**repurchase** Situation that occurs when an issuer buys its own securities. It is most frequent in *unit trust* holdings.

**repurchase agreement** (repo) Transaction between a *bond* dealer and a bank. The dealer sells government *securities* while at the same time agreeing to buy them back at a specified time at a price high enough to allow the bank a profit margin. In this way, the repo may be looked upon as a form of loan.

**resale price maintenance** Practice whereby a supplier refuses to sell goods to a retailer unless the retailer agrees to sell them at a certain price, or above a minimum price. Resale price maintenance may be applied to prevent retailers from using the product as a *loss leader*. Resale price maintenance is allowable under the 1976 Resale Prices Act if the supplier can prove that it is in the interests of the consumer, as in the case of books and some pharmaceuticals.

**research and development** (R & D)  Activity that aims to discover or invent new products or services. It covers pure scientific and technical research, applied research, product improvement and technological innovation.

**reserves**  That part of a company's profits that are put aside for a particular purpose.

**reserve for bad debts**  Money put aside against the possibility of unpaid debts.

**reserve for obsolescence**  Money put aside to cushion a company against the possibility of its *fixed assets* becoming obsolescent or uneconomic.

**reserve price**  Minimum price for shares sold by tender. See *offer for sale by tender*.

**resolution**  When a motion put before a meeting has been agreed upon, it becomes a resolution.

**restitution**  Either the giving back of something to someone or a compensatory payment.
*The court ordered the restitution of the property to its owner.*
*The court ordered the vandal to make restitution for the damage he caused to the building.*

**restraint order**  Court order preventing a person or organization from doing something.

**restrictive**  Describing something that sets limits on something else.

**restrictive covenant**  Agreement between two parties that restricts the activities of one, *e.g.* it may take the form of a *clause* in a *contract* to supply goods, that stops the supplier selling goods to a competitor of the second party. A restrictive covenant may not be upheld legally if it is seen to be against the general good (*e.g.* against the interests of free competition).

**restrictive endorsement**  Endorsement that restricts the negotiability of a document.

**restrictive (trade) practice**  Agreement made between two companies that aims to make restrictions regarding the supply of their goods, on such things as price, quantities, processes, geographical area, etc. On the whole, restrictive practices are assumed by the law to be against the public interest.

**retail** Sale of goods or services to the general public.

**retail price** Price at which a good or service is actually sold through a retailer.

**retail price index** (RPI) Analysis of trends in retail prices, expressed as an index number and used to evaluate changes in *retail prices* with reference to *inflation.*

**retained benefits** Pension benefits in respect of a previous period of employment or self-employment. It includes *deferred pensions, transfer plans* and *personal pensions.*

**retained earnings** That part of a company's post-tax earnings not distributed to shareholders, and thus retained by the firm to finance the day-to-day running of the company and any future expansion. Retained earnings are added to reserves and hence appear on the firm's *balance sheet.*

**retained profit** Profit remaining to a firm after the distribution of dividends and profit-sharing bonuses. Retained profit is generally used for the long-term expansion of the business, and is sometimes referred to as undistributed profit.

**retention** Holding back money to be used for a particular purpose. In reinsurance, it is the part of the risk that remains with the direct insurer.

**retention money** A buyer may hold back some of the payment due on completion of a contract, for a certain period of time, to allow him or her to check for possible defects in the work. The sum of money is known as retention money.

**retentions** Shortened form of either *retained earnings* or *retained profits.*

**retire a bill** To withdraw a *bill* from circulation by having the acceptor pay it, either on or before the due date.

**retirement annuity policy** (RAP) Individual pension arrangement that was the forerunner of a personal pension before 1 July 1988. Existing RAPSs can be increased but no new ones could be established after this date.

**Retirement Pension Forecast and Advice** (RPFA) Department of Social Security (DSS) service that provides advice to people about their forecast state pension entitlements.

**return** The comeback: profits and income from transactions or invest-ments. It may also be a document (usually describing a financial situa-tion) sent to an authority. *See return on capital; tax return.*

**return on capital** Measure of how well a company's capital is used, equal to 100 times the trading profit (before tax and interest) divided by the average capital used.

**revaluation** Practice whereby a company puts a new value on its *fixed assets*, because *nominal values* and *real values* of such assets as prop-erty and machines have changed. Revaluation is also a change in the exchange rate of a currency so that its value against other currencies increases. *See devaluation.*

**revaluation reserve** Reserve fund raised by a company by revaluing assets (at market price or replacement cost). Funds can also be raised by issuing shares at a premium above their par value.

**revenue** Money received from any transaction or sale, or money received by the government in the form of taxation.

**revenue account** Accounts of a business that state the amount of money received from sales, commission, etc.

**reversal** Change in a company's fortunes (from being profitable to being unprofitable, or vice versa).

**reverse arbitrage** Paying off a bank overdraft by borrowing from the money market. *See arbitrage.*

**reverse takeover** Purchase of control of a public company by a smaller, private company. This is often done in order that the private company may obtain a listing on the Stock Exchange.

**reverse yield gap** Situation in which low-risk assets provide greater returns than high-risk assets.

**reversion** Term with two meanings:
1. It is the return of property, goods or rights to their original owner.
2. It is the difference between the amount owing on a mortgage and the market value of the property (*i.e.*, the *equity* in the property).

**reversionary bonus** In life assurance, a bonus paid to the holders of a with-profits policy, related to the profitability of the assurance company. *See also annual bonus.*

**RICTA** Abbreviation of *renewable increasable convertible term assurance.*

**rider** Term with two meanings:

1. It is an addition to a document that follows logically from what has gone before. *See also* ***endorsement.***
2. It is an additional benefit added to a *life assurance* policy, *e.g.* disability rider.

**RIE** Abbreviation of *recognized investment exchange.*

**rigging the market** Action that influences a market, by overriding market forces, *e.g.* it may be done by one dealer buying a substantial number of shares or a significant quantity of a commodity, thus pushing the market up.

**right of resale** A seller may, in certain circumstances, reclaim goods from a buyer and resell them, *e.g.* if a stoppage in transaction or a *lien* occurs and the goods are likely to perish as a consequence. In this case, the seller may sell to another buyer and give a lawful title to the goods.

**rights issue** Practice of offering existing shareholders the opportunity to buy more shares (*i.e.* subscribe more ***capital***), in order to raise additional capital. Rights issues act as a protection for the shareholder, in that the total number of shares issued increases without decreasing the percentage holding of each shareholder.

**RINET** Abbreviation of *Reinsurance and Insurance Network.*

**ring** In general, a group of people who get together in order to illegally rig the market, *e.g.* by acting in concert to push prices up or down. *See also* ***bidding ring***; ***concert party***; ***rigging the market.***

A ring is also a method of trading on the London *futures* market or metals exchange. *See **ring trading.***

**ring trading** Method of trading adopted on the London Metals Exchange, whereby dealers sit in a ring and trade by open outcry. *See also **outcry market**; **ring.***

**risk** Amount a person or company potentially stands to lose by a transaction, used particularly of an insurance contract.

**risk arbitrage** Practice of buying in to a takeover bid in the expectation that share prices will rise.

**risk avoidance** Any action that removes the chance of an adverse outcome happening.

**R**

**risk capital** Capital invested in a company, or security, that presents a risk (*i.e.* the possibility of loss or, indeed, gain). The term is also used as an alternative term for *venture capital.*

**risk control**  In insurance, measures adopted to minimize the effect of an insurable *risk,* either before or after a *loss* occurs.

**risk excess**  In insurance, a working excess of loss cover, usually restored to cover risks written on a direct or facultative basis.

**risk identification**  Process of identifying all possible events or activities that could cause or enhance a loss.

**risk management**  Programme of identifying, measuring and controlling risk. It includes measures adopted to minimize financial risk (*e.g.,* through insurance, *hedging* or spreading the risk).

**risk manager**  Person working for a company or institution who organizes and administers its insurance cover, both within the company and in any dealings with clients or other people outside the company.

**risk measurement**  Assessment of the impact of possible losses.

**risk premium**  Term with two meanings:

1.  It is the difference between the forward *exchange rate* of a currency and the expected future *spot rate.*
2.  In reinsurance, it is a method of revising life business where only the death risk (not the reserve) is covered.

**risk reduction**  Measures that could reduce the chance of losses occurring or the size of such losses.

**risk retention insurance**  Policy of bearing a risk because it would cost more to insure against it than the loss itself.

**RITC**  Abbreviation of *reinsurance to close.*

**Road Traffic Act cover**  Minimum motor insurance cover required under the Road Traffic Act. It consists of insurance against third party and property damage.

**rollover**  Movement of an investment from one institution to the owner of another institution.

**roll-over relief**  Reduction in *capital gains tax* on the sale of a company's fixed assets if it is buying other assets in order to replace the first ones. *See also deferred taxation.*

**roll-up fund**  Offshore investment that reinvests interest so that it becomes part of the capital, thus conferring tax advantages.

**rotation of directors** Process whereby at each *annual general meeting* (AGM) of a public company, a certain proportion of the directors retire (normally one third), although they may then be re-elected to the board. This enables shareholders to change a director without having to dismiss him or her.

**round lot** Number of (possibly mixed) shares or bonds traded at the same time, as a lot. The *commission* charged on a round lot is usually slightly less than on an *odd lot*.

**round trip** On the futures market, the practice of buying and then selling the same investment or vice versa.

**round turn** An entire *futures* transaction from start to finish.

**royalty** Sum paid to an inventor, originator or author, or owner of something from which a product may be made (such as an oilfield), and calculated as a proportion of the income received from the sale of the product.
*She is still receiving royalties on a song she wrote ten years ago.*

**RPI** Abbreviation of *retail price index*.

**running ahead** Personal trading in a share by a broker immediately before following a client's instructions to do the same. It is illegal in the USA. *See also* **tailgating**.

**running broker** Someone who acts as an intermediary between those who issue *bills* and the *discount houses*.

**running costs** Alternative term for *operating costs*.

**running margin** Difference in rates of interest on money borrowed and on the same money invested.

**running the books** Job of a *lead manager*, at the head of a *syndicate*.

**running yield** Alternative term for *interest yield* or *flat yield*.

**run off** Term used to describe the situation where a reinsurance contract has ended, but a liability remains in respect of *cessions* accepted during the period of reinsurance.

# S

**SA** Abbreviation of *société anonyme.*

**safe investment** Investment certain to yield the expected *return.*

**salary** Money paid to an employee, normally expressed as so much per year, but usually paid by cheque or directly into the employee's bank account on a monthly basis. *See also wage.*

**salary sacrifice** In pensions, the giving up of remuneration in exchange for an employer's contribution to a pension scheme.

**sales audit** Method of calculating the state of the *retail* trade, by comparing the throughput of money against stock.

**sales journal** In book-keeping, an account book in which the record of a sale is first made.

**salvage** Rescuing people or property from a flood, fire, shipwreck or other disaster. A person who salvages goods may be paid compensation by their owners or insurers. The ownership of some salvaged goods can be a contentious issue.

**sandbag** Defensive tactics for a *takeover bid*, by which the *target company* agrees to negotiate a takeover, but lengthens talks in the hope that a *white knight* may ride by in the meantime.

**sans recours** *See without recourse*

**saturation** Situation in which something is completely full.

**save as you earn** (SAYE) UK government savings system whereby a proportion of a person's income is deducted at source and transferred to a *National Savings Bank* account.

**savings** Money put aside by individuals, often in a way that pays *interest.*

**savings and loan** US equivalent of a UK *building society.* It is also known as a *building and loan association.*

**savings certificates** *See National Savings Certificate.*

**SAYE** Abbreviation of *save as you earn.*

**S**

**scarce currency**  Alternative term for *hard currency*.

**schedule**  In insurance, a key part of an insurance contract that gives details of the insured, limit of liability, period of cover, premiums, and type of cover. It also states the policy number and any special conditions. *See also* **insurance policy**.

**scheduled territory**  Official name for those countries that have tied their currencies to sterling by keeping it as their *reserve currency*. It is also known as the sterling area.

**scorched earth**  Defensive tactics for a hostile *takeover bid* in which the *target* company sells its most attractive assets, or initiates adverse publicity about itself in an effort to make it seem a less than desirable acquisition.

**SCOUT**  Abbreviation of *shared currency option under tender*.

**scrip issue**  Practice of issuing extra shares to existing shareholders free of charge. This is done by transferring reserves into the company's share account. In this way, the company increases its capitalization while at the same time reducing its share price and increasing the number of shares on the market. It is also known as a bonus issue, capitalization issue or free issue.

**SDR**  Abbreviation of *Special Drawing Rights*.

**SEAF**  Abbreviation of *Stock Exchange Automatic Exchange Facility*.

**seasonal variations**  Statistical variations that occur during a particular season. These variations are often taken into account when calculating *e.g.* unemployment figures and trends. In these cases the figures are said to be seasonally adjusted.

**SEAQ**  Abbreviation of *Stock Exchange Automated Quotations*.

**SEATS**  Abbreviation of *Stock Exchange Alternative Trading Service*.

**SEC**  Abbreviation of *Securities and Exchange Commission*.

**secondary market**  Market in securities that have been listed for some time, rather than new issues. Secondary market trading occurs on the stock exchange. *See* **primary market**; **tertiary market**.

**second mortgage**  Additional *mortgage* on a property that is already mortgaged, granted only if the property has sufficient value to act as security for both loans.

**second via**  Second (duplicate) document in a *bill of exchange* in a set, that is sent by a different route to avoid loss. *See **bills in a set**.*

**secret ballot**  Vote conducted by having voters mark their ballot papers in secret, as opposed to a public show of hands or other form of ballot.

**secret reserves**  Alternative term for *hidden reserves.*

**sector**  Part of the national economy or any business activity.

**secured creditor**  Bank or other creditor that has a legal charge on one of the debtor's assets. *See also **preferential creditor**.*

**secured loan**  Loan that is advanced against some asset (the security) of the borrower. In the event that the loan is not repaid, the creditor has rights to the security.

**securities**  *See security.*

**Securities and Exchange Commission** (SEC)  Organization established in 1934 that regulates the securities market (brokers and stock exchanges) in the USA.

**Securities and Futures Authority** (SFA)  *Self-regulatory organization* (SRO) established in 1991 to regulate the conduct of people who deal in debentures, futures, options and shares. It was formed by combining the functions of the Securities Association (TSA) and the Association of Futures Brokers and Dealers (AFBD). It is to be incorporated into the *Financial Services Authority.*

**Securities and Investment Board** (SIB)  UK financial watchdog, set up in 1986 by the Department of Trade and Industry to oversee the UK's deregulated financial markets. It is due to be replaced by the Financial Services Authority. The US equivalent is the *Securities and Exchange Commission* (SEC).

**securities swill**  Informal US term for securities that are worth virtually nothing.

**security**  Term with two meanings:

1.  It is anything (usually property) pledged as *collateral* against a loan, or the document that sets out the terms of such collateral.

2.  It is any financial *instrument* that is traded on a stock exchange and that yields an income. Securities represent a loan that will be repaid

**S**

at some time in the future. In this sense the word is most often used in the plural, and securities include **bills of exchange, bonds, debentures, gilt-edged securities, options, shares** and **stocks**.

**SEDOL** Abbreviation of Stock Exchange Daily Official List. *See* **Official list**.

**seed capital** Capital used to determine whether a proposed project is viable.

**seed money** Money lent as *venture capital* to a company that is very young.

**self-administered pension scheme** Pension scheme that is administered by the company itself, rather than insured or third-party administered. Often larger schemes will be administered "in-house", although trustees may call in investment consultants or actuaries to give advice on certain aspects.

**self assessment** Scheme introduced in 1996 by the Inland Revenue that makes a tax payer responsible for calculating his or her liability for income tax. The calculation can, however, be delegated to the Revenue.

**self-employed retirement annuity** Type of deferred *annuity* available before July 1988 and restricted to self-employed people, proprietors of and partners in businesses, and employed people who are not eligible for a joint pension scheme. *See* **retirement annuity policy**.

**self-employment** Being in business on one's own account. The self-employed include those who run their own businesses, either alone or in partnership, and professional people such as doctors.

**self-insurance** Result of a decision to stand the risk of a loss than pay a *premium* to an insurance company to cover it. It is used by large organizations which set aside a fund to meet losses. It is not really insurance at all.

**self-invested personal pension** (SIPP) Type of *personal pension scheme* in which the investor makes his or her own investment decisions. It is run by a professional manager.

**self-liquidating** Describing something that has a predetermined life and liquidates itself at the end of that period. In the investment trust sector, for example, a *closed-end fund* with a stock exchange listing is self-liquidating.

**S**

**self-regulatory organization** (SRO) In the UK, a non-governmental organization that governs a particular area of business activity, laying down codes of practice and protecting consumers and investors. The SROs under the Financial Services Act include the *Investment Management Regulatory Authority* (IMRO), *Personal Investment Authority* (PIA) and *Securities and Futures Authority* (SFA).

**self-select personal equity plan** Type of *personal equity plan* (PEP) in which the investor selects the investments that make up the *portfolio*.

**sell at best** Instruction to a broker to sell shares or commodities at the best price possible. *I.e.* if the broker is selling, he or she must find the highest selling price. If the broker is buying, he or she must find the lowest price.

**seller's market** Market that is more favourable to sellers than to buyers. Such a market often arises when demand is greater than supply.

**seller's option** On the New York Stock Exchange, an option that enables the seller to deliver the relevant *security* at any time within a period of 6-60 days.

**selling out** If a person who has agreed to buy shares cannot close the deal, the seller is entitled to sell the shares for the best price possible and then charge the person who made the original tender the difference between the selling price and the original tender price, and any costs.

**selling short** Practice of making a bargain to sell securities or commodities the seller does not own. The seller does this in the hope that that before settlement is due, the price of the item will go down and he or she will be able to buy enough to cover the bargain at a lower price, thereby making a profit. The practice is also known as shorting or short selling. *See also* **short bear**.

**sell-side** Those people who are on the market to sell, rather than to buy.

**seller** Person who exchanges goods or services for money.

**sellers over** Market in which there are more sellers than buyers.

**sell price** Alternative term for *cash price*.

**senior debt** Oldest existing debt owed by a person or company, hence, the one that will be paid first, *ceteris paribus*.

**SEPON** Abbreviation of *stock exchange pool nominees*.

**sequestration** Act of seizure of property or other assets by the courts until a dispute has been settled.

**S**

**SERPS** Abbreviation of *State Earnings-Related Pension Scheme.*

**serious ill health** Describing a situation in which life expectancy is un-questionably short, normally less than 12 months. In such a case, an *occupational pension scheme* can pay all the member's pension benefits immediately as cash, subject to a tax charge of 20%.

**service** Something provided, usually for a fee, that may not be classed as manufacturing or production in any form (such as legal advice, broker-age, agency services, etc.).

**service a debt** To pay interest on a *debt.*

**service economy** The total output of the service, or tertiary, sector of an economy. It is also an economy that is based on services rather than manufacturing industries.

**service industry** Businesses engaged in the service, or tertiary sector, such as a shop, restaurant or hairdressing business.

**servicing a loan** Paying the interest due on a loan.

**set of bills** Alternative term for *bills in a set.*

**set-off** In accounting, two parties that have an indebtedness of the standing to each other may set off both debts against each other by assuming that one debt has paid off the other and *vice versa.* This is known as a set-off.

**settlement** Act of paying in full for goods or services received, or of repaying a debt.

**seven-day money** Funds that have been invested in the money market for seven days.

**SFA** Abbreviation of *Securities and Futures Authority.*

**share** *See shares.*

**share broker** Broker who charges commission on each share, rather than on a total transaction. *See also value broker.*

**share capital** Capital raised by a company through an issue of shares. *See also authorized capital; issued capital; uncalled capital.*

**share certificate** Document that proves a person's ownership of a com-pany's shares.

**shared currency option under tender** (SCOUT) In situations where a foreign currency contract is under tender from several companies,

SCOUT allows them to share a single *hedge* in the form of a currency *option*.

**share economy**  Aggregate value of companies quoted on the stock exchange. It is also known as "Quoted UK plc". It is also an economy in which many people are shareholders.

**share exchange**  Alternative term for *stock exchange*.

**share exchange scheme**  Arrangement by which investors can use an existing portfolio of shares (instead of cash) as an investment in an *investment trust* or *unit trust*.

**shareholder**  Person who holds *shares* in a company.

**shareholder democracy**  Either the notion that each shareholder is entitled to a vote, or the principle that as many people as possible hold shares in public companies and thus have a say in their management.

**shareholder derivative suit**  Legal action taken in the USA, by a share-holder or a group of shareholders, against the directors of a company for mismanagement or breaches of responsibility.

**shareholder relations**  Department within a US company, rather like customer relations, that concentrates on keeping shareholders up-to-date with company performance, etc.

**shareholder's equity**  Equity held by shareholders rather than by the company itself.

**shareholder's funds**  Money held by insurance companies that is not tied to liabilities to policyholders. It is also known as free reserves.

**share index**  Index that shows the average change in value of a number of individual shares. Share indexes therefore give an overall guide to movements in the financial markets. Examples include the Financial Times Stock Exchange 100 Index (FOOTSIE), the Nikkei-Dow Average and the Dow Jones Industrial Average.

**share issue**  A limited company wishing to raise *capital* may issue a number of shares, each worth a fraction of the company's total value. The shares are placed on the market by a *stockbroker* acting on behalf of the firm in question and many, in most cases, are purchased by financial institutions, other companies and private individuals. *See also* **issued capital**; **issuing bank**; **issuing house**.

**share option**  UK scheme that gives the employees the option to buy shares in their company at attractive prices (normally well below market price) at a specific future date. *See also **popular capitalism**.*

**share premium** On a new issue of shares, a premium charged on the *nominal value* of the shares if it seems that the *real value* is likely to be much higher.

**share pushing** Hard selling of shares that may be worthless to investors.

**share register** Register of shareholders that is held by a company, giving names, addresses, details of shareholding, etc.

**shares** Form of security that represents the shareholder's stake in a company. Income on shares is in the form of a dividend rather than interest and is declared depending on the company's performance over the year. In the USA shares are known as common stock.

**share shop** Government-appointed bank, building society or stockbroker which deals with shares in a newly privatized industry. For the duration of the public share offer, share shops sell shares directly to the public without a commission charge (which the government pays to the shop).

**share split** If the market price of a share is thought to be too high, a company may decide to issue extra shares to its holders (known as a *bonus issue*), increasing the number of shares on the market, and thus decreasing the price of each share. This process is known as a share split.

**share warrant** Certificate of ownership of shares, presented after shares are fully-paid.

**shark** Informal term for a person or company that may be preparing for a *takeover bid*.

**shark repellent** Informal term for a *defensive tactic* in the event of a *takeover bid*.

**shark watcher** Consultant who studies the buyers of a company's shares in an effort to identify possible *sharks*.

**shell company** Company that does not produce anything in the usual sense, but exists only in name. Shell companies may be set up and sold to people who are unfamiliar with the procedure for doing this, or may be the remnants of a defunct company that has been sold on to someone else. They may also be set up for use at some future time, or to operate as the holder of shares. *See also **paper company**.*

**shelter** Investment instrument that gives little in the way of return but allows the investor to reduce income tax liabilities.

**ship insurance**  Type of marine insurance, purchased by a shipowner, that covers a vessel and its machinery against such perils as collision, fire, stranding, storm damage, etc.

**short bond**  Bond with less than five years to maturity. *See also **long bond**; **medium bond**.*

**short credit**  Loan that must be repaid over a short timescale. *See also **extended credit**; **long credit**.*

**short covering**  When a person is **selling short**, the purchase of the security concerned in order to cover the bargain.

**short-dated gilt**  **Gilt-edged security** with a redemption term of less than five years.

**short-dated securities**  **Fixed-interest securities** that have a redemption date of less than five years.

**short end**  That part of the market that deals with securities with relatively little time to go before payment is due. The amount of time varies from a few days to up to five years, depending on which security is being traded.

**short hedge**  Hedge against a rise in interest rates on the **futures** market. *See also **long hedge**.*

**shorting**  Alternative term for **short selling**.

**short interest**  Interest rate charged on loans over a period of three months or less.

**shorts**  Alternative term for **short-dated securities**.

**short selling**  Alternative term for **selling short**.

**short-term**  Loosely, something (in the financial world, a security) with only a short time left before maturity. In the USA, short-term generally means something with less than a year to run. A US alternative is near-term.

**short-term capital**  Loan capital lent in the short-term, *i.e.* for less than five years. *See also **medium-term capital***

**short-term investment**  Investment for a short period. In the City, it refers to an investment for a period of days; elsewhere, the period may be up to three months. Short-term investments are usually made in return for interest rates slightly lower than those available on long-term investments. *See **long-term investment**.*

**S**

**short-termism** Policy of a *fund manager* who invests in companies whose performance is expected to improve in the short term, to adjust a *portfolio* for maximum gain, rather than taking a long-term view of how share prices are likely to change.

**show stopper** Informal term for a court injunction initiated by the target company and served against the raider in a *takeover*, stopping the hostile company party taking action any further.

**SIB** Abbreviation of *Securities and Investment Board.*

**SICAV** Abbreviation of *Société d'Investissement a Capital Variable.*

**sickness and accident insurance** *See personal sickness and accident insurance.*

**side-by-side trading** Prohibited practice in the USA of trading a share option at the same time as trading the underlying security on the same exchange.

**sight bill** Bill of exchange payable on presentation (i.e. on sight).

**sight deposit** Term with three meanings:

1. It is a *current account* at a bank or an instant access account at a building society, also known as a demand deposit. *See also time deposit.*

2. It is money *at call.*

3. It is money on deposit overnight.

**sight draft** *Bill of exchange* payable on presentation (*i.e.* on sight).

**simple debenture** Alternative term for *unsecured debenture.*

**simple interest** Rate of interest calculated by keeping interest that has already been paid separate from the capital sum. Thus, when calculating the next interest payment, the capital sum, but not the interest already paid, enters the calculation. *See also compound interest.*

**simple reversionary bonus** Type of reversionary bonus declared as a percentage of the sum assured only.

**single capacity** System that operated on the UK Stock Market before the *Big Bang*, whereby the functions of *jobber* and *stockbroker* were kept separate. A jobber was not allowed to deal with the general public and a stockbroker could not trade in shares except through a jobber. Since

Big Bang, the two functions may be amalgamated (*dual capacity*) and the people who perform these combined functions are known as *market makers*. *See also* **Chinese Wall**.

**single company personal equity plan** Type of *personal equity plan* (PEP) in which the entire fund is invested in a single company.

**single-currency peg** *Exchange rate* regime in which a country pegs it currency to the US dollar or some other stable currency and makes very few adjustments to the *parity*.

**single licence** Fact that an EU company needs only one authorization to offer insurance throughout the EU.

**single-life pension** Type of annuity or pension that is paid only for the lifetime of the beneficiary (and not that of any surviving spouse).

**single-premium assurance** Type of *life assurance* in which the *premium* is paid as a single lump sum (rather than as a series of payments).

**single-premium bond** Type of *bond* in which the investor pays a lump sum to a *life assurance* company, which uses the money to invest in a unit-linked fund.

**single-premium endowment policy** Type of *endowment policy* in which the *premium* is paid as a single lump sum (rather than as a series of payments).

**sinking fund** Sum of money set aside for a specific purpose and invested so that it produces the required amount at the right time.

**SIPP** Abbreviation of self-invested personal pension.

**six-month money** Funds invested on the money market for six months.

**skinny bid** Alternative term for *thin bid*.

**skittish** Popular term describing a market that is extremely volatile.

**slate bull** Non-profit making stock that is kept for a long time.

**sleeping economy** Informal term for an economy that contains substantial resources that are not fully exploited and having substantial unrealised trade potential. The People's Republic of China was usually quoted as an example of a sleeping economy.

**sleeping partner** Partner who invests capital in a firm but takes no active part in its management. He or she does, however, remain liable for the partnership's debts.

**slice (of the action)** Entitlement to a share in the profits of a company by being a shareholder, or of a transaction by taking a commission.

**sliding scale** Scale of charges that is based on the value of the thing upon which the charges are to be made. *See ad valorem.*

**slip** Document produced by a broker when insurance business is placed at *Lloyd's of London*. It includes such details as the name of the insured, the starting date and period of insurance, the property insured and the period of cover, the premium and commission payable, and any special conditions or limitations.

**slippage** Under-performance of a *start-up* company. Slippage may lead to the need for additional capital.

Alternatively, it is the fluctuation in the price of a contract on a futures exchange.

**slump** Period of time during which the economy is poor, with high levels of unemployment and reduced economic activity.

**small companies market** Republic of Ireland's equivalent of the alternative investment market.

**small company fund** Fund that puts unit trusts or other collective investments in the shares of various small companies.

**small self-administered scheme** (SSAS) Type of *occupational pension scheme* aimed at directors and giving its members control over investments. Small means fewer than 12 active members. These schemes are subject to strict Inland Revenue rules, including the requirement for a *pensioneer trustee.*

**snake** Popular term for the European system that links the following currencies: the Belgian and French francs, the Danish kroner, the Irish punt, the Dutch guilder, the German Deutschmark and the Italian lira.

*société anonyme* (SA) French equivalent of the UK *public limited company* (plc).

*société responsibilité limité* (SRL) French equivalent of the UK *private company.*

*Société d'Investissement a Capital Variable* (SICAV) French equivalent of a UK unit trust.

**society** Originally, in business and finance, a group of people who come together because they have the same interest or goal.

**S**

**soft arbitrage** Movement of funds between the money market and bank deposits to benefit from the difference in interest rates. *See also arbitrage*.

**soft loan**  Loan that carries an unusually low rate of *interest*, often advanced as a form of *foreign aid*.

**softs**  Popular name given to traded *commodities* other than metals; *e.g.* foodstuffs such as wheat and coffee.

**sola**  *Bill of exchange* that does not have a duplicate as in *bills in a set*.

**sold contract note**  Alternative term for *sold note*.

**sold note**  Document sent by a broker to his or her client, confirming that a sale has been made. It is also known as a sold contract note.

**sole agency**  Agreement by which only one party (*agent*) represents a principal either in a certain capacity or in a particular geographical area.

**sole trader**  Person who trades on his or her own behalf and has not registered as a business.

In the financial and stock exchange worlds, however, the term has three precise meanings:

1. It is a trader involved in buying and selling securities *short-term*, for his or her own account.
2. It is somebody who specializes in buying and selling securities on behalf of a broker or dealer, usually working as an employee.
3. It is a person who buys and sells contracts in financial *futures* without a *hedge* in the appropriate cash market.

**solicitor**  In the UK, a professional person who gives legal advice and initiates legal proceedings on a client's behalf.

**solvency**  State of a person or company that is cash positive, and able to pay all bills as they fall due; *i.e.* its assets are more than its liabilities. The converse is insolvency.

**solvency margin**  For an insurance company, the amount by which its assets must exceed its liabilities, as prescribed under the 1982 Insurance Companies Act.

**South Sea Bubble**  *See bubble*.

**space risks**  Risks that include material damage during testing of satellites, launch of satellites and damage while in orbit. Insurance against these risks is available in the marine market.

**S**

**special bonus** Additional benefit of some long-term *endowment assurances*, such as an extra percentage each year or a percentage of accrued bonuses.

**special condition of average** Condition in insurance that the pro rata *average* will be applied if the sum insured is less than 75% of the insured value at the time of loss.

**Special Drawing Rights** (SDR) Form of *credit* extended by the *International Monetary Fund* (IMF) to its member countries as an addition to the credit they already hold. SDRs do not represent actual money, they are simply a form of credit, but they do not have to be repaid to the IMF and thus form a permanent addition to the reserves of each member country. Originally, they were allocated to member countries in proportion to their subscription to the IMF, but since then additional allocations have been made. At first SDRs were valued in relation to the value of gold, but have since been valued in relation to the member country's own currency. SDRs may be exchanged between member countries or between those countries and the IMF.

**special manager** Person with the requisite experience who is appointed by the court to run a business that is in liquidation.

**special perils** Extra risk added to an insurance policy, *e.g.* explosion, storm and earthquake can be added to a standard fire policy.

**special reserve** Fund set aside by members of **Lloyd's of London** to pay tax liabilities.

**special resolution** *Resolution* to change the articles of association of a company which usually must be passed with a three-quarters majority.

**special situations fund** Fund that places *unit trusts* or other collective investments in a range of shares that are expected to rise sharply in value (perhaps because of a merger or takeover) or are believed to have bottomed out and are expected to recover.

**specification** In insurance, details of large risks added at the end of a policy.

**specific performance order** Order made by a court to one party to a contract to fulfil the obligations to which that party is contracted. It may be made, for example, in place of *damages*.

**speculation** Discussion about a possible future event. Broadly, in finance, it is the practice of making investments or going into a business that involves risk. The term is sometimes used with pejorative undertones to apply to investment for short-term gain. In certain markets, such as *commodities* and financial *futures*, speculation is clearly distinguished from transactions undertaken in the normal course of trading (physical buying or selling) or *hedging* (where the specific purpose is to minimize overall gains and losses arising from price movements).

**spin-off** A term with three meanings:

1. It is a company that has been formed from part of or separated from the ownership of a larger company.

2. It is merchandise that is produced to take advantage of one high-profile product, *e.g.* a television programme may have many spin-offs: a book; a recording of the theme tune; T-shirts; badges; etc.

3. It is a technology or product that arose as a by-product of another.

**split** Marketing exercise in which a company issues more shares to existing holders in order to reduce the price per share. *See also* **bonus issue**.

**split-capital trust** Type of trust that is issued by an *investment trust* company, with a fixed winding-up date on which investors are paid the surplus assets. Holders of income shares receive payment throughout the life of the trust.

**split-level trust** Type of trust issued by an *investment trust* company that uses its assets to pay holders of income shares. Capital shareholders are paid the capital value of the assets when the trust is wound up.

**spot** Something that is carried out at once, on the spot. The term is most often used on *futures* markets, where its opposite is *forward* or highest (as in highest prices).

**spot goods** As opposed to *futures*, spot goods are commodities available for immediate delivery, rather than forward delivery.

**spot market** Market in which the goods sold are available for immediate delivery. It is also known as the non-contract market. *See also* **futures**.

**spot price** Price quoted for goods available for immediate delivery, usually higher than the forward price because it takes into account all costs except delivery.

**spread** Broadly, the difference between two (or sometimes more) prices or values.

**springing warrant** Alternative US term for *exploding warrant*.

**squeeze** *See bear squeeze*.

**SRL** Abbreviation of *société responsibilité limité*.

**SRO** Abbreviation of *self-regulatory organization*.

**SSAS** Abbreviation of *small self-administered scheme*.

**SSP** Abbreviation of *statutory sick pay*.

**stag** Person who buys new issues of shares in the hope that he or she will be able to make a fast profit by selling them soon after trading on the stock exchange opens. With the UK privatization programme of the later 1980s, the number of stags increased. It is not to be confused with STAGS (short for sterling accruing government securities). *See also dolphin*.

**stagflation** US term for a combination of high inflation and economic stagnation.

**STAGS** Abbreviation of *sterling accruing government securities*.

**staircasing** *See equity sharing*.

**stale bull** Dealer who has bought in the expectation that prices will rise but cannot then sell at a profit, either because prices have remained static or fallen, or because nobody wants to buy.

**stamp duty** Duty levied on the completion of certain transfer documents, *e.g.* stamp duty is paid (on property over a certain value) when a person signs property transfer documents.

**standard** Broadly, a norm against which other things are measured.

**standard life** Describing a "life" accepted for **life assurance** which does not display evidence of ill health and which is acceptable at ordinary rates of *premium*.

**stand on velvet** Make a profit from speculation in *stocks*.

**standstill agreement** When bidding for shares in a *target* company, agreement that no more bids will be made for the time being.

**start-up** Normally used to describe a company that is beginning from scratch. A start-up often needs *venture capital* financing to help it on its way.

**stated account** Account that shows how much one party owes another. It is agreed upon by both parties and is legally binding unless it can be shown to be false.

**S**

**State Earnings-Related Pension Scheme** (SERPS) Non-compulsory UK government scheme established in 1978 to provide a pension for every employed person (as well as the basic flat-rate *state pension*), funded by payments from part of the National Insurance contributions paid by employers and employees. People contributing to a *personal pension plan* or and *occupational pension* may opt out of SERPS.

**statement** Written report often taken as an official or legal document.

**statement of account** Not to be confused with *stated account,* a document sent from a creditor to a debtor, detailing recent transactions and amounts owing, sometimes with terms for payment.

**statement in lieu of prospectus** If a company proposes to make a new issue of *shares* or *debentures* and does not issue a *prospectus,* it must pass a statement in lieu of prospectus to the registrar of companies at least three days before the issue is to take place.

**state pension** Pension paid by the UK government to people who have paid National Insurance contributions during their working lives. There are two categories of state pension: the basic pension and the *State Earnings-Related Pension* (SERPS). *See also old-age pension.*

**static risk** In insurance, any risk that results from natural causes.

**statute-barred debt** Debt that may no longer be called in because it has been outstanding too long.

**statutory company** Company set up by Act of Parliament to produce essential services such as the provision of power and water.

**statutory sick pay** (SSP) Benefit paid to an employee who is unable to work because of illness. It is paid (for a maximum of 28 weeks) by the employer, who can reclaim it from the government. It counts as income for tax purposes.

**stepped costs** Alternative term for *semi-variable costs.*

**sterling accruing government securities** (STAGS) Form of *zero coupon bond,* denominated in sterling and backed by Treasury stock.

**sterling area** *See scheduled territory.*

**stock** Term with four meanings:
1. It is a fixed-term security that is denominated in units of £100. *See fixed-interest security.*
2. In the USA it is an alternative term for *ordinary shares.*

3. It is sometimes also used in the UK to mean some types of *ordinary share*.

4. It is a collection of raw materials or goods held by a manufacturer, wholesaler, retailer or end-user. It is also known as stock-in-trade or inventory.

**stockbroker** Someone who gives advice and buys and sells *stocks* and *shares* on the stock exchange on behalf of clients.

**stock exchange** Essentially a place where *securities*, *stocks* and *shares* are bought and sold.

**Stock Exchange Alternative Trading Service** (SEATS) Service that displays quotations and orders for illiquid stock in which only one (or no) market maker is willing to trade.

**Stock Exchange Automated Quotations** (SEAQ) Electronic system on the London Stock exchange that displays in the offices of brokers and others up-to-date prices and information for all quoted securities. Only *market-makers* are permitted to quote prices on SEAQ, accepting certain obligations in return for the increased business that SEAQ offers.

**Stock Exchange Automatic Exchange Facility** (SEAF) Computerized system on the London stock Exchange that allows buying and selling of securities to be done at terminals in the broker's office. *See also* **CREST**; *Stock Exchange Automated Quotations* (SEAQ); *Stock Exchange Pool Nominees* (SEPON); *TALISMAN*.

**Stock Exchange Daily Official List** (SEDOL) *See Official List.*

**Stock Exchange Pool Nominees** (SEPON) Company that acted as a central pool for shares while they were being transferred from buyer to seller. Sold stock was deposited into SEPON and buy orders were fulfilled from it, through the *TALISMAN* system. In 1997 it was replaced by the Bank of England CREST system.

**stock-in-trade** Alternative term for *stock* (fourth meaning).\

**stockjobber** Alternative term for *jobber*.

**stop-loss** Type of insurance or reinsurance that covers a whole account over a period of time. No payment is made until the accumulated losses in the year exceed the stop-loss level.

**S**

**stop-loss order** Alternative term for *stop order*.

**stop-loss selling** Sale of shares or futures contracts in a declining market, usually at a predetermined price, in order to prevent further loss.

**stop order** Instruction given by a client to a *stockbroker*, to sell securities should they fall below a certain price.

**story** Security that is being actively traded on the US market at the present time, but which may lack underlying value.

**straddle** Practice of simultaneously buying forward and selling forward a *futures* contract or *option* in the same security in order to make a profit if the price of the security moves in either direction.

**straight bond** Also known as straight fixed-interest stock, a bond issued by a company.

**straight-line depreciation** Method of calculating the *depreciation rate*. A fixed proportion of the total original value of the *asset* is written off in each accounting period, making allowance for its current resale value, either as a useful asset or scrap. *See also write off.*

**straight-line method** In *accounting*, method of calculating *depreciation* by writing off the value of the *asset* in equal amounts in each year of the asset's lifetime.

**strangle** Practice of buying out-of-the-money call and put *options* that are close to expiry at a relatively low *premium*. If the price of the underlying *future* rises or falls suddenly, the buyer makes a profit.

**Street, The** Popular term for the New York Stock Exchange, referring to Wall Street.

**striking price** Also known as the exercise price, the price at which an *option* for the purchase or sale of a security is exercised.

**strip** Practice of taking US Treasury bonds, stripping the interest-bearing *coupon* and selling that and the principal separately. Such securities are said to have been stripped.

**strong bear hug** During a *takeover*, a situation in which there is a high level of publicity surrounding the bid, putting pressure on the *target* company.

**structural unemployment** Usually high level of unemployment caused by the change from a labour-intensive to a capital-intensive economy.

**subject bid (or offer)** Bid (or offer) that is subject to stated conditions. *See also firm bid.*

**subject matter of insurance** Property, item, person, limb, liability or event covered by an insurance policy.

**subject matter of contract** In insurance, the financial interest that the insured has in the subject matter of the insurance.

**subordinated loan** Loan that does not have repayment priority (compared to other loans).

**subrogation** Right of an insurer, having indemnified the insured, to avail himself or herself of any rights and remedies of the insured, *e.g.* salvage.

**subscribed capital** Alternative term for *issued capital*.

**subscriber** On the formation of a company, a person who signs the articles of association and memorandum of agreement. *See also* ***subscribed capital***.

**subscription** Sum paid to a company for shares in a new issue.

**subsidiary company** Company that is wholly or partly owned by another, called the *parent company*.

**subsidy** Sum paid (usually by government) to companies in certain industries to enable them to sell their goods or services at a price close to the prevailing market price. A subsidy is also used to provide financial support to a commercial or quasi-commercial activity that would otherwise not be viable in narrow profit-and-loss terms, usually in order to sustain broader economic or social benefits.

**substantial damages** Damages designed by the court to place the plaintiff in the financial position that he or she would have enjoyed had the loss or injury not occurred. If the monetary value of the loss or injury can be precisely calculated, the substantial damages awarded are said to be specific; if precise calculation is impossible, approximate (general) damages are awarded.

**sub-underwriter** Insurance company, bank, market maker or jobber who accepts part or all of the commitment made by an ***underwriter***.

**subvention** In the UK, a payment made from one company to another (related) company in order to give a better picture of the group's performance.

In the USA, a grant made by the government, a company or other institution, to a non-profit making organization.

**suicide clause** Clause in a *life assurance* policy that specifies no payment will be made if the assured commits suicide within a certain period (usually two years) of the date of the policy.

**suicide pill** Defensive tactics in the event of a *takeover bid*. If the raider manages to acquire a certain percentage of the *target* company's shares, the remaining shareholders are automatically entitled to exchange their shares for *debt* securities, thus exchanging the company's *equity* to debt and making it seem less attractive to the raider.

**sum insured** Limit of an insurance company's liability under a particular insurance policy.

**superannuation** Alternative name for company pension (an *occupational pension scheme*), paid to employees after retirement.

**supermajority** Between 70% and 80% of the voters. It is usual to demand a supermajority decision when deciding on such points as *mergers* and *takeovers*.

**superstock** Share issue in the USA that gives the existing holders a large number of votes per share. Normally used as a defensive tactic during a hostile *takeover bid*, superstock must be held for a certain period of time before the extra votes are credited to the holder.

**supplementary benefit** Payment made in the UK by the Department of Social Security (DSS) to someone who is either out of work but does not qualify for unemployment benefit, or is on a low wage.

**supplementary costs** Alternative term for *overheads*.

**supply** Provision of goods and services.

**supply and demand** Two market forces that in microeconomic theory determine the price of goods, services or investment instruments. If supply is low and demand high, the price increases. Conversely, if demand is low and supply high, the price falls (unless price controls are in operation).

**support** Practice of actively buying securities or foreign exchange by an "official" in order to stop their market value from falling. This most often happens when the *central bank* buys its own securities to stop the price falling and thus forestall a rise in interest rates.

**suppressed inflation** Inflationary trend that has been slowed down or completely halted, usually by extensive government intervention in the economy. It is also known as repressed inflation.

**S**

**SUPSI** Abbreviation of specific unpublished price-sensitive information. *See insider dealing*.

**surety** Alternative term for *guarantee*.

**suretyship** Type of pecuniary insurance that covers loss of money through fraud or dishonesty.

**surplus** Term with two meanings:

1. In life assurance, the excess of assets over liabilities as revealed in the annual valuation of the life fund.
2. In reinsurance, it is the amount by which the sum insured exceeds the ceding office's retention.

**surplus treaty** Reinsurance agreement whereby all risks that exceed a pre-determined amount are reinsured.

**surrender** To cash in a life assurance policy before benefits are due to be paid.

**surrender value** Value (realized on surrender) that certain kinds of *life assurance* policies may acquire after they have been in force for a certain period of time. Usually only *whole-life* and *endowment* policies accrue a surrender value, and the value can be little or nothing in the early years.

**surveyor** Person whose job is to examine buildings etc. and report on their condition, often employed by an insurance company (for buildings insurance) or a mortgage provider.

**suspension notice** Notice published by a company that wants, for a defined period, to suspend the facility of converting *loan stock* into *share capital*.

**swap** Means by which a borrower can exchange easily-raised funds for the type of funds required. A currency swap enables exchange of the currency in possession for the currency needed. An interest-rate swap exchanges a fixed rate for a floating rate.

**switching** Practice of transferring investment from one security to another (in a comparable class) in order to take advantage of price fluctuations or to improve a tax position.

**syndicate** Group of people that come together to work for a common aim, *e.g.* in underwriting large risks for *Lloyd's of London*. *See also consortium; underwriter*.

**syndication** Practice of dividing investment risk between several people in order to minimize individual risk.

Syndication is also the practice of distributing information (especially news information and newspaper and magazine articles) to several outlets.

**synergy** Additional benefits to be gained by the combination of hitherto separate activities. It is sometimes colloquially expressed as "2 + 2 = 5", and cited to justify the takeover or merger of companies with complementary or mutually reinforcing activities or resources.

**S**

# T

**tail-gating** Act of a broker who recommends purchase of a stock to one customer on the basis of another customer having just expressed faith in the stock by making a purchase. The term also includes the personal trading in a share by a broker immediately after taking an instruction from a client to do the same. *See also* **running ahead.**

**tailspin** Sudden plunge in market prices.

> *This week's crash sent equity prices on several European markets into a tailspin.*

**take back** When a US company is sold, the take back is a situation in which the owner must accept payment in something other than cash.

**take in** To accept *stocks* as loan security in order to postpone a sale until the next *settlement date.*

**takeover** Buying of a proportion of another company's shares so that the purchaser gains control of the company or its assets. *See also* **merger.**

**takeover bid** Offer by one company to buy all the shares of another, thereby gaining control of the target company. It is often shortened to "bid".

**takeover panel** Stock Exchange body responsible for seeing that the City Code on Takeovers and Mergers is observed by parties wishing to make a *takeover bid.*

**takeover stock** Shares that are bought by a raider during a takeover battle.

**taker-in** Person who is willing to take up a commitment made by a *bull* dealer, in the event of the dealer being unable or unwilling to pay for it at that time.

**TALISMAN** Abbreviation of Transfer Accounting, Lodgement for Investors, Stock Management for Jobbers. It was a central computerized system for settling equities, and also facilitated the transfer of stock from the central Stock Exchange pool and the issue of new certificates. In 1997 it was replaced by the Bank of England **CREST** system.

**talon** Slip that accompanies a sheet of coupons of *bearer bonds*, which may be sent to the issuing company when more coupons are required.

**tangible assets** Literally, assets that may be touched, such as buildings or stock. They may be contrasted with intangible (or invisible) assets, which are those that are not visible, such as a company's goodwill or the expertise of its staff. *See also* **invisible assets**.

**tangibles** Another term for *tangible assets*.

**tap** When the government makes a new issue on the gilt market, it is very rarely fully subscribed. The remaining gilts in the issue are gradually released by the *government broker* and this action is known as a tap. *See* **gilt-edged security**.

**tap buying** In certain circumstances, the government will buy back gilts before they have matured. This known as tap buying. *See* **gilt-edged security**.

**tape dancing** Unethical method of manipulating share prices in the USA in which a dealer reports a deal inclusive of his commission. This seems to make the share price rise.

**tap issue** Issue of government securities direct to government departments rather than onto the open market.

**tap stock** Gilt-edged stock released onto the market in a *tap*.

**target** Objective towards which somebody or an organization is working. In corporate finance, it is a company that is the object of a *takeover bid*.

*All the sales representatives met their sales targets for the year.*

*Having been made aware of the imminence of a hostile takeover bid, the board of the target company met to discuss defensive tactics.*

**target price** Average price for commodities fixed by the Common Agricultural Policy of the EU and achieved by purchasing goods at the *intervention price*.

**target risk** In insurance, a large, hazardous risk.

**tariff** List of charges made in return for goods or services. There are also three more particular meanings:

1.  It is the list of dutiable goods and duty payable, issued by Her Majesty's Customs.

2. It is a system of charges in which a certain rate is payable up to a certain point (*e.g.* a certain quantity of goods)˙ and then the rate changes beyond that point.
3. In insurance, it is a collective agreement by members to calculate and charge the same premium for a given risk or type of insurance.

**tariff barrier** Alternative term for *customs barrier*.

**tariff office** Insurance company that is bound with respect to the level of its premiums by membership of an organization (*e.g.* the Accident Offices Association).

**tariff rating** In insurance, an agreement by members to charge the same premiums for a given risk or insurance.

**TAURUS** Abbreviation of transfer and automated registration of uncertified stock, a computer system that was intended to enable *stocks* and *shares* to be transferred by computer, making contract notes and certificates unnecessary. After a series of failures, it was abandoned in 1993 and replaced three years later by **CREST**.

**tax** Money paid to central or local government to cover its expenditure. Various kinds of taxes are collected by the Inland Revenue (the Internal Revenue Service in the USA), HM Customs and Excise (in which case the tax is known as a duty) and local government authorities. *See also* **duty**; *rates*; *value-added tax*.

**taxable income** Income on which taxes are levied. It is calculated by deducting *personal allowances* from *gross* income.

**tax abatement** Reduction in the rate of tax. It should not be confused with a tax *rebate*.

**tax and price index** (TPI) Index launched in 1979 to compare levels of *taxation* with *retail prices* and relate them to average wage levels. The TPI is used to calculate the real spending power of the nation.

**taxation** Imposition and subsequent collection of a *tax*.

**taxation schedule** One of six categories into which income is divided for the purposes of calculating taxes.

**tax avoidance** Use of loopholes in tax legislation to minimize tax liability. Unlike *tax evasion*, tax avoidance is legal.

**tax base** The form of income upon which tax is calculated, *e.g.* the tax base for income tax is a person's taxable income.

**tax bracket** The percentage of one's income that one pays in tax depends on the level of income. Incomes are divided into brackets for the purpose of calculating tax. The term is also applied to people in that bracket.

*She is in a higher tax bracket than he is.*

**tax credit** That part of a *dividend* payment on which a company has already paid *tax*, thus relieving the *shareholder* of the necessity of doing so.

**tax concession** Allowance made by the Inland Revenue to taxpayers in certain categories, which means that these people or companies pay less tax than they would otherwise be liable for, *e.g.* tax concessions are often used by the government to induce companies to relocate in areas high in unemployment.

**tax deduction card** In *pay-as-you-earn* (PAYE) income tax, a record of all deductions made by the employer at source, submitted for each employee to the Inland Revenue annually.

**tax deductions** Money removed from a person's salary or wages to cover income tax. In the USA, however, tax deductions are expenses that are deductible against tax.

**tax evasion** Evasion of tax liabilities by providing false information to the *Inland Revenue*. Tax evasion is a criminal offence in the UK. *See also tax avoidance.*

**tax-exempt special savings account** (TESSA) Tax-free investment, introduced in 1990 to encourage people to save. Up to £9000 can be invested, and interest is tax free as long as no withdrawals are made for a period of five years. After five years, up to £9000 of the money may be invested in another TESSA. In 1997 the government announced that TESSAs would lose their tax-free status in 1999, to persuade investors to transfer to the planned new *Individual Savings Accounts* (ISAs).

**tax exemption** Not having to pay tax. In the USA, however, it is the proportion of income upon which tax is not payable.

**tax exile** Person who lives abroad in order to minimize liability for tax.

**tax gap** Difference between the amount somebody owes the Inland Revenue (the Inland Revenue Service in the USA), and the amount they actually pay.

**tax haven** Country with liberal tax and banking regulations. In some instances it benefits companies to set up their registered offices in such a country, to avoid paying taxes in their own country.

**tax holiday**  Period during which a start-up company need not pay taxes.

**tax loss**  Loss sustained by a person or business which may, once incurred, be offset against a demand for *income tax, capital gains tax* or *corporation tax*. Tax losses are frequently incurred deliberately in an attempt to reduce the real cost of tax-paying.

**tax point**  Point at which *value-added tax* (VAT) is payable.

**tax relief**  Concessions made to taxpayers in respect of certain liabilities.
*He expected to get tax relief on his mortgage.*

**tax return**  Document submitted to the *Inland Revenue* annually, stating an individual's earnings and expenses for the year and used to calculate that person's tax liabilities.

**tax shelter**  Investment instrument that does not attract tax.

**tax year**  Period of twelve months, specified to start at any calendar month, for tax and accounting purposes. It is also known as the *financial year. See also fiscal year.*

**T-bill**  Abbreviation of US *Treasury bill.*

**TCV**  Abbreviation of *total contract value.*

**teaser**  Initial low rate of interest offered on an adjustable rate mortgage (ARM), which may seem very attractive at the time of arrangement, but which inevitably rises.

**technical analysis**  Analysis of the changes in price of a company's *stock*, based on past movements in the value of its shares; also called chartism.

**technical market analyst**  Someone who studies the stock market and predicts changes on the basis of market trends and the state of the market as a whole.

**technical reserve**  Reserve that is held by an insurance company to meet any claims. *See also policyholder's funds.*

**teddy bear hug**  Situation in which the target company approves of a *takeover bid* in principle but requires a higher price.

**T**

**Ted spread**  Difference between the price of a US *Treasury bill* and the price of the Eurodollar.

**telebrokering** Selling of insurance services by telephone.

**telecommuting** Increasingly common practice whereby people work at home, "commuting" by computer link-up rather than by car or public transport. *See also electronic cottage.*

**telegraphic transfer** Method of transferring money to a transferee abroad. The transferor instructs his or her bank, who then contacts its agent in that country to pay the transferee.

**telemarketing** Advertising, selling and conducting market research over the telephone, person to person.

**telemarketing system** Computer system that canvasses people in their homes over the telephone. Dialling is done electronically and a voice-activated audio-tape carries on the "conversation".

**telesales** Selling a product over the telephone. It is a branch of *telemarketing.*

**teletext output price information computer** (TOPIC) Computerized system that provides stock dealers with up-to-the-minute information on market prices. *See also quote machine.*

**temporary assurance** *See term assurance.*

**tenancy in common** In principle, a situation in which two people are entitled to tenancy of the same property and may do as each wishes with their part of it. If one tenant dies, his share of the property is passed on to his or her heir, rather than to the other tenant(s). Now, however, tenancy in common applies only to groups of four or more people. *See also joint tenancy.*

**tender** Generally, an offer to supply goods or services at a certain price and under certain conditions. A tender is usually submitted in response to an invitation to do so and is normally made in competition with other potential suppliers. *See also estimate; quotation.*

**tender bills** *Treasury bills,* issued by the government each week to cover short-term finance. Tenders for these bills are made by discount houses and financial institutions. *See also tap.*

**tender offer** Offer for sale by *tender.* In the USA, it is an offer made to the shareholders of a public company to buy their holding at a certain price, normally above the current market price. This may be done by another company in order to effect a *takeover.*

**tender pool** One of a series of groups into which an acquisitive company may divide its target company's shareholders, in order more successfully to persuade them to take up a *tender offer*. It is a form of divide and conquer.

**tenor** Period of time before a *bill of exchange* has to be paid. In effect it is the "life" of the bill.

**term** Period of time during which something is valid.

**term assurance** *Life assurance* policy whereby a premium is paid to provide a policy which pays the sum insured on death within the term. If the insured survives the term, then nothing is paid on the policy. Term assurance can be used to cover loans. It is also known as temporary assurance.

**terminable annuity** Another name for *certain annuity*.

**terminal** The end of something. In computing, it is where data can be inputted or outputted from a system. *e.g.* a keyboard or VDU screen.

**terminal bonus** Bonus paid to the with-profits insurance policyholders as a lump sum on death or maturity of a participatory policy. It is not guaranteed.

**terminal date** Date of expiry of a *futures* contract.

**terminal market** Market in *futures*.

**terminate** To finish something, often used in regard to a contract or agreement.

*They terminated his contract of employment after he was caught trying to defraud the company.*

**term insurance** Life assurance provided for a fixed term only. See *term assurance*.

**term loan** Fixed loan made for a specified number of years.

**terms** Conditions attached to an agreement or contract.

**terms of business letter** Document that must be given to the client in all Financial Services Act transactions. It sets out the duties, responsibilities and status of the adviser in clear terms.

**term shares** Funds deposited with a building society for a number of years, to earn higher than usual interest.

**terms of trade** Indication of a country's trading position, based on a comparison of its imports and exports.

**territory** Geographical area covered by a sales representative or by a company's operations.

**tertiary market** Market in listed securities traded by non-exchange brokers on the over-the-counter market. *See also* *primary market.*

**The Opening** *Call-over* at the start of each trading session on some exchanges. Otherwise, the term is used as shorthand for *opening price.*

**thin bid** *Takeover bid* backed by an aggressor who holds only a small number of shares. It is also known as a skinny bid.

**third-class paper** Corporate debt issued by companies with a low *credit rating.* Third-class paper is a hazardous investment.

**third market** Stock Exchange market introduced in January 1987, with less stringent entry requirements than the *unlisted securities market* (USM). It was also known as the third tier. The USM was abolished at the end of 1990.

**third party** Person mentioned in a contract but not a party to the contract. Third-party insurance, *e.g.*, gives the insured cover against claims made by a third party (who is not named in the policy and not a party to it).

**third-party insurance** *See third party.*

**threshold** Limit or point at which something changes.

**threshold agreement** Agreement between an employer and employees (or the representative union) that wages will increase only if the rate of *inflation* reaches or exceeds a certain level, the threshold.

**threshold company** Company that has moved out of the *start-up* stage and is moving towards becoming secure and more profitable.

**threshold price** Price fixed under the Common Agricultural Policy (CAP) by the European Commission, below which the price of agricultural imports from non-member states is not allowed to fall.

**thrift** Shorthand in the USA for *thrift and loans.*

**thrift and loans** Financial institutions in the USA that are backed by an insurance fund and oriented towards the customer. They are also known as industrial banks. *See also* *savings and loan.*

**tick** Minimum price movement on a financial futures contract. *See also* *uptick.*

**T**

**tied agent** Person who gives advice about and sells financial products of one company only (unlike an *independent financial adviser*). It can be a salesperson of the company (a company representative) or an outside organization such as a building society, which decides to tie to an insurance company (appointed representative).

**tied loan** Loan made by one country to another on condition that the money concerned is spent on the lending nation. Tied loans are a common form of *foreign aid*, because they create employment and have no effect on the lending nation's *balance of payments*.

**tie-up** Arrangement whereby a large company helps to finance a smaller company, thus gaining rights in some or all of its developments. Tie-ups most often occur where the receiving company is developing in high-technology areas.

**tigers** *See Treasury Investment Growth Receipts* (TIGRs).

**tight money** Money only available at a high rate of *interest*. Tight money is created when the authorities reduce the *money supply* in an attempt to curtail the level of activity in the economy; funds therefore become scarce and thus attract high interest rates.

**TIGRs** Abbreviation of *Treasury Investment Growth Receipts*.

**time and motion** Study of the way in which a particular job is carried out, in an effort to streamline the physical actions involved and so save time.

**time bargain** Deal struck on the understanding that settlement will be postponed until the next *settlement date*.

**time deposit** Deposit or investment that cannot be withdrawn without giving notice. It is also an alternative US term for *fixed deposit*. *See also sight deposit*.

**time loss insurance** Type of insurance that gives cover for losses incurred while equipment or machinery is broken down and awaiting repair or replacement.

**time policy** Type of marine insurance that covers a vessel for a defined period of time (irrespective of where it is).

**time preference** Theory of interest that suggests that interest is the price paid by a borrower for immediate consumption, and a compensation to the lender, who loses the opportunity to use the articles or money lent for his or her own purposes. Therefore, time preference is a person's preference for current rather than future consumption, or *vice versa*.

**time value of money** Theory by which one's money is more valuable now than at any time in the future.

**tip** Cash given to someone who has rendered a service, over and above the payment agreed. Tipping customs vary from country to country, but those who are normally tipped include taxi-drivers, waiting staff, beauticians and hairdressers. It is also known as a gratuity. *See also* **perk.**

A tip may also be a piece of information passed to someone to whom it may be of advantage.

**tithe** Literally meaning "one-tenth", a tithe was originally a payment of that portion of one's income to the Church. Now, it has come to mean payment of a fixed sum at regular intervals.

**title** A person's right to something.

**title deed** Legal document giving the holder *title* to land or (more loosely) to property. Title deeds are often accepted as **collateral** for a **loan.** It is also known as deed of title.

**toehold purchase** First acquisition of up to 5% of a target company's shares in an attempted *takeover bid.*

**Tokyo Stock Exchange** (TSE) Most important and largest of Tokyo's eight stock exchanges.

**tombstone** Informal US term for an advertisement, placed in the press, giving details of those involved in a securities issue. A tombstone is not normally an offer to buy.

**tontine** Type of co-operative insurance, popular in the 17th century, in which a group of people paid for a life *annuity* with a lump sum. When somebody died, his or her money was shared among the other members. It ended when the last member died.

**top-hat pension** Extra pension provided to a senior important employee, taken out by his or her employer.

**TOPIC** Abbreviation of *teletext output price information computer.*

**top up** To improve the benefits gained from an existing arrangement, *e.g.* by increasing contributions to a pension or assurance scheme. *See additional voluntary contributions.*

**top-up mortgage** Alternative term for a *margin loan.*

**total contract value** (TCV) Figure applied to *futures* markets and calcu-

**T**

lated by multiplying the size of the contract (*e.g.* 10 tons of cocoa) by market price (*e.g.* £1,000/ton) to give the value of the contract (£10,000).

**total loss** In marine insurance, the loss of ship at sea or the total destruction of a ship and/or its cargo.

**touch** For any security, the difference between the best **bid price** of one market maker and the best **offer price** of another. *See also* **spread**.

**toxic waste** Informal US term rating a security as a very bad investment. *See also* **junk bond**.

**TPI** Abbreviation of **tax and price index**.

**tracker bond** Lump-sum account invested in equities that guarantees the capital and often guarantees also a minimum return.

**trade** Business of buying and selling in general in order to make a profit, or to buy or sell in a given market. In the USA, a trade may also be another term for a **bargain** or deal.

**trade agreement** Agreement between two or more countries or two groups of countries (*e.g.* the EU) regarding general terms of trade.

**trade balance** Alternative term for **balance of trade**.

**trade barrier** Something that restricts or discourages trade, such as high levels of import **duty** or low import **quotas**.
*The leaders of the car industry in the UK called for trade barriers to be set up to restrict foreign competition.*

**trade bill** **Bill of exchange** between traders, i.e. a bill used to pay for goods. The value and acceptability of a trade bill depends upon the standing of the accepting trader.

**trade credit** Credit one company or business gives to another, usually in the form of time to pay for goods or services supplied.

**trade creditor** Company or person who owes money for goods or services received. *See* **accounts payable**.

**trade debt** Debt incurred by a company during the normal course of business as the result of the non-payment of bills.

**trade debtor** Company or person who owes money for goods or servics received. *See* **accounts receivable**.

**trade investment** Investment in **capital goods** related to existing business, or in a new business in an established sector.

**traded option** Unlike traditional options, traded options are transferable and the terms of the option are fixed. Thus, it has been possible to form a market for trading the options themselves, as well as the underlying security, commodity or future.

**trade mark** Logo or name (trade name) used to distinguish one company's product from another's. Registered trade marks may not be used by another company in the country of registration.

**tradeoff** Exchanging one thing for another. Goods may be traded off against each other, but so may many other things such as the terms of an agreement.

*After five hours at the negotiating table they decided on a tradeoff of terms to break the stalemate.*

**trade references** List of trading partners to whom a company may refer if it wishes to confirm the creditworthiness of a potential customer.

**trade terms** Special conditions (usually discount prices) available to people working in the same industry or trade.

**trading** Activity of a trader in all its meanings.

**trading account** First section of a *profit-and-loss account*, in which income and expenditure concerned in a company's trading activities are detailed. The final figure on this account is the company's **gross profit**.

**trading day** Day on which trading takes place on a stock exchange. On the UK stock exchange, every day is a trading day with the exception of weekends and public holidays. *See also* **non-business days**.

**trading certificate** Certificate handed to a new company by the Registrar of Companies to enable it to begin trading.

**trading crowd** Group of dealers interested in trading in a particular security.

**trading floor** The area within an exchange building where trading takes place.

*There was panic on the trading floor of the Exchange today as prices began to fall sharply.*

**trading halt** Temporary stoppage in trading on a securities or options market.

**trading loss** Loss incurred while taking a principal (trading) position in a *market*. The loss must be recorded on a *profit-and-loss account* of a company. A trading loss is thus often disguised, where possible, by such tactics as "redefining" it as a *fixed asset* investment or including it as an extraordinary or *below-the-line* item in the accounts.

**trading post**  On the *trading floor* of the New York Stock Exchange, an area where dealers congregate to trade.

**traditional option**  Non-transferable option that has been available on a market for over a century, written on a variety of shares listed on the exchange. Each time a dealer wishes to buy a traditional option, the terms are re-written.

**tranche**  Slice or portion. In general, one of a series of payments which when put together add up to the total agreed.

*The author received his royalty advance as five tranches of £1000 each.*

More specifically, a tranche is a block of a stock issued before or after (and sometimes at a different price to) another block of identical stock.

**tranche funding**  Method of providing finance by which successive sums of money are forwarded, each dependent upon the financee attaining prearranged targets.

**tranchette**  Small block of *gilt-edged* stock issued to the market, as an addition to stock already on the market. *See also **tranche**.*

**transaction**  Act of carrying out a business deal.

*Considering the lengthy negotiations involved, they concluded the transaction surprisingly swiftly.*

**transaction charge**  Charge payable to the London International Financial Futures Exchange on each transaction made.

**transaction costs**  Costs incurred in buying and selling securities, such as the brokers' commissions, taxes, etc.

**transfer**  Legal movement of something (*e.g.* property, shares, etc.) from one owner to another.

**transfer deed**  Document proving the sale of a property or registered stock. To make the transfer official, the seller must sign the deed. In the case of a registered stock the document is also known as a stock transfer deed or a transfer form.

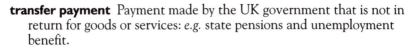

**transfer payment**  Payment made by the UK government that is not in return for goods or services: *e.g.* state pensions and unemployment benefit.

**transfer stamp duty** Duty levied on the transfer of securities on the stock exchange. It is therefore a form of capital transfer tax. Transfer stamp duty is not imposed upon government stocks, nor on securities bought and sold within one *account*.

**transfer value** In a pension plan, the amount available instead of *preserved benefits*, and able to be transferred to an alternative pension arrangement.

**transfer value analysis** Computer program designed to compare *preserved benefits* with taking on transfer value. *See critical yield*.

**travel insurance** Type of insurance that provides cover to travellers against personal accident, medical expenses, death, or the loss or damage to personal property and (sometimes) cash and credit cards.

**treasury** Government department that deals with national finance and government funding, and is responsible for the execution of the government's economic policy. Some large companies also have treasury departments.

**Treasury bill** In the UK, a government *bill of exchange* issued in £5,000 denominations to discount houses at a discount on its face value and repayable on a certain date (usually 91 days hence). In the USA, often abbreviated to T-bill, it is short-term *bill of exchange* issued by the US Treasury in $10,000 denominations.

**treasury bond** Alternative term for a *government bond*.

**treasury investment growth receipts** (TIGRs, pronounced tigers) Form of US *zero-coupon bond* in dollar denominations.

**treaty** In insurance, an agreement between a ceding company and a reinsurer in which the ceding company agrees to cede all risks as outlined in the treaty and the reinsurer must accept those cessions.

**trend** Direction of a price movement, which may be measured over periods of time.

**trial balance** In accounting, test that the books of account are accurate, by extracting a balance and checking that the debits equal the credits. This may take place monthly, but must be carried out at least annually, during an *audit*.

**tribunal** Special court set up to make a judgement on specific problems.

**triple-A** In the rating of US *stocks* and *bonds*, a triple-A rating is the highest rating a stock may achieve.

**T**

*Turnover was light in most bonds, but triple-A rated issues continued to be in demand.*

**triple-witching hour** Last hour before quarterly futures and options expire, during which turnover increases considerably, causing drastic changes in market prices.

**true and fair** Describes the ratification of an *account* in auditing. *See audit.*

**trust** Term with three meanings:

1. It is a group of companies that join forces to create a *cartel*, or in some cases a *monopoly*. In the latter sense it is more often used in the USA, *e.g.* in the term *anti-trust law*.

2. It is a sum of money or property placed into the care of a group of trustees, to be managed (although not necessarily invested) for the benefit of an individual or organization such as a charity.

3. In the securities industry, a trust is an investment operation that is managed by a group of trustees on behalf of other people, such as a unit trust.

**trust deed** Legal document that transfers property into the hands of trustees and sets out the terms of the trust.

**trustee** Person responsible for managing a *trust*, or the legal owner of the trust property.

**trust assurance** *Life assurance* policy placed into trust for the benefit of some other person.

**TSA** Abbreviation of The Securities Association., a former *self-regulatory organization* (SRO) now replaced by the *Securities and Futures Authority* (SFA).

**turn** Difference between the price at which a security is bought and the price at which it is sold. It is thus the profit on the transaction.

**turnover** Gross value of all sales made by a company during the accounting period. On the Stock Exchange, the turnover is the total number of shares changing hands during a certain period of time.

# U

**uberrima fides** Sometimes also quoted as uberrimae fidei, meaning "*utmost good faith*".

**UCITS** Abbreviation of *undertakings for collective investments in transferable securities.*

**ultimate net loss** In insurance, the total loss suffered by an insurer on his or her net account after all recoveries have been made.

**ultimo** Commercial Latin for "of the previous month", sometimes abbreviated to "ult".

**ultra vires** Latin for "beyond the power of", a phrase that denotes an act that goes beyond or against the acting company's objectives as defined in its articles of association.

**umpirage** In cases of *arbitration*, there may be more than one arbitrator. A group of arbitrators are governed by an umpire and in the event that the arbitrators are unable to reach a unanimous decision the umpire's decision is always final. The act of referring to the umpire in this way is known as umpirage.

**umpire** *See umpirage.*

**unbundling** Separation of a broker's prices from his services. It is also a term in the computer industry that denotes sales of parts (often software) separately from the main machine.

**uncalled capital** Money owing to a company on *partly-paid shares.* Uncalled capital exists as a reserve to be called upon at any time by the directors of a company.

**uncertificated units** In *unit trusts*, the dividends from the trust may be reinvested, to form new units. In most cases the dividends are too small to justify the issuing of a new certificate and so uncertificated units are held on behalf of the investor until the units are surrendered.

**undated stocks** Fixed interest security with no redemption date attached.

**under-average life** In *life assurance*, an insured person who has a physical defect or disability. Also known as an impaired life.

**undercapitalization** Situation of a company that does not have enough capital to take it through the initial burn-out period immediately after *start-up*. See also *burn rate*; *capitalization*.

**under contract** To be bound by the terms of a contract.

**underlying security** Security that is the subject of an *options* contract.

**underpin** To strengthen something, *e.g.* the current trend in market prices, a current way of thinking, etc.

*This month's government deficit data is expected to help underpin the gilt market.*

**undertaking** Agreement or promise to do something.

*They have given us a written undertaking to supply the goods within ten days.*

*They have undertaken the new brief for the job.*

**undertakings for collective investments in transferable securities** (UCITS) *Unit trusts* that may be traded in any of the EU countries.

**underwater** Describing shares that drop in value after the initial public offering. See also *discounted value*.

**underwater option** Stock *option* offered to US employees. The shares are normally offered at a discount on the market rate, but when the market price falls below the *grant price*, the option goes underwater.

**underwriter** Person or institution that agrees to take up a proportion of the risk of something, *e.g.* an underwriter may take up the shares of an issue that are not taken up by the public, in return for a commission (known as an underwriting commission). For the issuer, the underwriter represents the guarantee that the whole issue will be subscribed.

An insurance underwriter assess a risk and decides whether to accept or not and, if so, at what premium rate.

**underwriting** Process of assessing proposals/risks for insurance.

**underwriting cycle** Cyclical movement in the profitability of general insurance business over a period of time.

**underwriting result** Difference between insurance premiums earned and the total of claims plus expenses in a given year.

**undischarged bankruptcy** Occurs when the debts of the bankrupt have not been paid. In this case the individual has no property that may be called his or her own and is barred from public office, and from holding

**U**

management positions or directorships.

**undisclosed** Describes an action performed for various reasons without others knowing about it or without knowing the reasons behind it.

**undisclosed principal** Person represented in a business transaction by an agent or broker, and whose identity is therefore unknown to the person with whom the intermediary is conducting business.

**undistributed profit** Alternative term for *retained profit.*

**undue influence** If a party to a *contract* can be shown to have been influenced by a third party, such as a relative or close friend, so that the third party has some benefit from the contract (say, as the beneficiary of a *will*), then undue influence may be declared and the contract made void.

**unearned income** Income received from investments (and not from the provision of goods or services), including *dividends* and *interest* payments.

**unearned premium reserves** Money set aside by insurers to cover potential liabilities on insurance policies which are still in force at the end of an accounting year.

**unexpired risk reserves** Fund that an insurance company sets up to cover a shortfall in an insurance company's *unearned premium reserve.*

**unfunded debt** That portion of the *National Debt* that is in the form of fixed-term securities. It consists of the *floating debt*, listed securities and small-scale savings.

**unfunded pension scheme** Government scheme in which employed people make contributions to provide funds for paying pensions.

**unit** Term with three meanings:

1. It is one single item produced for sale. *See also* **unit cost.**

2. It is the name given to a single area of factory or retail space, especially on industrial estates.

3. In finance, it is a share (in the everyday sense) in an investment or series of investments. *See* **unit trust.**

**unitization** Conversion of an *investment trust* into a *unit trust.*

**unit-linked assurance policy** *Life assurance* policy for which the the premiums purchase units in a fund of the policyholder's choice. The value of the policy is directly linked to the performance of the underlying investments in that fund.

**unit-linked endowment**  Type of insurance often used alongside an *endowment mortgage.* Premiums are invested in a fund of the policyholder's choice and the fund value is directly linked to the performance of the fund. The policy aims to provide a sum to repay the mortgage loan at maturity, but there is no guarantee that it will do so. If the fund performs well, however, there may be a surplus available once the loan has been repaid. On death within the term, the policy pays a guaranteed minimum death benefit, which should be the amount of the loan.

**unit-linked personal pension**  Type of *personal pension plan* (PEP) in which contributions are invested in **unit trusts** to provide funds for paying the pension. The commonest kind of PEP, it can be purchased with a lump sum or by means of regular payments (with a maximum allowable investment of £6000 per year).

**unit trust**  Trust into which investors may buy by acquiring units. The capital thus collected is invested in various securities in a wide range of markets. Contributors to unit trusts benefit from the diverse nature of the *portfolio* built up, and from the expertise of a *fund manager.*

**unit trust personal equity plan**  See *unit-linked personal pension.*

**universal agent**  *Agent* with unlimited authority to close contracts on behalf of the principal. *See also* **power of attorney; warranty of authority.**

**utilized with profits**  Relatively new form of **with-profits** insurance that involves the premium buying units that are invested in the life office's with-profits fund. Bonuses are allocated in the form of additional units or increases to the unit price.

**universal whole-life**  Unit-linked whole-life assurance contract that offers flexibility in terms of varying the sum assured, and adding benefits such as **waiver of premium** or **permanent health insurance.**

**unlawful**  The formal difference between an act that is unlawful and an act that is illegal is that an illegal act is forbidden by law, whereas an unlawful act is not protected by law, *e.g.* most forms of wagering are unlawful.

**unlimited company**  Company that consists of members who are all liable for the total of the company's debts.

**unliquidated damages**  Amount of damages determined by a court, rather than specified by a contract.

**unlisted securities**  Those securities not listed on the stock exchange. *See Unlisted Securities Market.*

**Unlisted Securities Market** (USM)  Former market for shares in companies that do not fulfil the requirements for a full quotation on the Stock Exchange, or that do not wish to be quoted, but which do fulfil certain less stringent requirements. It closed in 1996 to be replaced by the *Alternative Investment Market* (AIM).

**unquoted**  Normally describing shares or debentures traded unofficially and not quoted on the Stock Market.

**unquoted company**  Company that does not have its shares quoted on a stock exchange.

**unquoted investments**  Alternative term for *unlisted securities.*

**unquoted securities**  Alternative term for *unlisted securities.*

**unsecured**  If something (normally a loan of some kind) is unsecured, perhaps because there are no assets to act as collateral, there is no guarantee it will be repaid.

**unsecured creditor**  Person who has made a loan but has no *security.*

**unsecured debenture**  *Debenture* that gives the holder no legal redress if full repayment has not been received by the specified repayment date. In such a case, the holder of an unsecured debenture must wait until the company has been wound up before claiming payment. For this reason, most debentures are secured against company property or financial assets. It is also known as a simple or naked debenture.

**unvalued policy**  Insurance policy that has a sum insured against each item of property, but not acknowledged by the insurer as true values. In the event of a claim, the insured must prove the actual value of the item. *See also valued policy.*

**up or out (position)**  High pressure job or position. In such a job an executive is either promoted very quickly or replaced equally speedily.
*The job of brand manager is an up or out position.*

**upstairs deal**  Deal arranged upstairs and behind closed doors – usually in the boardroom. Many *takeovers* are settled by upstairs deals.

**upstream** Movement, *e.g.* of funds, from a *subsidiary company* to its *parent company*. *See also* **downstream**.

**uptick** Describing a transaction (such as a sale of shares) that is made at a higher price than the one obtained immediately before. It is also known as a plus tick. Uptick is also used to denote a (short-lived) rise in a price or value.

*There was a small drop in sterling late in the day, which seemed to be caused by a slight uptick in the dollar.*

*See also* **downtick**; **tick**.

**uptrend** Improvement of some general kind, *e.g.* in market prices.

*The company's executives expected a small setback in profits in the short term, but were optimistic that the uptrend would continue.*

**usance** Term with three meanings:

1. It is the rate of interest charged on a loan.
2. It is **unearned income** derived from the ownership of wealth or capital.
3. It is the amount of time customarily allowed for payment of short-term **bills of exchange** between two foreign countries. The usual period is 60 days.

**user-friendly** Originally, describing computer software that is easily used, even by a novice. The term is now often used for anything that is easy to use.

**USM** Abbreviation of *unlisted securities market*.

**usufruct** The right to the use of property belonging to someone else, but not the right to diminish its value in such use.

**usury** Moneylending at an excessive rate of interest, not in itself illegal. *See* **moneylender**.

**utility stock** Share in a company providing utilities such as water, electricity and gas.

**utmost good faith** Phrase referring to contracts of insurance in which both parties must disclose all the facts that may influence the other's decision to enter into the contract, whether they are asked to do so or not. If either party has not acted in the utmost good faith, then the contract may become void.

# V

**valium picnic** Popular term for a quiet day on the New York Stock Exchange.

**valuation** Estimate of what something is worth. More particularly, it is a summary of the value of a *portfolio* of investments at a given time. In *life assurance*, a valuation of assets over liabilities is carried out annually.

**value** Term that is not as precise as it might seem. The value of something is the price a buyer is prepared to pay for it, but this can fluctuate according to all sorts of variables, *e.g.* whether it is a *buyer's market* or a *seller's market*, to what use the buyer will be putting the goods, etc. Usually the term is qualified, to minimize possible confusion.

**value-added tax** (VAT) Form of indirect taxation by which the producer, seller and consumer pay a percentage of the *added value* of the product or service, *e.g.* if a manufacturer buys raw materials at £10 per unit and sells each unit for £20, the added value is £10. The manufacturer is required to pay a percentage of the £20 in VAT, and can claim back the VAT paid on the £10-worth of materials. VAT for most things is 17.5% in the UK, although some goods and services are exempt and some *zero-rated*. *See also* **ad valorem**.

**value broker** Broker who charges a commission on a total transaction, rather than per share. *See also* **share broker**.

**valued policy** Insurance policy that has values assigned to insured items, the values being agreed by the insurer. In the event of a claim for total loss, that is the sum paid without the need for further negotiation. *See also* **unvalued policy**.

**variable-rate mortgage** *Mortgage* with a rate of interest that may be varied by the mortgagee to suit conditions on the money market.

**variation margin** When dealing in contracts on a *futures* market, the gain or loss at the end of a trading day that is recorded on a person's account. If the variation margin falls below the *initial margin* required, the trader is required to deposit more funds.

**VAT** Abbreviation of *value-added tax*.

**vendor** Person who sells goods or services.

**venture capital** Also known as risk capital, capital invested in a venture (usually a young company, often in high-technology areas) that presents a risk

**verba chartarum fortuis accipiuntur contra proferentem** Maxim used in legal circles, meaning that where the wording of a contract is imprecise and open to misinterpretation, it will be taken in the sense that goes against the party that drew up the contract. It is also known as the contra proferentem rule.

**verification** Checking that a statement is accurate. More particularly, the term refers to the checking of statements made by a company in its *prospectus*. Verification is undertaken by the company's solicitors in order to protect the company's directors. When a prospectus is sent for verification, it is often accompanied by verification notes, clarifying each statement.

**vertical diversification** Diversification into industries or businesses at different stages of production to the diversifying company. *See also horizontal diversification.*

**vertical integration** Amalgamation of companies involved in different stages of production in the same industry, *e.g.*, to produce one company capable of extracting raw materials, using them to produce goods and then distributing an selling the manufactured product.

**vested interest** Reason (*e.g.* an investment) or possible benefit that a person may have for maintaining a certain state of affairs.

**vigilantibus non dormientibus jura subveniunt** Maxim meaning that if people think they have a claim to make, they should go ahead and make the claim, as soon as possible. *See also laches.*

**viatical company** Company that buys *life assurance* policies from people with a long-term or terminal illness.

**voidable contract** Contract that may be voided by one or other of the parties to it, *e.g.* if one party fails to make known all information relevant to the contract, it may be deemed voidable. *See also void contract.*

**void contract** Contract that was drawn up on the basis of what turns out to be misunderstandings on both sides. Such a contract is deemed in law never to have existed. *See also voidable contract.*

**volatility** Measure of the stability of a particular instrument. If, say, a share price or a market index moves often and vacillates wildly, then it is said to be volatile.

**volume**  Term often confused with *turnover*, although in some instances they may be used to mean the same thing. Strictly, volume is the number of units traded, whereas turnover refers to the value of the units traded.

*The stock exchange saw today the third largest drop in terms of points, but volume was moderate at about 650 million shares.*

On the commodities market, however, volume refers to the quantity of *soft commodities* traded, and turnover refers to the *tonnage* of metals traded over a particular period of time (normally over a day of trading).

**voluntary liquidation**  Liquidation of a company that has decided to cease trading, rather one that has gone *bankrupt*.

**voting rights**  Right of a shareholder to vote at a company's *annual general meeting* (AGM). This right depends on which type of shares are held; generally, *ordinary shares* carry voting rights whereas *debentures* do not. The articles of association and the company's *prospectus* detail which shares carry voting rights and which do not.

**voyage policy**  In marine insurance, a policy that is valid for only a single, specific voyage.

**vulture capitalism**  Pejorative view of *venture capitalism*, whereby investors lure talented people away from established companies, encourage them to set up on their own, work hard and be ingenious and then face a demand for a high return on the investment.

# W

**wager** Bet. Essentially, a wager is a contract between two parties, that one will give the other something of value depending upon the outcome of some future event.

**waiter** Person on the London Stock Exchange or at Lloyds who runs errands, takes messages and looks after the day-to-day running of the exchange. Historically, the first waiters were those in the coffee houses at which dealings first took place.

**waiting time** Time an employee spends not working, *i.e.* waiting for a machine to warm up or be repaired, or waiting for another employee to finish the previous stage of a job.

**waive** To give up a right or remove or overrule conditions of an agree-ment.

**waiver of premium** Facility in which insurance premiums are treated as paid should the insured by unable to follow his or her own occupation through disability or sickness. It is available on life, personal health and pension policies.

**wallflower** Stock that is no longer favoured by stock market investors.

**Wall Street** Another name for the New York Stock Exchange (Wall Street is the street in Manhattan on which the exchange is located). Sometimes the name is further abbreviated to The Street.

**warehouse to warehouse** Clause in an insurance policy covering goods which states that they are insured while in transit.

**warehousing** On the stock market, using funds invested in insurance or unit trusts to buy shares that are falling in price, often as a precursor to a *takeover bid*. *See concert party*.

**warrant** Term with three meanings:
1. It is a receipt that describes goods held in a warehouse, transferable by endorsement. In this sense a *wharfinger warrant* (also known as a wharfinger receipt) is a similar receipt describing goods on a wharf. *See also wharfage*.

2. It is a long-date *option*.

3. It is a security of a specific market value that may be exchanged for a certain share at a predetermined price. The warrant's value lies in the difference between the predetermined conversion price and the *market price* of the share.

**warranty** Term with three meanings:

1. It is a statement or guarantee that goods are in working order or that workmanship is not faulty.

2. In a *contract*, it is an implicit or explicit guarantee that the premises upon which the contract is based are factual or true. If the warranty turns out to be false, the contract is not void, but the injured party may seek damages.

3. In insurance, it is an undertaking by an insured person that something will, or will not, be done; *e.g.* that an alarm system will be maintained and switched on. Breach of warranty allows an insurer to repudiate a claim.

**warranty of authority** Power given to an *agent* to act under the instructions of a principal.

**war risks insurance** In marine insurance, clause in a policy stipulating that a ship and its cargo are covered if loss results from a state of war between two countries.

**wash sale** Tax-avoiding fake "sale" of shares between two brokers (which also inflates the price). It is illegal.

**watered stock** Stock that has become a smaller percentage of a company's total share capital because of subsequent share issues.

**wealth** Total of a person's or country's *assets*, both tangible and intangible.

**wear and tear** Popular and legal term for *depreciation*. Wear and tear is the decrease in value of an item due to deterioration through normal use rather than through accident or negligence.

**weather insurance** Also known as *pluvius insurance*, insurance against losses caused by inclement weather (usually rain), available to farmers and the organizers of outdoor events.

**weighted ballot** Ballot (for shares) that is in some way biased towards a certain type of investor.

*The issuing house was instructed to weight the ballot for shares in favour of small investors.*

**whipsaw** Violent movement (or series of movements) in prices on any market.

*Today's whipsaw action reflects nervousness in the foreign-exchange market. Whipsawed by the dollar, blue-chip stocks managed to end another volatile session yesterday little changed, but many other stocks fell.*

**whistle blowing** Requirement under the 1995 Pensions Act that professional advisers notify the authorities if they become aware of any breach by an employer or trustee in connection with a pension scheme.

**white collar** Employee who does office work rather than factory work. *See also* **blue collar.**

**white knight** When a company finds itself the target of a **takeover bid**, it may seek an alternative company or person to whom it offers to sell itself in preference to being taken over by the original bidder. This friendly company is known as white knight and the tactic is known as a white knight defence. *See also* **grey knight; white squire defence.**

**white squire defence** In a **takeover** situation, a **target** company may place a significant number of its shares with a friendly party in order to prevent the **raider** from acquiring them. *See also* **white knight.**

**whole-life insurance** Type of **life assurance** that pays out on the death of the assured whenever it occurs. He or she pays premiums until death or (sometimes) retirement.

**wholesale broking** Insurance broking business that is obtained from other intermediaries rather than from the public.

**widow's pension** Pension paid in the UK to a married woman after her husband's death.

**will** Legal document drawn up by a person (usually under the advice of a solicitor) giving instructions as to how the person's estate is to be distributed after his or her death. The signature on a will has to be witnessed by two people, neither of whom is a beneficiary but can be an executor. *See also* **intestacy.**

**windbill** Alternative term for *accommodation bill.*

**windfall profit** Unexpected profit, usually sizeable, such as that caused by a rise in stock prices or an inheritance.

**winding-up** Cessation of business activity on the part of a company and the start of that company's liquidation.

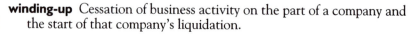

**windmill** Alternative term for *accommodation bill.*

**window-dressing** In *accounting*, a (legal) method of making a set of accounts seem better than they are by presenting them in such a way as to make the usual comparisons between figures difficult.

**wire house** Informal US term for a large stockbroking firm.

**withholding tax** Tax on the interest on a deposit or investment deducted at source (the depositor or investor receives net interest).

**without-profits policy** Type of *life assurance* policy whereby the policy-holder does not share in the assurance company's profits. *See also **with-profits policy**.*

**without recourse** Note on a ***bill of exchange*** indicating that in the event of non-payment of the bill, the current holder may not blame the person from whom he or she bought it. It is also sometimes written in French as sans recours.

**with particular average** (WPA) Describing an insurance policy that covers loss of part of a consignment of goods in transit.

**with-profits annuity** Annuity with income payments that are guaranteed to be not less than a certain sum. Each year, the annuity payment increases as bonuses are added; once increased, the annuity income cannot be reduced.

**with-profits policy** Type of *life assurance* policy whereby the policyholder receives a share of the assurance company's profits as annual bonuses during the term of the policy, and a terminal bonus on death or maturity.

**working assets** All the assets of a company except its *capital assets*. Working assets include outstanding debts, stocks of raw materials, stocks of finished product and cash in hand. It is also known as current assets.

**working capital** Capital available for the day-to-day running of a company, used to pay such expenses as salaries, purchases, etc.

**working cover** In reinsurance, the first *layer* of an *excess of loss treaty*.

**working director** Director who takes an active part in the management of a company.

**work in progress** In accounting, the value of goods currently under manufacture or services being supplied, but not completed at the end of the accounting period.

**worst-moment concept** In preparing financial projections and budgets, the worst moment concept takes into account the worst times in **cash-flow**, *e.g.* periods when large bills must be paid, as well as the easier times.

**writ** Notice served by a High Court, normally signalling the beginning of a court action, informing a person that he or she is either to appear in court at a certain date or that he or she must perform (or refrain from performing) a certain action. Failure to comply with a writ is punishable by the court.

**write** To write insurance business is to provide insurance cover.

**write down** In accounting, to take the cost of an *asset* and deduct the amount by which the asset has depreciated in capital terms. This is the write-down or **book value** of the asset.

**write off** (US **charge off**) To delete an *asset* from the accounts because it has depreciated (or been written-down) so far that it no longer has any book value. *See also* ***write down***.

**writing down allowance** Another term for *capital allowance*.

**written line** In reinsurance, the maximum amount that a reinsurer will accept on a slip.

**written premium** In insurance, the premium income received during the year.

**WT** Abbreviation of *warrant*.

**W**

# X

**XA** Abbreviation of ex all, denoting shares that have been bought minus rights to any benefits being offered, *e.g.* participation in a *rights issue*, rights to *dividends*, etc.

**XC** Abbreviation of ex capitalization, denoting a share that has been bought minus the right to participate in a forthcoming *scrip* issue.

**XD** Abbreviation of ex dividend, denoting a share that has been sold without the right to receive the next *dividend*.

**XR** Abbreviation of ex rights, denoting a *share* that has been sold, but does not entitle the new holder to participation in a forthcoming *rights issue*.

**X**

# Y

**yankee** Slang term on the London Stock Exchange for US *securities*.

**yankee bond** Bond that is issued in dollar denominations to attract US investors.

**yard** Slang term for a *billion*.

**year-earlier** Previous year.

*A & G Electronics posted a pre-tax profit up 20% on year-earlier pre-tax profits of $20 million.*

**year-later** Next year.

**yearling bond** UK fixed-interest security that has a life of under five years; such bonds are issued through banks and stockbrokers on a weekly basis.

**year's purchase** Method of calculating the value of a purchase (of, say, a company) by relating it to the anticipated year's *income* from the purchase; *i.e.*, the price of a business in relation to its average annual profits or the price of a property in relation to the average annual rent.

**Yellow book** Popular term for a publication entitled *Admission and Securities Listing*, issued by the London Stock Exchange Council, setting out regulations of admission to the Official list and the obligations of securities admitted.

**yield** Return on an investment, taking into account the annual income and the capital value of the investment, usually expressed as a percentage.

**yield gap** Difference in average yield between investments in ordinary *shares* and in *gilt-edged securities*.

**York-Antwerp rules** Voluntary code, drawn up in 1877, for those involved in shipping cargo by sea.

**yo-yo stock** Stock whose price fluctuates widely in an unpredictable way.

# Z

**zai-tech** Japanese and US stock market practice of borrowing money in order to invest in *stocks* and *bonds*.

**zebra** Form of *zero-coupon bond*.

**zero** Shorthand for *zero-coupon bond*.

**zero-balance account** Cheque account operated by a company by which cheques are drawn against the account balance, which at the start of the day is always zero. At the end of the day the value of all cheques drawn is totalled and the amount is transferred into the account, so that the account balance reverts from a *debt* to zero.

**zero-base budgeting** Method of *budget* management whereby each manager assigns a priority rating to each budget request. Zero-base budgeting forces each manager to justify every request.

**zero-coupon bond** US *bearer bond* that pays no *dividend*, but is issued at a substantial discount. A capital gain is made by the bearer when the bond matures, and so tax on the proceeds is paid at a lower rate than if the proceeds were in the form of dividends. Zero-coupon bonds are not issued in the UK. *See also* **bond washing**.

**zero-dividend preference share** Type of share sold by an *investment trust* that pays no dividend to the investor, who receives payment only when the trust is wound up.

**zero-rated** In the UK, describing an item that attracts no *value-added tax* (VAT).

*For the time being, books continue to be zero-rated.*

**Z**